The Practical
SQL
Handbook
Using Structured Query Language

The Practical
SQL
Handbook
Using Structured Query Language

**Sandra L. Emerson,
Marcy Darnovsky,
and Judith S. Bowman
of Sybase, Inc.**

ADDISON - WESLEY PUBLISHING COMPANY, INC.

Reading, Massachusetts   Menlo Park, California   New York
Don Mills, Ontario   Wokingham, England   Amsterdam   Bonn
Sydney   Singapore   Tokyo   Madrid   San Juan

Many of the designations used by manufacturers and sellers to distinguish their products are claimed as trademarks. Where those designations appear in this book, and Addison-Wesley was aware of a trademark claim, the designations have been printed in initial caps or all caps.

Transact-SQL is a trademark of Sybase Inc.

Library of Congress Cataloging-in-Publication Data

Emerson, Sandra L., 1947–
    The practical SQL handbook : using structured query language /
  Sandra L. Emerson, Marcy Darnovsky, and Judith S. Bowman.
      p.   cm.
    Bibliography: p.
    Includes index.
    ISBN 0-201-51738-8
    1. SQL (Computer program language)   2. Relational databases.
  I. Darnovsky, Marcy.   II. Bowman, Judith S.   III. Title.
  QA76.73.S67E54   1989
  005.75'6 — dc19

88–34177
CIP

Cover design by Doliber Skeffington
Text design by Sally Carson
Set in 10-point Trump Mediaeval by Chiron Inc.

ISBN 0-201-51738-8
ABCDEFGHIJ-AL-89
First Printing, April, 1989

The Practical SQL Handbook

ACKNOWLEDGEMENTS

We would like to thank the following people for their contributions to this book:

Donna Jeker and Stu Schuster for supplying timely support and encouragement;

Jeff Lichtman and Howard Torf for offering advice, examples, anecdotes, and reality checks;

Tom Bondur, Susie Bowman, John Cooper, and Wayne Duquesne for providing resource materials and other information;

Paul Winsberg for reviewing the database design chapter.

Table of Contents

Foreword

FOREWORD

I've come to praise SQL—not to bury it!

Although the SQL language has become an essential part of relational database management on all types of computers, it is frequently presented in the trade press in a less than favorable light. This is a mistake—and I should know, because I've made it myself.

Back at the beginning of relational time, when SQL was being designed at the IBM Research Laboratory, I was involved in implementing a database language meant to compete with SQL. Our language could handle more complex queries than SQL could, and had fewer special cases, but it was harder to learn. After seven years and two complete product developments with the non-SQL language, I became an enthusiastic convert to SQL.

The reasons were simple: SQL is easy to learn, powerful enough and getting more powerful all the time, and—most important—will soon be implemented by every surviving DBMS vendor. Therefore, my third DBMS design (at Sybase) was based entirely on SQL.

It's easy to lose sight of the fact that as recently as five years ago nearly every database was non-relational, and each had its own special language. Implementation costs were prohibitive, and learning to use another database management system was an ordeal.

We have now entered an age in which all DBMS's support either a complete relational language or a retrieval-only relational interface. In the late 1980's, "relational" implies SQL. A working knowledge of the SQL language is now crucial, no matter which DBMS you ultimately use.

Given its academic origins, it's easy to understand why many people are intimidated by SQL and relational database management systems. Terms such as "normal forms," "correlation variables," and "referential integrity" are not intuitive, and do nothing to convey the meaning of what are basically simple concepts. They make database management seem like a branch of higher mathematics—which only makes for more doctoral dissertations and more Ph.D.'s (myself included).

Despite its simplicity, SQL is a powerful language. Such power can produce unexpected pitfalls: even DP professionals are sometimes fooled. Several years ago, for example, I was involved in a competitive benchmark with another DBMS company. We performed well in every case except one, in which we took 60 hours (yes, *hours*) to perform a command that a different system completed in two minutes.

We agonized over the situation for days, until someone asked the customer to tell us in English what question the query was supposed to answer. That exercise made it clear that the customer's SQL statement had a right parenthesis in the wrong place. When the parenthesis was moved, the query ran in under a minute (down from 60 hours!).

I'll never forget the customer's lament: "Relational languages are more sensitive to parentheses than FORTRAN!" Today, I could rescue such a customer, and save a lot of wear and tear on the benchmarkers, with a copy of *The Practical SQL Handbook*.

Having worked with relational database management systems since 1976, I was quite happy to read *The Practical SQL Handbook*. It covers not only SQL, but also database design and normalization in a manner which can be described—as the title says—as practical. That means that this book will get you up and running in a hurry.

The examples in *The Practical SQL Handbook* always make clear the practical significance of the concepts being explained. For example, *The Practical SQL Handbook* makes it clear that enforcing "referential integrity" can mean something as straightforward as putting a "no vaporware rule" into your DBMS application: the system will then refuse to allow you to ship a product that doesn't exist. Nor will it let you ship to a customer who doesn't exist (this could be called the "no-fraud rule").

The Practical SQL Handbook also prepares you for the SQL future. While many critics of SQL concern themselves with things SQL can't do, a more appropriate approach would be to ask what SQL can't do *yet*. SQL is not a static language, and both DBMS vendors and the SQL standards committees are busy extending it. Many of the changes are being driven by the need to develop increasingly complicated systems that require the database to play a stronger role in governing application programs. SQL extensions to enforce central database administration are particularly important for systems in which personal computers and workstations communicate with the DBMS over a network architecture known as client-server computing. *The Practical SQL Handbook* covers some of these extensions to SQL, as seen in the Transact-SQL language developed by Sybase for the SQL Server.

In summary, this is the book for the "intelligent amateur." It is for someone who has little or no knowledge of SQL and who needs a broad introduction to relational database management. This book provides a vendor-independent introduction to everything you need to know to start using SQL and relational databases.

Robert Epstein
Executive Vice-President
Sybase, Inc.

Introduction

THE BEGINNINGS OF SQL

In the beginning was IBM, and IBM created SQL.

SQL, originally an acronym for "Structured Query Language," is a unified language for defining, querying, modifying, and controlling the data in a relational database. Its name is officially pronounced "ess-cue-ell" (according to the American National Standards Institute), but many people say "sequel." In this book, we use the term SQL as if it were pronounced "sequel."

The relational model of database management was proposed in 1970 by Dr. E. F. Codd at the IBM Research Laboratory in San Jose, California, and developed during the following decade in universities and research laboratories. SQL, one of several languages that grew out of this early work, has now almost completely taken over the world of relational database languages. Vendors of relational database management systems that initially chose other languages have flocked to SQL; national and international standards organizations have proposed a codified version of the language.

During the early years (roughly 1970-1980), the poor performance of relational database management systems hampered their commercial viability. The relational model's important strengths—mathematical soundness and intuitive appeal—could not overcome the fact that the management of large databases with early relational systems was slow and difficult—practically speaking, sometimes impossible. Two factors changed this situation: the availability of faster, larger-capacity computers, and the development of superior data retrieval, data storage, and data access methods to support the "back end" functions of relational systems.

In 1981, IBM announced its first commercial SQL-based product, SQL/DS. Oracle, Relational Technology, and several other vendors also announced SQL-based relational database management systems during the

1

early 1980s. Currently, more than 75 SQL or SQL-like database management systems are available, running on computers of all sizes and shapes—from single-user micros to machines that handle hundreds of users. About 200,000 people are using SQL in 1988, and that number will double every year for several years. These are serious users: SQL is now entrusted with "mission-critical" information management and data processing tasks in corporate, government, and public interest organizations.

The emergence of a highly competitive marketplace for relational database management systems has produced an array of SQL implementations, representing years of effort to develop a complete and highly expressive language for the relational model. But a problem remains: there are as many dialects of SQL as there are relational systems on the market. Although all the dialects are recognizably SQL, none is identical to another in syntax or semantics. Furthermore, many vendors regularly extend their versions of SQL, which makes the language a moving target as well as a multiple target.

SQL will continue to evolve—in part because its original design was vague in a number of areas (and the database industry didn't wait for those fuzzy areas to be cleared up), and in part because the industry is striving to develop database systems that fulfill more of the capabilities of the relational model.

The flexibility of SQL and the ease with which it can be extended means that it will keep on changing to meet the demands of the market.

The Beginnings of the SQL Standard

One response to the divergence among SQL dialects has been an attempt by U.S. and international standards organizations to come up with an official version of the language. Since the early 1980s, academics and relational database industry figures have joined forces under the auspices of these standards organizations. While they are not trying to impose the equivalent of the standard-gauge railroad on the relational database industry, they are making a valiant effort to capture the essential elements of SQL.

As a result of these standardization efforts, there have been several major drafts of a document proposing the details of a SQL standard (1983, 1986, and 1988). The 1988 version of the proposed SQL standard was released as "ISO-ANSI SQL2" by the American National Standards Institute (ANSI) and the International Organization for Standardization (ISO).

The starting point for the ISO-ANSI effort was the original IBM SQL. Thus, the standard was based from the beginning on an existing implementation rather than on an abstract design. As the standard matures, it continues to evolve on the basis of experience gained in both the theoretical and commercial arenas of relational database management. The 1988 proposal differs notably both in scope and in functionality from the earlier drafts, and SQL3 (which incorporates further extensions) has already appeared on the horizon.

Notwithstanding the difficulty of documenting a moving target, the participants in the joint ISO-ANSI effort are trying to produce a comprehensive set of guidelines that all self-respecting SQL implementations must meet. The existence of a standard that defines a basic minimum SQL has the obvious advantages of:

- Reducing retraining time when users move from one SQL to another
- Making applications portable from one SQL to another
- Making applications long-lived
- Promoting cross-system communication

Even when a stable standard emerges, however, it will still be a framework rather than a recipe. Inevitably, commercial vendors will continue to extend and improve SQL and adapt it to the perceived needs of their customers.

The Commercialization of SQL

The first commercial implementations of SQL had much the same experimental flavor as the research versions developed in university settings and industry labs, in part because the pioneer SQL vendors were working without the benefit of a finished standard. Early implementations such as Oracle, SQL/DS, and DB2 have grown and changed remarkably since their first appearance. Still, commercial SQL implementations tend to lead the standard rather than to follow it, and continue to differ from each other— and from the standard—in many respects. They also seem to respond more rapidly to their customers and to their competitors than to the meetings of the standards organizations.

The situation could become a Babel of mutually incomprehensible SQL dialects competing for market share. Fortunately, however, market forces, as well as the standards movement, encourage commercial implementations to become more and more like each other as time goes on. Developers of database management systems pay as much attention to what the competition is doing as to what the standards committee says.

Competition promotes cross-fertilization and imitation on the commercial SQL scene for two reasons. First, companies try to offer prospective customers the same "checklist" of functions and extensions (for example, interactive support for rapid prototyping of SQL-based applications). Second, companies are constantly trying to attract customers of other relational systems and need to minimize the cost of converting from one SQL-based system to another.

In 1989, these forces are pushing commercial implementations closer together. After all, both commercial interests and the standards committees hope to define a SQL that:

- Implements an increasingly complete relational model
- Minimizes incompatibility and implementation-dependence
- Adds language for new functions carefully, in order to maintain compatibility with early versions of SQL

The shape and the flavor of SQL are already well established. During the last decade of this century, as relational database management sales keep growing and the expected shakeout occurs, the scope of the remaining SQLs and many of their details will also converge.

This book, in fact, is a harbinger of that day. With it, you can teach yourself to use whatever SQL dialect you happen to have access to. Along the way, you'll learn how the hallmarks of a modern and mature relational database management system are reflected in its implementation of SQL.

WHO SHOULD USE THIS BOOK

The Practical SQL Handbook is meant for you if you use a relational database system—whether you're sharing that system with other users or going it alone on a single-user personal computer (PC). It assumes that you're an intelligent amateur—whether you're an end user in a large company, government office, or nonprofit agency; the owner of a small business; the manager of a small organization; a home computer user working on a personal project; or a student learning about database technology. You may be moving to a relational database system from a PC file manager, making the transition to SQL from a non-SQL-based database management system, or taking up database management for the first time.

We do take for granted that you have a nodding acquaintance with computers and computer tools. Of course, some degree of familiarity with database systems will help.

If you're planning to develop a sophisticated database application, you'll need to embed SQL in a programming language or use it with a "fourth-generation application language" (4GL). But you need never have written a single line of programming code in order to use *The Practical SQL Handbook* successfully to learn both the basics of SQL and to get a good grasp on a variety of more advanced topics.

Theoreticians are not our intended audience; we assume that the fine points of relational theory and the intricacies of the ISO-ANSI debates are not of primary interest to our readers. On the other hand, we think you should be aware of the major SQL controversies—at least in their broad outlines—so that you'll be alert to the tricky areas of SQL use. In short, we think you want to know what really works, or at least the fastest way to find that out.

Accordingly, this book concentrates on teaching you to use SQL interactively—typing the commands and receiving results directly on a screen, as opposed to embedding them in a programming language. Every commercial implementation of SQL has an interactive interface for use in learning the language initially and writing *ad hoc* queries. Many provide report writers or 4GLs that can be used in association with SQL to develop applications of moderate complexity.

THE FOCUS OF THIS BOOK

With the long deliberations of the standards committees in the background, and the commercial battle for database management customers in the foreground, should a SQL book such as this one focus on the proposed ISO-ANSI standard, or should it attempt to capture the fast-moving world of the relational industry? The ISO-ANSI proposal describes an identifiable entity, but an entirely mythical one—there is no existing implementation of "ISO-ANSI SQL." Real-world SQL implementations, on the other hand, have an actual existence—in a variety of forms.

In spite of the messiness involved, this book focuses on the real world of commercial SQLs—which we also refer to as "industry SQLs." We made this choice because the industry SQLs provide a better teaching tool in the areas of notation, target audience, and overall functionality:

- The syntax notation used to document most industry SQLs is reasonably clear and intuitively understandable. The ISO-ANSI publications, on the other hand, use BNF (Backus Naur Form) notation, which is very precise but difficult to read and understand.
- All the industry SQLs support an interactive interface for the beginning or casual user; the ISO-ANSI standard is largely concerned with the embedded SQL interface for programmers and applications developers.
- Vendors of relational database systems are eager to include in their SQL implementations facilities needed in the real world (such as commands for creating and dropping indexes), which the ISO-ANSI standard has so far neglected to provide.

The 1988 ISO-ANSI proposed standard, like its predecessors, is a forbidding document, bristling with clauses, caveats, and footnotes; its BNF notation is best suited for capturing the function of each language element, rather than its exact syntax. If you want to undertake your own investigations, we recommend that you take a guide along—C.J. Date's *A Guide to the SQL Standard*. Date is one of the major theoreticians of the relational model and one of the most prolific writers on relational matters. His book explains how to read BNF and serves as a useful collection of his opinions on the merits and deficiencies of the 1986 standard and of SQL in general.

The 1988 proposed standard, a much larger and more comprehensive document than the 1986 draft, clearly shows the influence of developments in the commercial SQLs. The 1988 proposed standard is much more pragmatic and mature, and it provides new functions that address many of the issues raised by Date and other critics.

After ruminating on the ISO-ANSI document for a while, even with the assistance of Date's *Guide*, you're likely to turn for enlightenment to the closest relational database management system's user's manual. But user's manuals have their own drawbacks and limitations.

While some user's manuals are adequate for learning the basics of SQL, a great many are either overly simplistic or overly obscure. Perhaps more problematic, user's manuals (including several written by the authors of this book) unavoidably focus on the details of syntax and the eccentricities of one particular dialect—often at the expense of the conceptual picture.

The Practical SQL Handbook is meant to take up where even the best SQL user's manual leaves off. It takes you step by step through the basics of SQL and then introduces you to the issues involved in designing SQL-based database applications. *The Practical SQL Handbook* covers topics that are usually neglected or given short shrift in user's manuals: database design, indexes, nulls, joins, subqueries, views, performance, and data integrity.

Because SQL-based database management systems have grown so fast in number and in popularity, and because of the proliferation of SQL dialects, the available learning resources are still meager. *The Practical SQL Handbook* is the first complete, practical guide to today's most popular database language. With it, you'll learn to navigate with ease through the world of relational database management.

HOW TO LEARN SQL WITH THIS BOOK

Let's begin with a few expectations. First of all, we expect you to read large parts of this book while sitting at your terminal. Second, we expect you to study and reproduce the examples. Third, we expect you to practice, test, and explore. There's no substitute for interactive practice, even if your ultimate intention may be to program a highly sophisticated application.

From there, a lot is up to you. Learning styles differ: some people absorb new material through carefully considering prose explanations; others take in concepts just by looking at pictures. We expect this book to be equally helpful whether you choose to read every word of it or to briefly scan the text and rely mainly on the examples. Words and phrases in **boldface** indicate the first significant mention of an important term. Many of these terms are defined in the Glossary.

Some of the hundreds of examples in *The Practical SQL Handbook* are deliberately simple in order to illustrate basic concepts. Others are more difficult. At the most complex end of the range you'll find SQL statements that may serve as models for your own applications. Wherever their complexity warrants it, examples are dissected and explained in detail.

The fact that every version of SQL is different from every other version, at least in some details, means that no general-purpose book on SQL can guarantee all of its examples to work exactly as presented. The good news is that our decision to base *The Practical SQL Handbook* on the industry SQLs rather than on the official SQL standard will make the "translation" process more straightforward. With the reference materials supplied with your SQL product, the lists of cross-system analogies in keywords and operators in Appendix B, and a little detective work, you'll be able to test most of our examples on whatever SQL or SQL-like system you're using.

All the examples in *The Practical SQL Handbook* are guaranteed to work in the language with which they were developed—Sybase's Transact-SQL. We deliberately postpone discussion of Transact-SQL's non-standard features and enhancements until the last chapter of the book, including them in order to illustrate some typical extensions of SQL. We don't claim to represent in depth any implementation of SQL other than Transact-SQL, nor to cover any other dialect's strengths or limitations. We do cover (in broad strokes) the major areas of commonality among industry SQLs.

With very few exceptions, all examples are derived from our sample database, called the *bookbiz* database. Chapters 2 and 3 explain the sample database, and show you step-by-step how to re-create its structure on your system and insert the sample data in it. You don't have to use the same sample data we do, but that's the best approach—it will help you see more quickly whether your results are correct.

The *bookbiz* database is very small database. Its size and simplicity will allow you to re-create it on your own system. On the other hand, it is complex enough to illustrate important points about the significant relational issues.

Structure of This Book

Each chapter of *The Practical SQL Handbook* presents one SQL feature or a cluster of related features. The discussion follows a pattern, beginning with:

- Definition—what does it do
- Minimal syntax—a simple "vanilla" version of the command (one that is stripped of most optional clauses and extensions, that tend to vary from SQL to SQL)
- A simple example

Following this initial description of syntax and usage, we elaborate on the role of this feature in the relational model, and its possible use in database applications.

If necessary, we then provide additional syntax—optional clauses providing additional functions or fine-tuning capabilities—and more complex examples. In this way, each new feature has a complete description and example.

Where possible, each example builds on previous ones. However, the examples in each chapter stand alone, so that you can complete a chapter at one sitting. Remember to refresh your sample database in order to keep it in a useful state. You will need to start with a clean copy of the sample database at the beginning of each chapter. Learning SQL is like learning any other foreign language: the learning process begins with imitation, proceeds through comprehension, and should end with fluency. At each of these stages, the key to success is *practice*.

Interactive practice of SQL will be more pleasant and efficient if you follow some simple, time-saving procedures:

- Save your practice SQL statements in operating system files. (Your system should provide a method for doing this.) If you are not certain that a SQL query (data retrieval operation) is producing the desired results, save the results for off-line examination. Keep some log or record of what worked and what didn't, and save the error message, too, if you can.

- Save your successes. Keep elegant SQL solutions on file: you may want to imitate them for other purposes later on.

- Structure an application's queries into separate modules or subroutines. Like modern structured programming, good SQL applications should be made of many subroutines and be open to constant reapplication and recycling.

- Make yourself a crib sheet. Even if your system has provided you with a quick reference card, make your own list and quick sketches of favorite commands. This will reinforce learning. You will soon find that you use some SQL commands much more often than others.

- Improve on our solutions. In our experience, the more you work at expressing yourself in SQL, the simpler and more elegant your statements become.

The point of learning SQL and practicing it interactively is to be able to express any desired operation properly, so that you get the results you want. In order to achieve this proficiency, you'll have to explore and test-drive your relational system's SQL until you're sure you can trust it. You don't want to find out when you're running at fifty transactions per second that your results have been invalidated by a SQL error (or a logic error).

SQL requires practice because it's a foreign language, and the entity that speaks it best—your system's parser—isn't human. Although SQL has a limited number of keywords and operators and is relatively easy to read, there are areas that are tricky. Like many other high-level languages for computers, SQL has a definite grammar and structure and a fair number of specific syntax rules. SQL may be English-like, but it's still far from being a natural language. Sooner or later, you'll come across some operations that SQL simply cannot perform.

The Practical SQL Handbook will help you understand SQL's strengths and limits. It will assist in heading off potential disasters caused by poor database design or unwieldy and unmaintainable SQL-based applications, and make the learning of SQL as quick and painless as possible.

OVERVIEW OF THE BOOK

Chapter 1: SQL and Relational Database Management. This chapter briefly defines and informally illustrates the relational model, and presents the chief features of the SQL language as the voice of the relational model.

Chapter 2: Designing Databases. Database design is often an intimidating prospect. This chapter surveys the most helpful techniques, using the sample database to illustrate the analysis of data and the decision-making involved in database design. It discusses primary and foreign keys, entity-relationship modeling, and the normalization rules, which can act as guidelines for good database design.

Chapter 3: Creating and Filling a Database. The design proposed in the previous chapter becomes a reality here, as the SQL commands for creating databases, tables, and indexes, and for adding, changing, and deleting data are examined in detail. An explanation of our SQL syntax conventions accompanies this initiation into hands-on use of the SQL language.

Chapter 4: Selecting Data from the Database. This chapter, which assumes that you now have an on-line database with which to practice, presents the basic elements of the SELECT command. It explains how to retrieve particular rows and columns from a single table, and covers computed values, comparison operators, and logical (Boolean) operators.

Chapter 5: Sorting Data and Other Selection Techniques. Other clauses in the SELECT statement allow you to sort your data, eliminate duplicates from the results, or use aggregate functions to report averages, sums, or counts.

Chapter 6: Grouping Data and Reporting From It. The SELECT statement also includes language for grouping data and reporting from it using the aggregate functions described in the previous chapter. This chapter covers these SQL features, and also returns to the controversial topic of how a relational database management system should handle null values (missing information).

Chapter 7: Joining Tables for Comprehensive Data Analysis. The join operation is one of the hallmarks of the relational model. This chapter explains how to use the join operation to retrieve data from one or more tables. A complex variant on simple selection, joins confront users with significant issues in analyzing and verifying the results of data retrieval.

Chapter 8: Structuring Queries with Subqueries. This chapter deals with the proper use and application of nested queries, or subqueries. The correlated subquery (notorious for causing confusion) is explained, with many examples.

Chapter 9: Creating and Using Views. This chapter discusses views (virtual tables) and their use in providing customized access to data. Views can also provide data security, since you can grant other users access to specified portions of a table for specified operations. The thorny issue of updating views is described in some detail.

Chapter 10: Security, Transactions, Performance, and Integrity. This chapter is devoted to considerations encountered in real-world database management. It explains the SQL commands for specifying permissions, returns to the subject of indexing to discuss its use in boosting performance, and covers mechanisms for transaction management. It also describes extensions to the SQL language that provide database consistency and referential integrity. Some of the features discussed here are specific to Sybase's implementation of SQL.

Appendix A: Syntax Summary for the SQL Used in this Book

Appendix B: Industry SQL Equivalents

Appendix C: Glossary

Appendix D: The *bookbiz* Sample Database (chart of tables with data, data structure diagram, and CREATE and INSERT statements)

Appendix E: Bibliography

Chapter 1

SQL and Relational Database Management

RELATIONAL DATABASE MANAGEMENT

SQL is the language in which one "speaks" relational database. But just what is a relational database management system?

All database management systems store and manipulate information. The relational approach to database management is based on a mathematical model that includes formidable-sounding components such as relational algebra and relational calculus. Most working definitions of relational database management, however, rely on descriptions and functional specifications rather than on theoretical precision.

C.J. Date gives this informal definition of a relational database management system:

- It represents all information in the database as tables
- It supports the three relational operations known as **selection**, **projection**, and **join**, for specifying exactly what data you want to see (and it can carry out these operations without requiring the system to physically store its data in any particular form)

Dr. E.F. Codd, the inventor of the relational model, has developed a detailed list of criteria that implementations of the relational model must meet. A comprehensive explanation of this list, often called "Codd's rules," would introduce terminology and theoretical issues not really within the scope of this book. We do touch on many of these issues, however, in subsequent chapters. Here, we summarize the features of Codd's twelve –rule test for relational systems and use these, in combination with Date's more basic definition, to come up with a general definition. To be considered fully relational, a relational database management system must:

- Represent all information in the database as tables
- Keep the logical representation of data independent from its physical storage characteristics
- Use one high-level language for structuring, querying, and changing the information in the database (theoretically, any number of database languages could fit this bill; in practice, SQL is *the* relational language)
- Support the main relational operations (selection, projection, join); it must also support set operations such as union, intersection, difference, division
- Support views, which allow the user to specify alternative ways of looking at data in tables
- Provide a method for differentiating between unknown values (**nulls**) and zero or blank
- Supports mechanisms for integrity, authorization, transactions, and recovery

The rest of this chapter gives an overview of these points; most of them are further discussed in subsequent chapters. After reading the brief explanations here, you'll begin to understand the lay of the relational land.

The Relational Model: It's All Tables

Codd's very first rule says that all information in a relational database is represented by values in **tables**. In a relational system, tables have (horizontal) **rows** and (vertical) **columns**. A note on terminology: since table, row, and column are the common terms used in commercial relational database management systems, they're the ones we'll use in this book. However, you may come across references to **relation**, **tuple**, and **attribute**. They are very nearly synonymous with table, row, and column respectively; so are **file**, **record**, and **field**. The first three are academic terms; the second three stem from general data processing vocabulary. All data is represented in table format—there's no other way to see the information in the database.

```
                    columns

              Name          Address
          +-----------------+------------------------------+
          |                 |                              |
  rows    | Jane Doe        | 127 Elm St.                  |
          +-----------------+------------------------------+
          |                 |                              |
          | Richard Roe     | 10 Trenholm Place            |
          +-----------------+------------------------------+
          |                 |                              |
          | Edgar Poe       | 1533 Usher House Rd.         |
          +-----------------+------------------------------+
```

Figure 1–1: The Personnel Table

A set of related tables forms a **database**. The tables in a relational database are separate but equal. There is no hierarchical ranking of tables and, in fact, no physical necessary relationship among them.

Each table consists of a set of rows and columns. Each row describes one occurrence of an **entity**—a person, a company, a sale, or some other thing. Each column describes one characteristic of the entity—a person's name or address, a company's phone number or president, a sale's items sold or quantity or date.

Each data element, or **value**, can be identified as the intersection of a row (the x axis) and a column (the y axis). To zero in on the exact data element you want, you need to know the name of its table and what column it's in, and the value of its row's **primary key**, or unique identifier. (As we'll discuss in Chapter 2, it is necessary that each row be uniquely identified by one of its values.)

For example, suppose you want to know Jane Doe's address. To instruct the system to show you that particular piece of information, you tell it to fetch Jane Doe's address from the table called *personnel*. (See Figure 1-1.) The column name is *address* (or some such thing); the name *Jane Doe* is the primary key value identifying that row.

There are two types of tables in a relational database: **user tables** and **system tables**. User tables contain the information that is the database management system's *raison d'être*—information on sales, orders, personnel schedules, and the like. The system tables, also known as the **system catalog**, contain the database description. An active system catalog that provides additional database management functions is called a **data dictionary**. System tables are usually kept up to date by the DBMS itself, but they can be accessed just like any other table. Being able to access the system tables as if they were any other table is another of Codd's rules for relational systems.

To reiterate: all the information in the database, whether it's system data or user data, is represented as tables.

Independence Forever

In database management, as in so many other aspects of life, independence is seen as something to strive for. Data independence is a crucial aspect of database management: it lets applications change without affecting database design, and it lets database design change without affecting applications. A database management system should not force you to make irrevocable decisions about what data you'll store, how you'll access it, or what your users will require. You don't want to be stuck with a system that's become obsolete because your work requirements have changed.

The relational model provides data independence on two important levels—*physical* and *logical*. **Physical data independence** means that the representation of the data—the user's eye view—is completely independent of how the data is physically stored. As a consequence, physical storage can be changed or rearranged without affecting either your view of the data or the logical database design.

Such changes can become necessary or desirable, especially in large multi-user systems. For example, when you run out of storage space, you'll need to add physical storage. When a storage device breaks down, you'll have to replace it—in a hurry. Usually less urgently, you may want to improve performance, efficiency, or ease of use by changing the method by which the system locates the physical data. (These methods are referred to generically as **access strategies**, which often make use of **indexes**.)

A second type of independence provided by relational systems, known as **logical independence**, means that relationships among tables, columns, and rows can change without impairing the function of application programs and *ad hoc* queries. You can split tables between rows, or between columns, without impairing applications or queries. You can also get an answer to any *ad hoc* question that you ask the system about the database, even though its logical design has changed.

Physical and logical data independence account for two more of Codd's twelve rules.

A High-Level Language

The definition of a relational system (and Codd's rules) require that a single language—sometimes called a **comprehensive data sublanguage**—be able to handle all communications with the database. In the commercial world of relational database management, that language is SQL.

SQL is used for **data manipulation** (retrieval and modification), **data definition**, and **data administration**. Every retrieval, modification, definition, or administrative operation is expressed as a SQL **statement** or **command**.

There are two varieties of data manipulation operations—**data retrieval** and **data modification**. Retrieval means finding the particular data you want; modification means adding, removing, or changing the data.

Data retrieval operations (often called **queries**) search the database, fetch information you've requested in the most efficient way possible, and display it. All SQL queries are expressed using the keyword SELECT.

The rest of this chapter includes some simple SQL queries. Don't worry about the syntax right now: it'll be fully explained in Chapter 3, before you're expected to sit down at a computer terminal and replicate anything you see here. For now, just glance at the examples and results to get the flavor of SQL and an impression of what the statement is doing.

Here's a SELECT statement that shows you all the data in the *publishers* table, which is part of the *bookbiz* database:

```
SQL:
select *
from publishers
```

The asterisk (*) is a shorthand device for asking for every column in the table. Here are the results the query would produce:

```
Results:
pub_id pub_name                address      city         state
------ ---------------------   -----------  -----------  -----
0736   New Age Books           1 1st St     Boston       MA
0877   Binnet & Hardley        2 2nd Ave.   Washington   DC
1389   Algodata Infosystems    3 3rd Dr.    Berkeley     CA

(3 rows affected)
```

Data modification operations are accomplished using the INSERT, DELETE, and UPDATE keywords, respectively. You can add a row to the *publishers* table like this:

```
SQL:
insert into publishers
values ("0010", "Pragmatics", "4 4th Ln.", "Chicago", "IL")
```

When you look at the data again with a SELECT statement, you see the new row:

```
SQL:
select *
from publishers
```

```
Results:
pub_id pub_name                 address      city           state
------ ----------------------   ----------   -------------  -----
0010   Pragmatics               4 4th Ln.    Chicago        IL
0736   New Age Books            1 1st St     Boston         MA
0877   Binnet & Hardley         2 2nd Ave.   Washington     DC
1389   Algodata Infosystems     3 3rd Dr.    Berkeley       CA
```

Other SQL commands perform data definition operations, such as creating or removing objects like tables, indexes, and views. This statement sets up a table called *test*, with two columns—one called *id* that holds integers, and another called *name* that holds up to 15 characters.

```
SQL:
create table test
(id int,
name char(15))
```

You can SELECT from the *test* table, even before it has any data in it:

```
SQL:
select *
from test
```

Here's what the system shows you:

```
Results:
id      name
------  ---------------
```

```
(0 rows affected)
```

In the final category of SQL statements are data administration or **data control** commands. They allow you to coordinate the use of the database and maintain it in its most efficient state.

One important aspect of administration in a shared database system is the ability to control access to the data. The SQL keyword GRANT, which controls which users can access data, is a good example of an administrative command. Here's a GRANT statement that gives a user named *karen* permission to select data from the *test* table:

```
SQL:
grant select
on test
to karen
```

Before we go on to consider the relational operations, remember that these remarks are strictly introductory—don't try to learn the details of SQL syntax yet.

Relational Operations

Three specific data retrieval (or query) operations are part of the definition of a relational database management system. The relational operations—projection, selection (also called **restriction**), and join—allow you to tell the system exactly what data you want to see. Projection selects columns, selection selects rows, and join brings together data in related tables.

The physical and logical independence described earlier in this chapter means that you don't have to worry about where the data is physically stored, or how to find it—that's the database management system's problem. SQL is considered a **non-procedural** language because it allows you to express what you want without specifying any of the details about where it's located or how to get it.

All three of the data retrieval operations are expressed with the SQL keyword SELECT. This can be confusing: in SQL, you use SELECT not only for the selection operation, but also for projections and joins.

To give you a bit more of the flavor of the all-important SELECT statement, here's a simplified version of its syntax:

```
SQL:
SELECT select_list
FROM table_list
WHERE search_conditions
```

The next sub-sections explain how this deceptively simple-looking statement is used to express all three relational operations.

Projection.   The projection, or project, operation allows you to list (in the select_list) which *columns* you want to see. For example, if you want to see all the rows in the table that contains information about publishers, but only the columns that contain the publishers' names and identification numbers, you'd write this data retrieval statement:

```
SQL:
select pub_id, pub_name
from publishers
```

Here are the results you would get:

```
Results:
 pub_id pub_name
 ------ -----------------------
 0010    Pragmatics
 0736    New Age Books
 0877    Binnet & Hardley
 1389    Algodata Infosystems

(3 rows affected)
```

Once again, don't concern yourself with the SQL syntax at this point. Focus on understanding the conceptual point: *a projection specifies a subset of the columns in the table.* Note that the results of this projection (or any other relational operation) are displayed as a table. Result tables are sometimes referred to as **derived tables** to distinguish them from the **base tables** that contain the raw data.

Selection.   The selection, or select, operation allows you to retrieve a subset of the rows in a table. To specify the rows you want, you put conditions in a WHERE clause. The SELECT statement's WHERE clause specifies the criteria that a row must meet in order to be included in the selection. For example, if you want information about publishers located in California only, here's what you'd type:

```
SQL:
select *
from publishers
where state = "CA"
```

Here are the results you would get:

```
Results:
pub_id pub_name              address       city            state
------ --------------------- ------------- --------------- -----
  1389  Algodata Infosystems  3 3rd Dr.     Berkeley        CA

(1 row affected)
```

You can combine projection and selection in many ways to zero in on just the columns and rows in a table you want to see.

Join.   The join operation works on two or more tables at a time. It combines the data from two or more tables, allowing you to compare and contrast information in your database. The join operation gives SQL and the relational model a good deal of their power and flexibility. You can find any relationship that exists among data elements, not just the relationships you anticipated when you designed your database.

When you "join" two tables, it's as if you're melding them together for the duration of the query. The join operation combines data by comparing values in specified columns and displaying the results.

The easiest way to understand the join operation is with an example. Let's suppose you want to know the name and publisher of all the books in the database. The name of each book is stored in the *titles* table. So is a good deal of other information about each book, including the identification number of its publisher. However, the publisher's name isn't in the *titles* table—that information is in the *publishers* table.

The problem can be solved because both the *publishers* table and the *titles* table contain the publishers' identification numbers: you can join the two tables in order to display the publisher's name along with the book's title. The system tests for every instance in which the two *pub_id* columns are the same; whenever there is a match, it creates a new row—containing columns from both the tables—as the result of the join. Here's the query:

```
SQL:
select title, pub_name
from titles, publishers
where publishers.pub_id = titles.pub_id
```

The *title* column in the SELECT clause comes from the *titles* table; the *pub_name* column from the *publishers* table. Projection can specify columns from several tables in the select list. The FROM clause indicates the two tables that are to be joined; the WHERE clause says that rows in these tables are to be linked when the identification numbers in the two *pub_id* columns are the same.

Here are the results:

```
Results:

title                                  pub_name
-----------------------------          ---------------------
You Can Combat Computer Stress!        New Age Books
Computer Phobic and Non-Phobic
   Individuals: Behavior Variations    New Age Books
Is Anger the Enemy?                    New Age Books
Life Without Fear                      New Age Books
Prolonged Data Deprivation: Four
   Case Studies                        New Age Books
Emotional Security: A New Algorithm    New Age Books
Silicon Valley Gastronomic Treats      Binnet & Hardley
The Gourmet Microwave                  Binnet & Hardley
The Psychology of Computer Cooking     Binnet & Hardley
Onions, Leeks, and Garlic: Cooking
   Secrets of the Mediterranean        Binnet & Hardley
Fifty Years in Buckingham Palace
   Kitchens                            Binnet & Hardley
Sushi, Anyone?                         Binnet & Hardley
The Busy Executive's Database Guide    Algodata Infosystems
Cooking with Computers: Surreptitious
   Balance Sheets                      Algodata Infosystems
```

```
Straight Talk About Computers        Algodata Infosystems
But Is It User Friendly?             Algodata Infosystems
Secrets of Silicon Valley            Algodata Infosystems
Net Etiquette                        Algodata Infosystems

(18 rows affected)
```

At this point in the discussion, you might wonder if we're not overselling the importance of the join operation. Why not just put all those columns in the same table in the first place? you might ask. If the table gets big and unwieldy, why not simply use the projection operation to limit the number of columns that are displayed at one time?

Those are reasonable questions; the answer is that the number of columns in a table must often be limited for reasons of both consistency and convenience. The discussion of database design in the next chapter sets out guidelines for deciding which columns to put into which tables.

Alternatives for Viewing Data

A **view** is an alternative way of looking at the data in one or more tables. Views are sometimes called **virtual tables** or **derived tables**. Another term for the table(s) on which a view is based is **base table(s)**. A view is a shiftable frame through which you can see only the particular data that concerns you. You can derive a view from one or more database tables (or, for that matter, from other views), using any desired selection, projection, and join operations. Views allow you to create customized tables tailored to special needs. In effect, you capture a cluster of selection, projection, and join operations to use as the foundation for future queries.

The data you see when you look at a view (or "through" a view, as it's often put) is not actually stored in the database the way data in "real" or base tables are. It's important to realize that a view is not a copy of the data in another table. When you change data through a view, you're changing the real thing. Like selection results, a view looks like an ordinary database table.

Views are set up with the SQL CREATE VIEW statement. You can make virtually any SELECT statement into a view simply by incorporating it into a CREATE VIEW command. To make the previous example into a view, you would use the CREATE VIEW command shown here:

```
SQL:
create view Books_and_Pubs as
```

```
select title, pub_name
from titles, publishers
where publishers.pub_id = titles.pub_id
```

When you select from the view, it displays results from the query that you used to create it.

In the ideal relational system, you would be able to display a view and operate on it almost exactly as you could any other table. In the real world, different versions of SQL place limitations on view manipulation, in particular with respect to updates. One of Codd's rules explicitly addresses view updatability, stipulating that a true relational system should allow all updates that are "theoretically" possible. Most relational database management systems fall short of his standards on this one.

Chapter 9 is devoted to views, and includes a discussion of what a "theoretically updatable" view means.

Nulls

In the real world of information management, data is often missing or incomplete: you forgot to ask for a phone number, a respondent to a questionnaire refuses to divulge his age, a book has been contracted but the publication date has not been set. Such missing information would leave a gaping hole in your set of tidy tables.

The unsightliness of these holes is not the real problem, of course. The danger is that they might introduce inconsistencies into your database. In order to preserve the integrity of your data, the relational model (and Codd's rules) use the concept of nulls to handle missing information.

Null does not mean zero or blank. Rather, it indicates that a value is unknown, unavailable, or inapplicable. Essentially, the use of nulls changes double-valued logic (yes/no or something/nothing) into triple-valued logic (yes/no/maybe or something/nothing/not sure).

In the opinion of relational expert C.J. Date, nulls are not the perfect solution to the problem of missing information. However, they are an integral part of both the official SQL standard and the *de facto* industry standard. Nulls are such an important topic that they are covered in several chapters: Chapter 3 explains how to set up tables that allow nulls in certain columns; Chapter 4 touches on issues in selecting nulls; Chapter 5 considers nulls with ordering and aggregate functions; and Chapter 6 summarizes the issues regarding nulls in database management.

Security

The security issue can be summarized as the need to control who can use what data, and for what purpose. The SQL GRANT and REVOKE commands allow certain privileged users to choose who will be authorized to look at or change database information. In most SQL implementations, access and data modification permissions can be controlled both on the level of tables and columns.

The privileged users who bestow these permissions are the **owners** of databases and database objects. A user owns a database or one of its objects by virtue of having created it with one of the SQL CREATE commands; some systems allow ownership to be transferred from the creator to another user.

Most multi-user systems designate another privileged user, even higher on the totem pole than owners, who is often referred to as the **system administrator** or **database administrator**. The user in this role often possesses wide powers to grant and revoke permissions (and is also responsible for a variety of other maintenance and administrative tasks).

Views can be used as an additional security mechanism—users can be granted permission to access only the particular subset of data that's included in a view. Views are covered in Chapter 9; the GRANT and REVOKE commands are covered in Chapter 10.

Integrity

Integrity is a serious and complex issue in relational database management. In general, it means the consistency of the data in the database.

Inconsistencies in data arise in several ways. One kind of inconsistency can be introduced by system failure—a hardware problem, a software bug, or a logical error in an application program. Relational database management systems that protect data from this type of inconsistency do so by guaranteeing that SQL commands either run to completion or are canceled. The processes by which this guarantee is enforced is often referred to as **transaction management**. Transactions and SQL's method of handling them are discussed in Chapter 10.

Another kind of integrity, called **entity integrity**, is a design issue. Entity integrity requires that no primary key be allowed to have a null value.

A third variety of data integrity, called **referential integrity**, means consistency among pieces of information that are repeated in more than one table. For example, if you correct an employee's improperly entered social security number in one table, other tables that include employee information probably still reference the old number, so you have to update them, too. *It's vital that when information is changed in one place, it is also changed in every other place it appears.*

Codd's rules firmly state that relational database management systems should support not only entity and referential integrity, but also the ability "to specify additional integrity constraints reflecting either business policies or government regulations." Furthermore, Codd says, integrity constraints must be:

- Definable in the same high-level language used by the rest of the system
- Stored in the data dictionary, not in application programs

At present, only a few implementations of SQL meet Codd's integrity criteria.

Beginning Database Design

Now that you have a basic understanding of relational database systems, you may be impatient to get started. But before you can do any data retrieval or modification, you have to get data into the database. And before you can do that, you have to decide what the database looks like. We cover database design in chapter 2.

Chapter 2

Designing Databases

DATABASE DESIGN

The process of deciding what the database looks like is called **database design**. Informally speaking, designing a database means deciding on the tables that belong in the database and the columns that belong in each table. The design determines how objects interact with each other. This interaction is critical for satisfactory performance and integrity.

Database design is concerned with the *logical* structure of the database. In the relational model, decisions about logical design are completely independent of the database's *physical* storage and structure. The logical structure is also independent of what the end user eventually sees: the designer can customize that by creating views (see Chapter 9 for details) or through the use of front-end application programs.

Database design using the relational model offers several important advantages over the design process used in other database models. The independence of the logical design from both the physical design and the end user's view is one. The intuitiveness of the design process, at least for simple databases, is another. Perhaps most significant, the relational model leaves you with a database design that is flexible—design decisions don't limit the questions you can ask about the data in the future. In other words, since the relational model does not require you to define access paths among your data at design time, you can query about any kind of logical relationship the database contains, not just the relationships for which you originally planned. (In this chapter, we assume that "you" are the database designer.)

On the other hand, relational systems have no *built-in* protections against poor design decisions—no automatic way to distinguish a good design from a bad one. There is simply no set of automated tools that can substitute for your understanding of relational design principles and procedures.

Database design, like some of the other issues touched on in this book, is a very large subject. Professional careers have been devoted to it, and hundreds of articles and dozens of books have been written about it—some of them extremely technical and bristling with jargon and abstract terminology, others aimed at casual users of personal computers. (The ones we've found most helpful are listed in the bibliography.)

While the discussion in this chapter is brief, and decidedly practical rather than theoretical, it is meant to give you enough understanding to design a moderately complex database. It will acquaint you with the jargon and the issues so that you'll be able to tackle more technical discussions of database design if you need to do so. The basic principles are the same whether the database you're designing is simple or complex.

If you're working with a single-user system, of course, you're on your own: there's no design guru to turn to, nor can the system software do the design work for you. On the other hand, a single-user database is likely to be straightforward enough so that, with the help of this chapter, you can bootstrap yourself to design competence.

If you're working in a multi-user situation, on the other hand, the design and creation of the database is usually the job of a specialist. This is especially true if your application is critical to the mission of your organization and involves sharing data with other users. This specialist—whose role may be called system administrator, database administrator, or MIS specialist—is qualified by his or her experience and understanding of the local computing environment, the organization's business policies, and the rules of relational database design. A database designer who is knowledgeable about all of these factors is more likely to provide a database that is easy to use and maintain, as well as conducive to efficiency and consistency.

Even if you'll be relying on an expert for database design, this chapter will help you become a better SQL user by showing you how to analyze the relationships among the data. A grasp of relational design issues is invaluable both in learning and practicing SQL, and in maintaining, updating, or querying a database that someone else has set up. Furthermore, when it comes time to ask the design guru for help, knowledge of the ground rules will make your questions and requests more intelligent.

Like the rest of *The Practical SQL Handbook*, this chapter takes the *bookbiz* database as its main example. Once you've worked your way through this chapter and come to understand how *bookbiz* is designed, you'll need to know how to put it on-line with the SQL CREATE commands—a process called data definition. We discuss data definition in Chapter 3.

Other issues connected to database design and data definition include customization (setting up views tailored to each end user's needs—see Chapter 9), security (deciding who to authorize for what operations on what data—see Chapter 10), and integrity (guaranteeing the consistency of related data items—see Chapter 10).

How to Approach Database Design

Discussions of database design for relational systems—this one included—often seem schizophrenic. On the one hand, you're told that the relational model makes database design intuitive and easy; on the other hand, you're told that unless your database is "simple" (whatever that is), you'll either have to refer to other sources (sounds ominous), or let the gurus do it for you (so why bother to wade through endless explanations?).

Recognizing this confusion, relational theorist C.J. Date postulates that "database design has the property that (in simple cases at least) it is often easier just to do it than to try and articulate exactly what it was you did." Our attempt to explain exactly what to do when you design a database combines encouragement and education for your intuitive impulses with brief (and sketchy) discussions of two design aids—**entity-relationship modeling** and **normalization**.

Educating the intuition is mostly a matter of demonstrating a few mistakes that beginning designers are likely to make. Once the flaws have been pointed out, the correct structures should become obvious by comparison.

As for the formal design methodologies, most experts stress that they are guidelines rather than rigid rules. The best way to describe the existence of real-world objects and the relationships among them is to some degree a subjective matter—almost as much in database design as in natural language. Often there's more than one correct solution to a design problem, and there is sometimes good reason to violate even the most basic design rule.

But this doesn't mean that the theories of database design are not useful. Even as a beginner it's important that you understand the basics. As your experience grows you will probably rely on the formal methodologies more and more, but don't let them tyrannize you.

Getting Started.   Many discussions of relational database design focus almost entirely on how to apply the normalization rules. Basically, normalization means splitting tables that initially seem to "make sense" into two or more related tables that can be "put back together" with the join operation. The technical term for this process is **non-loss decomposition**, which simply means splitting a table into several smaller tables without the loss of information.

The normalization guidelines are most valuable as an *ex post facto* check on your work: once you have a pretty good idea which columns go into which tables, you can analyze them according to the normalization rules in order to make sure you haven't committed any database design *faux pas*. An understanding of normalization can also guide you as you build your design, but it's not a recipe for creating a database structure from scratch.

So how do you figure out what columns go where in the first place? What *is* the recipe? The answer is that there isn't a very precise one. But you can get a good deal of help from entity-relationship modeling— analyzing the data in terms of the **entities** (objects or things) it describes and the relationships (one-to-one, one-to-many, or many-to-many) between those entities. Different kinds of entities and different kinds of relationships are represented differently in the database.

In practice, designing a database requires combining a thorough understanding of the world you're trying to model with intuition and at least a nodding acquaintance with entity-relationship modeling and normalization. Then, you do it again. In other words, database design is usually an iterative process, in which you keep getting closer and closer to what you want, but often move back a step or two and redo earlier work as you refine your idea of what you need.

To give you a more concrete idea, here's an example of some steps you might follow when you design a database:

1. The first step in the design process, and perhaps the most important and time-consuming one, has nothing to do with the database management system *per se*. It involves investigating and thinking about the information environment you're modeling. Where will the information come from and in what form? How will it be entered into the system and by whom? How frequently will it change? What is most critical in terms of response time and availability?

    Examine all paper and/or on-line files and forms that are currently used to store and track the organization's data; consider also what kind of output is needed from the database—reports, purchase orders, statistical information—and for whom. In a shared database environment, you'll need to collect information by interviewing other people in the organization, either individually or in groups. Don't forget anyone who will be involved in any way with the data—generating it, handling it, changing it, querying it, making reports from it.

2. Make a list of the entities (things that are the subjects of the database), along with their properties or attributes. The entities are likely to wind up being tables (each table describing one thing, like a person or company or book); the properties are likely to be represented as columns in a table (the person's salary, the company's address, the book's price).

3. Now comes the task of checking how the columns are grouped. Do the entities work as tables, or do some columns need to be moved from one group to another? This is the heart of the design process, and naturally enough this task is the one that relies most heavily on the formal methodologies.

4. As you work, find a systematic way to record the design decisions you're making, either on paper or with a text editor. You might make a list of the tables, columns, keys, and so on; or you might prefer drawing sketches of the tables and the relationships among them. This chapter includes examples of both. You can also record some of your design decisions with the SQL CREATE statements (which collectively are sometimes called DDL, or data definition language, statements). The advantage of using SQL is that you have to write the data definition statements anyway. Its disadvantage is that most implementations of SQL do not include syntax for some crucial design concepts (more on that later). C.J. Date recommends using what he calls *pseudoDDL*, by which he means the SQL DDL statements coupled with additional language that he has invented for recording the missing concepts.

5. Once you have a draft of the database design, look at it as a whole and analyze it according to the normalization guidelines to find logical errors. Correct any violations of the normal forms—or make a conscious decision to override the normalization guidelines in the interests of ease of comprehension or performance. Document the reasons for such decisions.

6. Now you're ready to put the database on line and to add some prototype data, using SQL for both steps. Try out some of the queries

and reports you think you'll need. You may want to make some benchmark tests (see Chapter 10) to try out a few variations on the design or on the indexes you choose.

7. Re-evaluate what you've done in the light of how satisfied you are with the results.

Most of the rest of this chapter is devoted to an explanation of how we approached the design of the *bookbiz* database. This detailed step-by-step discussion should help you understand the database design process.

Characteristics of a Good Design

What is meant by a good database design—a "clean" design, as the jargon has it? Broadly speaking, a good design:

- Makes your interactions with the database easier to understand
- Guarantees the consistency of the database
- Paves the way for the highest performance your system can deliver

Some factors that make a database easy to understand are not technically part of database design. However, tables wider than a terminal screen are inescapably clumsy and can contribute to user misunderstanding and error. On the other hand, splitting data into many small tables makes it hard to see relationships among columns when you're looking at data on your terminal screen or in a printout. Settling on the right number of columns is sometimes a compromise between ease of comprehension and adherence to the normalization guidelines.

A well-designed database helps prevent (or at least minimize) the introduction of inconsistent information and the unintentional deletion of information. It accomplishes these ends by minimizing the unnecessary duplication of data within tables and by providing mechanisms to support referential integrity among tables. The perils of data inconsistency are explained in more detail later in this chapter.

Finally, a well-designed database is a prerequisite for satisfactory performance. Again, the number of columns in a table is important: the retrieval of data can be slower if results have to come from many tables rather than from one table. On the other hand, huge tables can require the system to handle more data than may be absolutely necessary to answer a particular query. In other words, number and size of tables affects performance. (Also crucial for performance purposes are appropriate choices about which columns to index, and what kind of indexes to put on them. Indexing is a matter of physical design rather than of logical database design. Indexing is discussed in Chapter 3 and in Chapter 10.)

Those are some of the benefits of good database design. A bad design, on the other hand, can foster misunderstandings of query results, increase the risk of introducing inconsistencies in the data, force redundant data entry, and make life difficult if you need to change the structure of the tables that you've built and filled with data. In some installations, the effect of a bad design on performance is the most worrisome aspect: long waits on data updates or retrievals can be caused by too many indexes (or too few of them), or by leaving tables unnecessarily large (or making them unnecessarily small). When relational systems are used with very large databases and high volumes of transactions, the performance implications of a poor design are magnified.

No single solution can fully satisfy all the objectives of good design. Frequently, the question for a database designer is one of a tradeoff, and the tradeoff may ultimately depend on the needs and uses of the application for which the database is being designed.

Introducing the Sample Database

The first characteristic to note about the *bookbiz* database is that it is not a real-world database, but simply a learning tool. Its primary purpose is to provide you with a small collection of interesting data to manipulate as you study SQL syntax and semantics. Outside of its size, it's not very different from a database that someone might actually set up and use.

The *bookbiz* database is about a fictional publishing company that has three subsidiary publishing lines. The database stores information that editors, administrators, and executives might want about books, their authors, their editors, and the company's financial arrangements. It can produce many kinds of reports summarizing current sales, comparing different book lines, discovering which editors work with which authors, and so on. In real life, the database would probably support many other kinds of uses and many more kinds of reports.

Users of the *bookbiz* database can pose many different questions, including these:

- Which authors live in California?
- Which business books cost more than $9.95?
- Who has written the greatest number of books?

- How much do we owe the author of *Life Without Fear*?
- What's the average advance paid for all the psychology books?
- How would increasing the price of all the cookbooks by ten percent affect royalty payments?
- How are sales of the computer subsidiary doing?

As the database designer, don't try to just imagine what questions are most important to the future users of the database you're designing. You need to research their needs by reviewing current data collection and retrieval methods and by interviewing your users individually and/or in groups.

One important area of investigation is the business rules and policies of the organization that affect the data. The policies of the publisher for which *bookbiz* is being designed include these:

- An author may have written more than one book.
- A book may have been a collaborative project of more than one author.
- The order of the authors' names on the title page is critical information, as is the percentage of the royalties each will collect.
- An editor may be working on more than one book, and a single book may be assigned more than one editor.

DATA ENTITIES AND RELATIONSHIPS

We begin the consideration of designing *bookbiz* with a somewhat simplified version of entity-relationship modeling. At the most basic level, entity-relationship modeling (also called **entity modeling**) means identifying the important things—entities—about which information will be stored in the database system, identifying the important properties of these things, and identifying the important relationships among them. Then you apply the rules of entity-relationship modeling for representing entities, properties, relationships (and a few other elements) in the database.

Entities: Things with an Independent Existence

Let's start by considering the entities that make up a subset of the *bookbiz* database. Ignoring for the moment most of the financial information that *bookbiz* tracks, a preliminary list of entities might be:

- The authors who have written books published by the company
- The books themselves
- The editors working for the company
- The subsidiary publishing houses owned by the company

Each item in this list is an entity with an independent existence in the world under consideration—the world of the *bookbiz* database. Each is represented in the database by a table. (Other kinds of data elements are also represented by tables, but that's jumping ahead of the story.)
    Each of these entity types has certain properties that are to be recorded in the database. Among the properties are:

```
book's name
book's price
book's publication date
author's name
author's address
author's telephone number
editor's name
editor's address
editor's phone number
publisher's name
publisher's address
```

Each item in this list refers to one property or attribute of the entity in question (the author, book, editor, or publishing subsidiary); each is a potential column in the database. Column names should be selected for clarity (to describe the kinds of values the column names) and brevity (to minimize both typing and the width of displays). The **domain** of a column, or the set of values from which the column's values can be drawn, is specified in different ways in different database systems. Some systems allow you to designate only the column's datatype (such as alphabetic or numeric) and null status. Others let you specify the domain much more precisely. Domains are discussed in detail in the section on integrity in Chapter 10.
    The list of entities and their properties we've identified might be taken as a first tentative step in deciding on the tables and columns to be included in the database. You might sketch these decisions like this:

```
titles table
name                 price                   pub_date
--------------        ----------------------  -----------
```

```
authors table
name                 address          phone
--------------        --------------   ------------
```

```
editors table
name                 address          phone
--------------        --------------   ------------
```

```
publishers table
name                 address
--------------        --------------
```

This sketch of four tables, each with several columns, is a first stab at the structure of the database; you can imagine that each table will contain multiple rows of data. Each row in a table represents an **occurrence** (or **instance**) of the entity—a single book, author, editor, or publishing company.

One of the jobs of the database design is to provide a way to distinguish among entity occurrences, so that the system can retrieve a particular row. As you might have guessed, rows (representing occurrences of entities) are distinguished from each other by the values of the table's primary key. In fact, the (informal) definition of a primary key is the column or combination of columns that uniquely identifies the row.

Primary Keys.   What is the primary key for each of these tables? Consider the *authors* table. Of the columns identified so far, *name* is the obvious candidate for the primary key: an author's name distinguishes him or her from other authors. But the *name* column is problematic as a primary key for several reasons. First, the value in *name* is made up of the author's first name and last name. Combining first and last names is usually a bad idea, if only because it would be difficult (in many systems, impossible) to sort authors alphabetically by last name. So the first necessary change is to split the *name* column into two columns, like this:

```
authors table
au_lname             au_fname          address            phone
--------------        --------------   --------------     -------
```

(Setting up separate columns for the authors' first and last names also satisfies the first normalization rule, which states in part that each column in a row must contain only one value, and that the value cannot be broken down into smaller meaningful values. A composite datatype such as *datetime* could permit a column value that is composite.)

Now, getting back to the question of identifying the primary key of the *authors* table, it might seem as though the combination of the columns *au_lname* and *au_fname* is the right choice. In fact, that combination would work pretty well—until the table grew large enough to contain duplicate names. Once there are two Mary Smiths, for example, the *au_lname-au_fname* combination would no longer uniquely identify each author.

Another problem with using values like names as unique identifiers is the frequency with which they are entered incorrectly. It's easy to misspell names: imagine a data entry clerk on the phone entering a new record about Anne Ringer—or is it Ann Ringer? Other kinds of proper names, like names of companies or organizations, are even worse. How many variations might there be on the name of the phone company, for example: AT&T, A.T. and T., Ma Bell, and so on. To a computer, these are all different companies.

For these reasons, it's usually a good idea to create a separate column explicitly designed to serve as the primary key. Real-world examples of such unique identifiers are common: social security numbers, employee identification numbers, license plate numbers, purchase order numbers, student identification numbers, airline flight numbers, and so on. Theoretically, any datatype can be used for a primary key column, but in practice primary keys are often created as character columns.

In the *authors* table, arbitrarily assigned codes could have served as unique identifiers. Instead, we chose to use social security numbers, a common practice. With its new primary key column, the structure of the *authors* table looks like this:

```
authors table
au_id       au_lname        au_fname        address      phone
----------  --------------  --------------  -----------  -------
```

Choosing and setting up the column(s) for a table's primary key is one of the crucial steps in database design. Despite the importance of primary keys, however, there is no SQL syntax for designating them. (SQL has been roundly criticized for this omission, and a few implementations of the language have corrected the problem).

Although most SQLs do not explicitly support primary keys, you can enforce the uniqueness of values in the primary key column(s) by creating a unique index on it (or them). The presence of a unique index guarantees that INSERT or UPDATE commands that would introduce a duplicate value in the primary key column(s) are rejected.

There's one more guarantee related to primary keys that you can enforce in all versions of SQL that support nulls. When you define the primary key column(s), you can specify that it (or they) not allow null values. Since the primary key is an identifier that must exist, it never makes sense for its value to be null.

Here are the other *bookbiz* tables under consideration, with primary key columns added:

```
titles table
title_id         name              price        pub_date
---------------  ---------------   ----------   ------------------

editors table
ed_id            name              address      phone
---------------  ---------------   ---------------  -------------

publishers table
pub_id           name              address
---------------  ---------------   ---------------
```

The primary key values for editors (in the *ed_id* column) are social security numbers. Publishers' IDs (in *pub_id*) are arbitrary four-digit codes, and book IDs (in *title_id*) are two uppercase letters representing the book's type followed by four digits.

As previously mentioned, it's a good idea to keep track of your decisions about tables, their columns, and their primary keys as you go. In the case of tables and columns (indexes too), these decisions will eventually be reflected in SQL data definition statements. They are also recorded in the data dictionary, where structural and other information about the database is centrally stored (largely for use by the system itself and by application programs).

Your choices of primary keys, however, won't appear explicitly in any SQL statements or in the data dictionary (at least, not in the majority of SQL dialects). This makes it all the more important to record these design decisions somehow: in a chart, in a picture, in system files, or in comments in the data definition statements.

One-to-Many Relationships

At this point we have structures for four tables in the *bookbiz* database: *authors*, *titles*, *editors*, and *publishers*. Some of the properties of each of the entities described by the tables have been specified, and a primary key has been identified for each table.

However, you may have noticed that certain important relationships among the data are not yet represented in the proposed design. For example, there's nothing in these four tables that tells you about the relationship between a particular publisher and the books it puts out.

The relationship between publishers and books can be described as **one-to-many**: each book has only one publisher, while each publisher can put out many books. One-to-many relationships among data are often written as 1-to-N (or 1-to-M) or 1:N (or 1:M). Such relationships are sometimes called **designations**.

How can this one-to-many relationship be represented in the database? In the *bookbiz* database, a first impulse might be to put the books in the *publishers* table. The first cut (with only a few columns and a couple rows of data shown) might look like this:

```
publishers table

pub_id pub_name              title
------ --------------------- -------------------------
0736   New Age Books         Is Anger the Enemy?
1389   Algodata Infosystems  But Is It User Friendly
```

Unfortunately, this proposed table sends your database design off in the wrong direction. Remember the data relationship we're modeling—one publisher, many books—and consider what happens when one of the publishers, say New Age Books, publishes another book. Where does title number two go? Do we add it to the same column as the first title?

```
publishers table

pub_id pub_name             title
------ -------------------- ---------------------------------------------
0736   New Age Books        Is Anger the Enemy?       Life Without Fear
1389   Algodata Infosystems But Is It User Friendly?
```

Although only a small number of rows are shown for the sake of readability, it's already possible to see some of the problems this plan would
create:

- Since SQL refers to columns by name, there is no simple way to distinguish one value in the *title* column from another.
- There's no obvious place to put all the other information about
  books—their prices, publication dates, and so on. It would be very
  difficult to store that data in this table while maintaining a clear
  relationship between each book and its properties.
- The absence of a second value in some rows—whenever a publisher
  has only one book to its name—is confusing.

Multi-valued columns like the one shown here—also known as repeating
groups—are often found in non-relational database management systems.
In relational database systems, multi-valued columns are (by definition)
not allowed: at each row-and-column intersection, there must be one and
only one value.

This requirement also happens to be the first of the normalization
rules. Informally, the first normalization rule states that:

- Each column in a row can have only one value, and that value must
  be **atomic**—that is, it cannot be broken down into smaller meaningful values.
- Each row has a fixed number of columns (that is, the table takes on
  a "rectangular" shape, with each row having the same number of
  columns).

The requirements of the first normalization rule (also known as **first
normal form**) are actually part of the definition of the relational model.

Now, what is the correct way of overcoming this violation of first normal form, this problem of repeating groups? You can't just create a table
with more than one *title* column:

```
publishers table
pub_id pub_name               title1                    title2
------ -------------------     ------------------------  ------------------
0736   New Age Books           Is Anger the Enemy?       Life Without Fear
1389   Algodata Infosystems    But Is It User Friendly?
```

This scheme doesn't change the situation—it's just a disguise for repeating groups, and leaves you with the same problems. It's not a great solution practically speaking, either; as soon as a publisher produces a third book, you'll have to restructure the table again, adding a *title3* column.

Where there is a one-to-many relationship (one publisher, many books) the correct design involves a separate row for each book:

```
publishers table
pub_id  pub_name                 title
------  --------------------     --------------------------
0736    New Age Books            Is Anger the Enemy?
0736    New Age Books            Life Without Fear
1389    Algodata Infosystems     But Is It User Friendly?
```

The *publishers* table is now in first normal form. Here's what it looks like when we add additional information about each publisher and substitute title ID numbers for the names of the books:

```
publishers table
pub_id  pub_name                 city      state  title_id
------  --------------------     --------  -----  --------
0736    New Age Books            Boston    MA     PS2091
0736    New Age Books            Boston    MA     PS2106
1389    Algodata Infosystems     Berkeley  CA     PC1035
```

Another problem can now be seen, even with only a small amount of data. Think about what happens when more books are added: since each publisher is associated with many books, the publishers' names, and all the other publisher information, will be repeated in many rows of the table.

Recall that one of the goals of database design is to control redundancy, because redundancy introduces opportunities for error. In this situation, the redundancy can be eliminated by associating publishers and their books in the *titles* table rather than in the *publishers* table. Here's what the two tables would look like (for the sake of readability, only some of the columns in the *titles* table, and some of the rows of both tables, are shown here):

```
publishers table
pub_id  pub_name                 city       state
-------  --------------------     ---------  ------
0736    New Age Books            Boston     MA
1389    Algodata Infosystems     Berkeley   CA

titles table
title_id  title                        type            pub_id   price
--------  --------------------------   -------------   -------  -------
PS2091    Is Anger the Enemy?          psychology      0736     $10.95
PS2106    Life Without Fear            psychology      0736     $ 7.00
PC1035    But Is It User Friendly?     popular_comp    1389     $22.95
```

Now the *publishers* table has one row for each publisher; the name and address of each publisher appear once in the database. The *titles* table has one row for each book and information about each book appears only once in the database. Each row in the *titles* table includes the book publisher's ID number. There are many books for each publisher, a fact that is reflected in the repetition of publisher ID numbers in more than one row in the *titles* table—but that's far less redundancy than would occur with any of the other options.

The one-to-many relationship between publishers and books is represented in this scheme by the logical connection between the *pub_id* columns in the two tables—a connection that can be made in the database by joining the two tables. *In other words, this design has been planned with the join operation in mind, in order to allow any user to retrieve information about both publishers and titles with just one query.*

In the *publishers* table, *pub_id* is the primary key. In the *titles* table, the *pub_id* column is called the **foreign key**. The relational model requires that one-to-many relationships be represented by means of primary key-foreign key pairings.

Foreign Keys.   Like the concept of primary key, the concept of foreign key is crucial in database design. Informally, a foreign key is a column (or combination of columns) in one table whose values match those of the primary key in some other table.

SQL provides no explicit support for foreign keys; as with primary keys, it's a good idea to record your design decisions about foreign keys. Unlike primary keys, foreign keys sometimes can have null values. In the case of books and publishers, it doesn't make much sense to allow the *titles.pub_id* column to be null. If a book didn't have a publisher, it probably wouldn't be part of the *bookbiz* database at all. Based on this real-world assumption, the designer of the database would probably specify that the *titles.pub_id* column should not allow null values.

But there are other cases in which allowing null values in a foreign key does make sense. For example, the *bookbiz* database includes information about editors, and about which editors are working on which books. The identity of the book's editor might be stored in the *titles* table in a foreign key column that matched the primary key of the *editors* table. (That's not the final design of the *bookbiz* database, but imagine it for the sake of this example.) If company policy allowed for a book to be listed without an assigned editor, then the foreign key containing the editor's identity (name or ID number or whatever) should allow null values.

Note that the decision about whether to allow nulls in a foreign key depends not on theoretical considerations, but on the logical meaning of the relationship between the information in the primary and foreign key columns—and that depends on the real-world situation: a company policy, an organization's rule, etc.

A consideration of the logical relationship between the information in the primary and foreign key columns introduces some further questions. What happens in the *pub_id* column of the *titles* table if the row describing the publisher is deleted from or changed in the *publishers* table? Should the description of a book be allowed to refer to a publisher ID number if that publisher no longer exists in the database? It doesn't make sense logically, and it violates the definition of a foreign key, which requires the value in a foreign key column(s) to match the value in a primary key column somewhere in the database.

A complete database design should include planning for primary key/foreign key consistency (or referential integrity). Unfortunately, in most implementations of SQL the planner is hampered by the absence of syntax for designating keys and/or maintaining referential integrity.

There are three basic ways to handle the referential integrity problem, as illustrated by the relationship between a book and its publisher:

- When a publisher's ID number is updated in or deleted from the *publishers* table, the system should automatically reproduce the change in the *titles* table, either by updating all corresponding values in the *titles.pub_id* column or by deleting any rows that reference it. (The latter solution is probably too drastic in this case, but would make sense in certain situations).
- Instead of deleting an entire row in *titles* or updating *titles.pub_id* with the new publisher ID, the system could first set *titles.pub_id* to null, and then delete from or update the *publishers* table.

- When a SQL command that would update or delete a value in *publishers.pub_id* is submitted, the command can be rejected by the database system.

Most SQL dialects don't have special facilities for implementing these solutions. The best you can do in many database systems is to prohibit the data modification operations that could potentially violate referential integrity, using the GRANT and REVOKE commands. (See Chapter 10 for a discussion of GRANT and REVOKE.)

Most database systems rely on application programs to provide special-purpose guarantees of referential integrity. This lack of centralization becomes particularly problematic when more than one application runs on the same database. (We return to this issue in Chapter 10, and explain the Transact-SQL extension that handles referential integrity in the database system itself.)

Many-to-Many Relationships

After identifying all the one-to-many relationships in the *bookbiz* database, and representing them with primary key-foreign key pairings, the next step is to consider other kinds of data relationships. For example, how are authors and books related?

Some books are written by more than one author and some authors have written more than one book. In other words, authors and books have a **many-to-many** relationship (often written as N-to-N, M-to-M, N:N, or M:M, and sometimes called an **association**). According to entity-relationship theory, associations in relational databases are represented as tables of their own. In other words, the *bookbiz* database needs a table for authors, a table for titles, and a table to represent the association between them, like this:

titles table

title_id	title	type	pub_id	price
PS2091	Is Anger the Enemy?	psychology	0736	$10.95
PS2106	Life Without Fear	psychology	0736	$ 7.00
PC1035	But Is It User Friendly?	popular_comp	1389	$22.95
MC3021	The Gourmet Microwave	mod_cook	0877	$ 2.99

authors table:

au_id	au_lname	au_fname	city	state
238-95-7766	Carson	Cheryl	Berkeley	CA
998-72-3567	Ringer	Albert	Salt Lake City	UT
899-46-2035	Ringer	Anne	Salt Lake City	UT
722-51-5454	DeFrance	Michel	Gary	IN

titleauthors table:

au_id	title_id	au_ord	royaltyshare
238-95-7766	PC1035	1	1.00
998-72-3567	PS2091	1	.50
899-46-2035	PS2091	2	.50
899-46-2035	MC3021	2	.25
722-51-5454	MC3021	1	.75
998-72-3567	PS2106	1	1.00

(Again, for the sake of readability, not all of the columns and rows of the *titles*, *authors*, and *titleauthors* tables are shown.)

The *titleauthors* table represents the many-to-many relationship between authors and books. It is a base table just like *titles* and *authors*, but it represents an association rather than an independent entity. When a user of the *bookbiz* database wants information about who wrote which books, he or she writes a join query that uses the *titleauthors* table as a connecting table between *titles* and *authors*.

The *titleauthors* and *titles* table join on their respective *title_id* columns; *titleauthors* and *authors* join on each table's *au_id* column. In other words, *titleauthors.title_id* is the foreign key whose matching primary key is *titles.title_id*; *titleauthors.au_id* is the foreign key whose matching primary key is *authors.au_id*. The general principle, as stated by C.J. Date, is that "in the relational model, participants in an association are identified by foreign keys with the table representing that association."

What is the primary key in *titleauthors*? Neither the author ID nor the title ID uniquely identifies rows in *titleauthors*: the IDs of titles with more than one author are repeated, as are the IDs of authors who have written more than one book. However, each title ID-author ID combination *is* unique. As Date puts it, "for a given association, it will often be the case that the combination of all foreign keys for participants in that association will have the uniqueness property." The primary key of *titleauthors*, then, is the combination of *title_id* and *au_id*.

The Entity-Relationship Approach Summarized. Entity-relationship modeling is much larger, more precise, and more detailed than the procedures discussed so briefly here indicate. However, the approach just outlined can help you design a good database that checks out against the next design methodology to be considered, the normalization rules. Before turning to that topic, here is a review list of the basic steps discussed so far:

1. Represent each independent entity (book, author, publisher, editor, employee, department, student, course, company, etc.) as a base table. Designate its primary key.

2. Represent each many-to-many relationship (or association) as a "connecting table" between the two tables representing the independent entities that participate in the association. Include in this connecting table foreign keys that point to the entity tables. The primary key of the connecting table is probably the combination of those foreign keys.

3. One-to-many relationships are not represented as tables. Instead, represent each one-to-many relationship by making sure there is a foreign key column(s) in the "many" table pointing to the primary key column(s) in the "one" table. Plan for the referential integrity constraints associated with each foreign key.

4. Represent each property of an entity (author's address, book's type, etc.) as a column of the entity's table.

THE NORMALIZATION GUIDELINES

The entity-relationship approach instigated the decision to represent the association among *publishers* and *authors* as a separate table. You might have reached the same decision on the basis of the normalization rules.

The references made so far in this chapter to the normalization rules may have made them sound somewhat mysterious. Therefore, before illustrating what they say, here are a few general words about them.

Basically, the normalization guidelines are a set of data design standards called the **normal forms**. Five normal forms are widely accepted, although many more than that have been proposed. Making your tables match these standards is called normalization.

The normal forms progress in order from first through fifth. Each form implies that the requirements of the previous forms have been met. If you follow normalization rule number one, your data will be in first normal form. If you follow normalization rule number three, your data will be in **third normal form** (and also in first and **second normal form**).

Following the normalization guidelines usually means splitting tables into two or more tables with fewer columns. Primary key-foreign key relationships are designed into the new smaller tables, so that they can be reconnected with the join operation.

One of the main advantages of splitting tables according to the normalization guidelines is the reduction of data redundancy within tables. This statement may seem confusing when you realize that the existence of matching primary key-foreign key hooks means that data among tables is unavoidably duplicated. But *intentional duplication* is not the same thing as redundancy. In fact, the maintenance of intentional duplication (that is, consistency) between primary and foreign keys is the whole point of referential integrity.

The normalization guidelines, like entity-relationship modeling, were developed as part of the academic work on database theory. While they are extremely useful, they can be followed too slavishly. Most database designers find that putting their data in third or fourth normal form is usually as far as they need to go.

First Normal Form

As we learned when we discussed one-to-many relationships, first normal form requires that *at each row-and-column intersection, there must be one and only one value.* In other words, each column in a row can have only one value, and that value must be atomic. Another way of stating the same thing: there can be no repeating groups in a table that satisfies first normal form.

Second Normal Form

To illustrate second normal form and the rationale for it, look at this version of the *authors* table:

authors2 table

au_id	title_id	au_lname	au_fname	city	state
238-95-7766	PC1035	Carson	Cheryl	Berkeley	CA
998-72-3567	PS2091	Ringer	Albert	Salt Lake City	UT
899-46-2035	PS2091	Ringer	Anne	Salt Lake City	UT
899-46-2035	MC3021	Ringer	Anne	Salt Lake City	UT
998-72-3567	PS2106	Ringer	Albert	Salt Lake City	UT
722-51-5454	MC3021	DeFrance	Michel	Gary	IN

This table is in first normal form, since it has only one value at each row-and-column intersection. Its primary key is the combination of the *au_id* and *title_id* columns, since neither one by itself has the property of uniqueness. But a problem is immediately obvious: the repetition of information about the author threatens data consistency. Each time an author's ID appears, his or her name and address information (in the finished design, street address and phone number would be included too) are repeated. If, for example, Albert Ringer moved to a new city, it would be all too easy to change one occurrence and forget to change the others. This is the problem that second normal form addresses.

The second normalization rule states that *every non-key column must depend on the entire primary key*. Therefore, a table must not contain a non-key column that pertains to only *part* of a composite primary key. Putting a table into second normal form requires making sure that all the non-primary key columns (the columns that give information about the subject but do not uniquely define it) relate to the entire primary key and not just to one of its components.

In the language of normalization, the problem with the *authors2* table is that an author's name, city, and state are facts only about the author ID, and not about all parts of the author ID-title ID key. Thus, the second normalization rule dictates that *authors2* be split into two tables, one for titles and one for authors. The normalization rules do not explicitly suggest the design of a third table, *titleauthors*, to represent the many-to-many relationship among the titles and authors. But if you analyze the three tables—*titles*, *authors*, and *titleauthors*—according to the normalization rules, you'll find that all of them pass with flying colors.

In sum, second normal form requires that *no non-key column be a fact about a subset of the primary key*. It applies when the primary key is made up of more than one column, and is irrelevant when the primary key is one column only.

Third Normal Form

Third normal form applies the principle addressed by second normal form in a more general way: it's not limited to *composite* primary keys. Third normal form requires that *no non-key column depend on another non-key column*. Each non-key column must be a fact about the primary key column.

Here's an example. This table contains information about books and their editors. Its primary key is the *title_id* column.

```
title_id  type             ed_lname              phone
--------  --------------   -------------------   ------------
MC2222    mod_cook         Rutherford-Hayes      301 468-3909
MC3021    mod_cook         Rutherford-Hayes      301 468-3909
PC1035    popular_comp     Samuelson             415 843-6990
PC8888    popular_comp     Samuelson             415 843-6990
TC3218    trad_cook        Rutherford-Hayes      301 468-3909
TC4203    trad_cook        Rutherford-Hayes      301 468-3909
TC7777    trad_cook        Rutherford-Hayes      301 468-3909
```

The type of a book is a fact about the primary key, as is the editor's name. However, the editor's phone number depends on the editor, and not directly on the title.

A violation of third normal form can lead to inconsistencies because the editor's phone number is repeated each time the editor's name appears, and must be updated in many places each time it changes. You can correct the situation by (again) splitting the table into two tables, one to store information about editors and one to store information about titles.

Actually, the relationship among titles and editors is an association, just like the relationship among titles and authors: more than one editor can be assigned to a book, and each editor can be responsible for more than one book. Therefore, the situation calls for three tables: *titles*, *editors*, and *titleditors*.

```
titles table
title_id    title                            type
pub_id      price            advance          ytd_sales
contract    pub_date         notes
----------  ---------------  --------------   ----------
```

```
editors table
ed_id          ed_lname           ed_fname           ed_pos
phone          address            city               state       zip
-----------    ------------------ ----------------   ----------  ------


titleditors table
ed_id          title_id ed_ord
-----------    -------- ------
```

Analyzing the structures of these three tables, you'll see that they all satisfy both second and third normal forms. They satisfy second normal form because every non-key column is a fact about the entire primary key. The satisfy third normal form because no non-key column is a fact about another non-key column. To summarize, in William Kent's memorable phrase: *every non-key column provides a fact about the key, the whole key, and nothing but the key.*

Fourth and Fifth Normal Forms

Fourth normal form *forbids independent one-to-many relationships between primary key columns and non-key columns.* Using a rather unlikely example as illustration, one author can have many cars and many pets, but there is no connection between cars and pets even though each is legitimately related to a particular author.

```
au_lname   car                           pet
---------- ----------------------------- --------
Ringer     1987 Chevy Nova               Rover
Ringer     1977 Volvo Station Wagon
Bennet     1984 VW Rabbit                Spot
Green      1985 Toyota Corolla           Fluffy
Green      Valiant
Green                                    Sam
```

Putting these two different kinds of information in the same table can lead to unsightly blanks where there are more pets than cars (as in Green's case) or more cars than pets (as in Ringer's case). Deleting a car or a pet (if a car dies or a pet moves to another home) could also cause blanks in rows.

The problem here is with the spurious relationship that seems to exist between cars and pets by virtue of their positional association in the row. It is better to put each of these entities in a separate table, and record their relationship to an author by using the author ID as a foreign key column. For example:

```
pet       author_id
------    --------------------
Rover     998-72-3567
Spot      409-56-7008
Fluffy    213-46-8915
Valiant   213-46-8915
Sam       213-46-8915
```

Fifth normal formal takes the process to its logical end, *breaking tables into the smallest possible pieces in order to eliminate all redundancy within a table*. Tables normalized to this extent consist of little more than the primary key. Here's an example:

```
titles table
title_id  titlename

authors table
author_id authorname

authors&titles table
author_id title_id

prices table
title_id  price

advances table
title_id  advance

pets table
pet       author_id
```

One advantage in putting a database into fifth normal form is control of database integrity. Since you are assured that each piece of non-key data (data that is not a primary key or a foreign key) is likely to occur only once in the database, it's relatively easy to update that kind of data without worrying about keeping all the duplicates up to date. If a book's price changes, for example, you make an entry in the *prices* table only. You don't have to scan the other tables to see if the price appears there.

However, since each table has so few columns, you have to repeat the same keys over and over in order to be able to join the tables and get meaningful information out of them. Changing the value of a single key (a particular *title_id*, for example) is a consistency problem of a different order. You still have to identify every place where that value exists and make sure it gets updated. Fortunately, the values in primary key columns tend to change much less frequently than those in non-key, dependent columns.

The moral is moderation: strive to reach a balance between redundant data and redundant keys.

SKETCHING THE DATABASE

Let's review the process by which the design of the *bookbiz* database was developed. We started by proposing four tables: *authors*, *titles*, *publishers*, and *editors*. It seems intuitive to design a table for each of these things; the entity-relationship approach states explicitly that each independent entity be represented by a base table. Entity-relationship theory also called for two more base tables—one to model the association among *titles* and *authors* (*titleauthors*), and one for the association among *titles* and *editors* (*titleditors*).

The rest of the *bookbiz* database consists of:

- The *roysched* table, which lists the royalty rates to which authors are entitled as a percentage that increases as the number of books sold increases. The *roysched* table is used primarily for reference purposes. Its data will not change (there will be no new rows, no deletions of rows, not even any modification of existing rows) unless the royalty schedule itself changes—which would happen only if an author's contract were to be renegotiated or a new title added.

- Two tables, *sales* and *salesdetails*, for keeping track of sales.

That makes nine tables in all.

Before we go into more detail about the full *bookbiz* database, take a look at this picture of it.

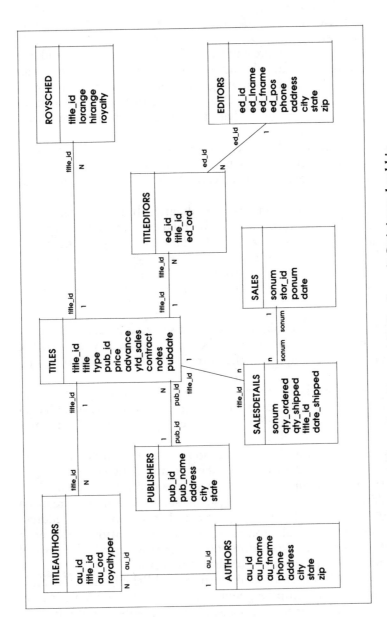

Data Structure Diagram for the Sample Database *bookbiz*

This kind of database design sketch is often called a **data structure diagram**. It shows the tables, the columns in each table, and the relationships among the tables.

Each box in the diagram represents a table, with its name and the names of its columns inside it. The lines connecting the boxes represent relationships among the tables, showing the anticipated joins between them. (Other joins are also possible—these are just the explicitly planned ones.) For example, *titles* and *publishers* have been planned so that they can join on the *pub_id* column.

The *N* and *1* on either end of the line between *titles* and *publishers* indicate a many-to-one relationship between the tables. There can be many titles to one publisher but there can't be many publishers to one title.

It's a good idea to sketch a data structure diagram like this one. A picture makes it easier to to determine that the relationships between tables seem reasonable. Take a final look for redundant data. If you find a one-to-one (1:1) relationship between two tables, you might be better off collapsing them into one table. A many-to-many relationship (N:N), as noted earlier, calls for another table to represent the association between the two entity tables.

Summarizing the *bookbiz* **Database.**   Now let's take a closer look at the nine tables in the *bookbiz* database, to better familiarize you with the material on which the examples in the rest of *The Practical SQL Handbook* are based.

The *bookbiz* database keeps track of the activities of three subsidiary publishing companies. Since the fiscal arrangements of the subsidiaries are not independent, the parent publisher has chosen to maintain a single database.

The *publishers* table contains information about the three subsidiary publishing lines—their identification numbers, names, and addresses.

For each author under contract with any of the publishers, the *authors* table contains an identification number (social security numbers are often used as unique identifiers for people), first and last name, and address information. The *editors* table contains similar information about each editor, with the addition of a position column that describes the type of work the editor does (acquisitions or project management).

For each book that has been or is about to be published, the *titles* table contains an identification number, name, type, publisher identification number, price, advance, year-to-date sales, contract status, comments, and publication date. The numbers in the *ytd_sales* column, which will change as more books are sold, might be kept current in one of several ways:

- By making periodic entries using the data modification commands.
- By coding logic into an application program that automatically updates *ytd_sales* whenever a sale is entered into the *salesdetails* table.
- By using SQL to define a **trigger** that accomplishes the same automatic updating. (Triggers are provided by only a few of the more sophisticated relational database management systems. See Chapter 10.)

The titles and authors are represented in separate tables that can be linked together with a third table, the *titleauthors* table. For each book, *titleauthors* contains a row for every author involved, with information on the title ID, the author ID, the author cover credit order (which name comes first), and the royalty split among the authors of a book. The *titleditors* table similarly links the titles and their editors. Instead of cover credit order, it lists editing order, so that it's possible to find who was the first or last editor.

The *roysched* table lists the unit sales ranges and the royalty connected with each range. The royalty is some percentage of the net receipts from sales. The percentage is used to calculate the amount due each author based on sales of his or her book.

The *sales* table has top-level information about each purchase order received from bookstores: sales order number (assigned by the publisher), store identification, purchase order number (assigned by the store), and date. The *salesdetails* table contains information about each line in the purchase order (assuming any purchase order may involve more than one book): title, quantity ordered, quantity shipped, and date shipped.

Of course, a real publisher's database would be much more complex, with tables for stores, employees, distributors, production costs, vendors, subcontractors, and the like. (As an exercise, you might try sketching some of these tables and deciding how they would relate to the tables already in *bookbiz*.) However, these nine tables do present enough material to work with for learning SQL, and they are used throughout this book.

Testing Your Database Design

Once you've come up with a proposed design for your database, you should create the tables and insert some data. (The next chapter gives detailed information on these procedures.) Then you should test your design by running some queries and updating the data. Your tests may reveal oversights in the design.

Database designs are seldom satisfactory when based entirely on theory. It's essential to play with your design interactively before undertaking serious production efforts—even if you plan to use it in an application that will involve thousands of lines of programming code and tens of thousands of rows of data. Don't wait until you've invested hundreds of hours in a flawed design. You can avoid problems by working interactively with a prototype of the database.

Other Database Definition Considerations

If you were about to put a real-world database on-line, you'd have several additional critical issues to consider before proceeding: indexing, security, and integrity.

Deciding which columns to index, and what kind of index is best for each column, is an important part of database design. You might want to include indexes in your design sketch. Primary keys are nearly always uniquely indexed. Other columns that are frequently searched, sorted, or joined are usually indexed. See Chapter 3 for more on indexes.

Determining permissions (privileges) is another vital part of the design process; they too might be included in your design sketch. Consider in more detail who is going to use the database and why. Is there information that should be available to everybody, available to certain people only, or available exclusively to the system administrator? Most relational systems allow you to assign permissions to individual users on a database, table, view, and even column level. You'll find a complete treatment of the subject in Chapter 10.

Ordinarily, planning for data integrity is a major part of database design. It involves setting up a system to make sure changes to one piece of data apply to all copies of that data anywhere in the database so that you won't end up with orphans or inaccuracies. An example using *bookbiz* might be discovering that an author's ID number was incorrect. If you changed it in the *authors* table only, you'd never again be able to find out what books that author had written, because that author's ID number in *titleauthors* would no longer match the ID number in *authors*. In order to access the information in *titleauthors*, you'd have to make sure that when the author ID changed in *authors*, it also changed in *titleauthors*.

However, since some relational systems consider data integrity an application task while others embed these functions in the database, discussion of this issue is deferred to Chapter 10.

PUTTING A DATABASE ON LINE

The next chapter will help you install the sample database, using your own relational database management system and its SQL dialect. Once you've designed your database on paper, using the techniques and guidelines discussed in the previous chapter, you're ready to put it on line.

Chapter 3

Creating and Filling a Database

CREATING DATABASES AND OBJECTS WITH SQL

SQL CREATE commands tell your relational database management system the name, structure, and other characteristics of your database and database objects.

Since all the examples in *The Practical SQL Handbook* rely on the *bookbiz* database, we strongly recommend that you replicate its structure and data for use with the book. The SQL statements for creating *bookbiz* are given in this chapter, as are examples of the INSERT statements for entering its sample data. The complete structure of *bookbiz* and statements for entering all of its data are repeated in Appendix D. (We recommend that you put these statements into an operating system file so that you can use them repeatedly, as we explain at the end of this chapter.)

You can make up your own data for the sample database if you wish, but you'll have an easier time following the examples and understanding your results if you use the data we have supplied.

SQL dialects vary quite a bit in their CREATE statements, so check your system's reference guide for the exact syntax you should use. Before you try to create any tables, be sure you're familiar with

- The datatypes available to you
- Conventions for naming tables, columns, and indexes
- The types of indexes available
- How your system deals with nulls (missing or inapplicable information)

If you're working in a multi-user environment, you will also need to investigate whether you have permission to create database objects. You can experiment—give a CREATE command and see if your system obeys—or you can check with your system administrator. It's usually a good idea to go through channels because the system administrator may want you to create your test database in a particular location, or to create the database objects in a database that's already been set up.

SQL SYNTAX

Since this is the first chapter for which you'll actually be sitting at a terminal and typing commands, now is the time to get familiar with the conventions used in this book to represent SQL examples and syntax. The difference between an example and syntax is that the former is a SQL command that you might actually type, just as it appears; syntax is more like a prototype—a template that tells you how exactly what is required (and what's permitted) for the command in question.

You've already seen both examples and syntax. Here are some repeats:

```
SQL example:
select pub_id, pub_name, address, city, state
from publishers
where state = "CA"
```

```
SQL syntax:
SELECT select_list
FROM table_list
WHERE search_conditions
```

Notice that:

- SQL examples are given entirely in lower case letters, while syntax is a combination of upper and lower case. Upper case is for **keywords**—names reserved for use by the system. Lower case is for values that you supply, such as names of columns or names of tables.
- Examples contain actual data values and names of actual database objects, while syntax refers to categories of database objects ("table_list", "select_list") and place-holders for data values.

The text that precedes an example or syntax will always indicate which one it is. If you're ever confused, the presence of SQL keywords (words with a special meaning in SQL, such as SELECT, WHERE, and FROM) in upper case letters is a dead giveaway: that's syntax. But be aware that in most implementations of SQL, database objects can have names that include—or consist entirely of—upper case letters. In this book, we use only lower case names for database objects in order to minimize confusion.

A SQL statement must follow precise syntactical and structural rules, and may include only these elements:

- Keywords are words that have a special meaning to SQL. In many implementations of SQL, all keywords are reserved—they cannot be used to name database objects. Syntax in this book shows keywords in upper case letters, but case is not significant when you use a keyword in a statement.

- **Identifiers** are names of databases, tables, or other database objects. Each SQL dialect has slightly different rules about identifiers— minimum and maximum length, characters that cannot be used, etc. Embedded blanks in identifiers are never allowed; in many implementations, characters like the asterisk (*), underbar (_), or period (.) are not permitted.

  In most SQL implementations, case is significant when you're typing identifiers. Once you give a database object a name, always type it just that way. In other words, if you name a table *MYfriends* when you create it, SQL won't be able to locate it if you mistakenly type *Myfriends*, with the second character lower case.

- Operators and functions provide mathematical and computational capabilities. Most implementations of SQL provide **arithmetic operators** such as + (plus) and - (minus), **comparison operators** such as > (greater than) and <= (less than or equal to), **logical operators** (AND, OR, and NOT), and **aggregate functions** such as SUM, AVG, COUNT, COUNT(*), MAX, and MIN.

Some of the SQL syntax may appear confusing at first. That's because a lot of rules about what is permitted and what is required are packed into a single statement. However, in terms of how you type commands on your terminal screen, SQL is a **free-form language**, meaning there are no requirements for how many words you put on a line or where you break a line. For readability and consistency, the examples and syntax in this book are usually formatted so that each clause of a statement begins on a new line. Long or complex clauses extend to additional lines; these lines are indented for readability.

Once you understand the conventions for reading SQL statements, you'll find them convenient references. The best way to learn the conventions is to read them carefully, and then to compare SQL examples and the syntax that goes with them.

Here are the conventions we have adopted for SQL syntax:

- Words or phrases the user should supply—expressions, constant values, identifiers, etc.—are always in lower case letters. Here's a repeat of the SELECT syntax given earlier in this chapter:

```
SELECT select_list
FROM table_list
WHERE search_conditions
```

Here, "select_list," "table_list," and "search_conditions" represent values or database objects whose names you would substitute when you actually submitted a command to SQL.

- SQL keywords are always shown in upper case letters, though in most versions of SQL, you may type them in any case. The keywords in the syntax above are SELECT, FROM, and WHERE; the ability to type them in any case means that "SELECT" is the same as "select" is the same as "SeLeCt".

In some versions of SQL, certain keywords can be abbreviated. In Transact-SQL, for example, some keywords are shown partly in upper case and partly in lower case letters, like this:

```
BEGIN TRANsaction
```

This means you can use either the full word or only the upper case part of it.

- Braces ({ }) around words or phrases mean that you must choose at least one of the enclosed options. The options inside a set of braces may be separated from each other by a vertical bar (|), which means "or."

```
{cash | check | credit}
```

This means that you must choose *one and only one* of the options when you type your SQL statement.

The enclosed options may also be separated by commas (,):

```
{die_on_your_feet , live_on_your_knees ,
 stay_on_your_toes , get_off_your_bum}
```

This means you *must* choose *one or more* of the options. If you choose more than one, separate your choices with commas. The braces are not part of the statement, so don't type them when you enter a SQL command:

```
select live_on_your_knees, die_on_your_feet
from life
where choice = "not the greatest"
```

• Brackets ([ ]) mean that choosing one or more of the enclosed item(s) is optional. When you see something like this, it means you don't have to choose it:

```
[severe_depression]
```

If there is more than one optional item inside a set of brackets and the options are separated by a vertical bar, you can choose none or only one of them:

```
[beans | rice | sweet_potatoes]
```

If the enclosed options are separated by commas, you can choose none, one, or more of them.

```
[extra_cheese , avocado , sour_cream]
```

If you choose more than one, separate your choices with commas. The brackets are not part of the statement, so don't type them when you enter a statement.

• Ellipses (...) mean that you can repeat the last unit as many times as you like. Here's an example of how they might be used in syntax:

```
BUY thing_name = price AS {cash | check | credit}
    [, thing_name = price AS {cash | check | credit} ]...
```

In this statement, "BUY" and "AS" are required keywords. The items inside braces and separated by vertical bars indicate that you must choose one (and only one) of the methods of payment. You may also choose to buy additional things—as many of them as you like. For each thing you buy, give its name, its price, and a method of payment.

- When you see parentheses (( )) in syntax, they are actually part of what you type (unlike brackets and braces). Don't forget them.

A SQL statement generally requires a **terminator**, which sends the SQL command to the database management system for processing. Different SQL dialects use different terminators; common terminators include the semicolon (;) and the word "go." Since the possibilities vary, we generally have not included terminators in the examples or syntax.

Coping with Failure

Errors in SQL statements occur for many reasons. Among the most common are:

- Typing mistakes:

```
slect name
from authers
(''select'' and ''authers'' are misspelled)
```

- Syntax errors:

```
select name, phone
where state = "CA"
from authors
```

(the FROM clause should precede the WHERE clause)

- Forgetting to enclose character data in single or double quotes:

```
select name
from authors
where state = CA
```

(CA should be in quotes)

• Lapses of (your) memory about the names of database objects:

```
select title
from documents
```

(the name of the table is *titles*)

When you type a statement that your version of SQL does not understand, the command will not be executed. Instead, the system displays some sort of error message on your screen, the helpfulness of which varies a great deal from system to system (and even within systems). A good error message tells you as much as possible about where you went wrong, including the type of error that has been detected and the line on which the mistake is located.

Here are a couple of examples from Transact-SQL, a system that displays a message number, a severity level, and the state of each error along with the error message itself:

```
select * from pulbihsers

    Msg 208, Level 16, State 1:
    Invalid object (table) name  pulbihsers

slect * from publishers

    Msg 101, Level 15, State 1:
    Line 1: SQL syntax error.
    Msg 102, Level 15, State 1:
    Incorrect syntax near '*'.
```

After looking at the message, you can correct the error and re-submit your SQL statement. (The error messages in other versions of SQL may look quite different.)

CREATING DATABASES

A database is a named allocation of storage space that will contain tables, views, indexes, and other database objects. You begin by creating the database; then you create each of the objects in it.

Since a significant amount of storage space may have to be set aside for each new database (even if the database will never contain much data), permission to create databases is often jealously guarded in multi-user environments. If this is the case in your situation, you won't have to learn about the SQL command to create a database—you can go on to the sections that discuss creating database objects. However, you will have to talk with your system administrator, and get him or her to issue the command to create a database for you. Let the system administrator know that your database will be a small one used for learning purposes, and won't require much storage space.

In a single-user system, it's up to you to be aware of your storage needs and capacities. You'll usually have to rely on operating system facilities for determining them.

In most multi-user versions of SQL, each database is controlled or owned by a specified user. The **database owner** is charged with certain responsibilities and bestowed certain rights. These rights and responsibilities vary widely among database management systems, but often include:

- Setting up permissions for other users within the database
- Making backup copies of the database on a regular basis and running the recovery procedures in case of system failure
- Enlarging the database if more space becomes necessary

Typically, a database is owned by the user that created it. But since the system administrator often maintains a monopoly on database creation, some relational database management systems provide a facility that allows him or her to transfer ownership to other users.

Depending on both the database software and the hardware you're using, databases may be physically stored either on disks, on disk partitions, or in operating system files. The generic term is **database device**.

Generally, database devices are assigned logical names in order to preserve physical data independence. In most database system installations, only the system administrator worries about physical storage. Users who will be issuing the SQL commands to create databases need know only the logical names of the database devices, so that they can allocate the correct amount of storage space on the correct device (often according to instructions from the system administrator).

The ISO-ANSI standard does not include a CREATE DATABASE statement. Instead, ISO-ANSI provides a CREATE SCHEMA command for defining the portion of a database that a specific user owns. Typically, a database consists of more than one **schema**.

Among commercial versions of SQL, however, there's not a lot of variation when it comes to the CREATE DATABASE command. In its most vanilla form (that is, without any optional clauses and extensions), its syntax looks like this:

```
CREATE DATABASE database_name
```

To create the *bookbiz* database, type this command:

```
create database bookbiz
```

Depending on the implementation, the syntax may include other clauses that let you (or the system administrator) control the location of the database (the database device on which the database will be physically stored) and its size (how much device space the database can use before the system stops it). The syntax for the Transact-SQL CREATE DATABASE command, for example, looks like this:

```
CREATE DATABASE database_name
[ON {DEFAULT [= size] | device_name [= size]}
  [, device_name [= size]]...]
```

Choosing a Database

Creating a database does not usually imply moving to it. Depending on the version of SQL you're using, you may have to type a command like one of the following after you create a database (but before you create any of its objects):

1   USE database_name

        or

2   DATABASE database_name

Commands like these are used any time you want to move from one database to another. (In a relational database management system, you're always in some database: it may be a system database that's part of the data dictionary, or it may be a user database.) If you're outside a database, you're also outside the database system.

Altering a Database

Some SQL versions include a command that allows you to change the size of a database (usually to make it bigger). The keyword ALTER is often associated with SQL commands that affect space on database devices.

The ability to add database device space for a database is extremely important for any application that will grow over time. Less important, and less frequently included in SQL implementations, is the ability to shrink a database in order to reclaim unused database device space.

CREATING TABLES

Once you've created a database and moved to it, you can begin creating tables.

Tables are the basic building blocks of any database. They hold the rows and columns of your data. With SQL's data definition commands, you can create tables, drop tables, and **alter** them (add, remove, rearrange, or change the characteristics of columns).

In most SQL implementations, the user who creates a table is its owner, and is responsible for granting permissions for its use to other users. When you create a table with SQL, you:

- Name it
- Name the columns it contains
- Specify the datatype of each column
- Specify the **null status** of each column—whether that column permits or forbids null values in most versions of SQL.

The SQL command for setting up a table is called CREATE TABLE. (Make sure you're using the correct database before you enter a CREATE TABLE statement.) A slightly simplified form of the CREATE TABLE syntax is:

```
CREATE TABLE table_name
(column_name datatype [NULL | NOT NULL]
[, column_name datatype [NULL | NOT NULL] ]...)
```

Let's examine this syntax, since it's more complicated than any introduced so far. The first clause, the CREATE TABLE clause, is straightforward—just make sure the table names you choose follow your system's rules for identifiers. The second line of the syntax begins with an opening parenthesis, which you must be sure to type. Then give the name of the first column, followed by a space and the name of its datatype. (For some datatypes, you must specify a length—usually by putting an integer in parentheses immediately following the datatype.)

The keywords NULL and NOT NULL inside square brackets indicate that they are optional. The vertical bar between them means you can use only one or the other, not both. The system makes the choice if the user doesn't. Some systems default to allowing nulls in columns whose null status isn't made explicit; some default to not allowing nulls. The ISO-ANSI standard default is to permit nulls.

The third line of the syntax, also enclosed in square brackets, repeats the definition of a column, and is followed by an ellipsis. The brackets mean that defining a second column is optional; the ellipsis means that you can define as many columns as you like (within the limitations of your system—check your reference guide). Note that each column definition is separated from the next by a comma; and don't forget the parenthesis at the end of the list of columns.

In addition to system-specific limits on the number of columns that you may include in a single table, each system has a limit on the length of a row (the total bytes that all the columns use). Usually, the limit is large enough so that you won't have to think about it. But if you're defining a table with lots of columns or with very large columns, you may have to compute exactly how long each row will be. To figure this out, add together the lengths of the longest data value each column can hold—determined by the column's assigned length (if it has one) or by the length that applies to its datatype.

Following the rules given in the syntax, here's an example of a SQL command that creates a table named *authors* with two columns: *au_id* (author identification code) and *au_lname* (author's last name):

```
create table authors
(au_id char(11) not null,
au_lname char(20) null)
```

Choosing a Datatype

In the example above, *char* is the datatype for both columns, indicating that both the *au_id* and *au_name* columns will contain characters.

The datatype of a column specifies what kind of information the column will hold (characters, numbers, dates, and so on), so that the system will know how the data is to be physically stored, and how it can be manipulated. For example, a character datatype holds letters, numbers, and special characters, while an integer datatype holds whole numbers only. Data in integer columns can be manipulated with arithmetic operators, while character data cannot.

Relational systems can handle a wide variety of datatypes. But be careful in making assumptions—even when two systems use the same datatype name, their meaning may be different. You'll want to check your system's reference manuals to find out what datatypes are available to you, and when and how to use them.

Choosing the proper datatypes is more binding than many other design decisions, since in many versions of SQL it is difficult to change a column's datatype identity. However, most SQLs provide datatype conversion functions so that data stored as one type can be treated as if it were another type. For example, even if you have stored only numbers in a character column, it may be difficult or impossible to change the datatype of the column. But you may be able, with the help of a data conversion function, to perform arithmetic operations on those numbers, even though those operations are incompatible with character columns.

Here's a summary of some possible datatypes, along with some hints on the kind of data for which each typically is used:

- **Character datatypes**—hold letters, numbers, and special characters. They are known variously as *character, char, varchar* (variable-length character), *text,* and *string.* A few relational database management systems provide special functions for text values (searching, substituting, etc.).

  Character datatypes are the best choice in some situations that may seem surprising at first—such as zip codes and phone numbers. Zip codes are best stored in character columns because they often need to be sorted—and codes that begin with zero may not sort properly if they are stored as numbers. Some systems, in fact, simply strip leading zeroes off all numbers. (Sort order varies from implementation to implementation.)

  Special characters often used in phone numbers (hyphens and parentheses) are rejected unless a column is stored as characters.

- **Whole number datatypes**—hold integers only (no fractions or decimals). They are often known by such names as *integer, int,* *smallint*, and *tinyint*. All commercial versions of SQL provide arithmetic operations for use with whole numbers; almost all provide aggregate functions that allow you to find the maximum, minimum, average, total, and count of the values in a column of whole numbers. Some SQLs provide other functions, such as statistical operations.

- **Decimal datatypes**—hold numbers with fractions. They are usually known as *decimal* or *float*. Their precision and the number of significant digits varies among database management systems; sometimes it depends on the particular hardware you're using.
- **Money datatypes**—hold currency values. Arithmetic operations are usually provided for them.
- **Date** and **time datatypes**—record date, time, and combinations of date and time. Special date functions for determining the interval between two dates, and for adding or subtracting a given amount of time to a date, are sometimes provided.
- **Binary datatypes**—hold code, images, and hexadecimal data.
- **Bit datatypes**—hold yes/no, true/false, and on/off data (rarely used).

Become familiar with the characteristics of your system's datatypes so that you can use them effectively.

Choosing a Datatype Length.   For certain datatypes, especially character datatypes, you may be required to supply a length. The number in parentheses after the datatype defines the maximum number of characters that can be stored in the column. Most systems require explicit lengths for character datatypes but not for numeric or date datatypes.

Be sure to check on how your system handles the physical storage of datatypes. Find out which datatypes are **fixed length**—in other words, those for which the amount of storage space specified in the CREATE TABLE statement is allocated for each value in the column, no matter how much data is actually entered. For example, a column defined as *char(10)* would be allocated ten bytes or characters of storage space, no matter what value you enter in the column. Longer values may be truncated; values shorter than ten characters may be padded with blanks at the end, like this:

```
name
----------
Greenjeans
Kangaroo__
```

```
Ho_____
Rumpelstil
```

Datatypes that don't take length specifications are often fixed-length. If your implementation allocates eight bytes of storage for integer columns, for example, all eight bytes would be used regardless of whether the value you enter in the column is "3" or "300000."

The data in variable-length datatypes is stored as its actual length, not as its defined length. For example, say your system supplies a variable-length character datatype and you've defined a column like the one shown earlier as *varchar(10)* instead of *char(10)*. The "10" still represents the maximum length, but shorter values are not blank-padded. The first value, (Greenjeans) would take ten bytes of storage, but the second (Kangaroo) would take only eight, the third (Ho) would take two, and so on.

Using fixed-length datatypes when much of the actual data is a great deal shorter than the length specified can waste storage space.

Assigning Null Status

Most systems allow you to assign null or not null status to each column when you create a table. A few systems do not support null values at all—they always insert some default value other than null (such as zero or blank) when a column has no entered value.

Assigning null status to a column instructs the system to insert a null in that column if the user does not enter a value. As we've explained, a null represents some unknown, unavailable, or inapplicable value—it's not the same as blank or zero.

Assigning not null status to a column means that non-entries in that column are not allowed. If you don't specify a value for that column, the system will reject the entry and display an error message. (In systems that provide the capability of specifying default values for a column, the default is automatically entered if you don't specify a value for a not null column.)

How should you decide the null status of columns when you're designing a table? You should not permit nulls in columns in which known values are essential to the utility of the database. Primary key columns should never allow nulls because they uniquely identify the row. For example, without the *title_id* column, you'd have no way to find a book's author(s) or editor(s) in the *bookbiz* database. The database was designed so that the *authors* and *editors* tables can be linked to *titles* by joining on the *title_id* column.

You may decide that other columns should forbid null entries too: perhaps you should disallow nulls in the *au_lname* and *au_fname* columns, on the grounds that it doesn't make sense to enter an author's address or phone number without entering his or her name.

However, when you know or suspect that a column will contain some unknown or inapplicable data, it should permit nulls. Missing addresses and phone numbers are common, so these columns should allow nulls. And, the first name column in an *authors* table should permit nulls since an author's *nom de plume* could consist of a single name (*e.g.*, *Colette*).

In the *titles* table, the *title_id* and *title* columns do not allow nulls; most of the other columns do. (See the illustration of the *titles* table in Appendix D). Nulls are forbidden because *title_id* is the primary key—each title identification number indicates a unique book. On the other hand, the *advance* column does permit null values. While an advance with a null title ID would make no sense at all, a title ID with a null advance might simply mean the publisher and author haven't agreed on the exact amount yet or the clerk hasn't entered it.

While null would mean "not yet known" in the case of an advance not yet decided upon, it can have slightly different meanings in other situations. Null can mean that the value will never be known. For example, if you added a *phone* field to the *authors* table, and some authors' telephone numbers were unlisted, you'd have to reconcile yourself to a permanent null. Then again, null might mean something like "not applicable"—for example, if the author didn't have a telephone.

Here's an example that shows how to assign null status. The keywords NOT NULL come directly after the datatype and length:

```
create table authors
(au_id char(11) not null)
```

In many systems, null is the default. Check your system to see if that's the case.

The Table Creation Process

Creating a table, like creating a database, involves a series of steps that begins with design and ends with issuing a SQL command. Here's an outline of the process. It assumes you've already designed and normalized your database, and therefore know which columns will be in each table.

- Decide on the datatype (and length, if required) of each column.
- Decide which columns should accept null values, and which should not.
- Decide which columns need indexes, and what kind each should be (assuming your system supports more than one kind). Indexes are discussed in this chapter and in Chapter 10.
- If you're in a multi-user environment, make sure you have permission to create tables and indexes. If not, see your system administrator or the owner of the database in which you're working.
- Create the table (and any indexes it needs) with the CREATE TABLE and CREATE INDEX statements.

Here's a chart showing the structure of the *titles* table: column names, datatypes, null status, and the indexes that will go with each column.

Column	Datatype	Null?	Index
title_id	varchar(11)	not null	titleidind
title	varchar(80)	not null	titleind
type	char(12)	null	
pub_id	char(4)	null	
price	money	null	
advance	money	null	
ytd_sale	int	null	
contract	bit	not null	
notes	varchar	null	
pubdate	datetime	null	

When you're designing a table for a real application (rather than doing an exercise), there are a few other issues to consider, such as permissions. If other users can use your database at all, which of them do you want to be able to SELECT from your table? Who should be able to change it with the INSERT, UPDATE, and DELETE commands? (You control permissions with the GRANT and REVOKE commands, discussed in Chapter 8.)

Some relational database systems provide two other facilities that the creator of a table should consider.

- A **default** is a value that the system automatically supplies when the user entering data doesn't give one explicitly. For example, you might define a default for the *type* column of the *titles* table. If a book hasn't yet been categorized, and the data entry clerk therefore can't make an entry in the *type* column, the system would automatically insert whatever default value you've chosen—

perhaps the word "UNCLASSIFIED." (If no default is defined, and the *type* column permits null values, the system will automatically insert the value "NULL.")

- A **rule** specifies what data may be entered in a particular column: it is a way of defining the domain of the column. Rules are sometimes referred to as **validation rules**, since they allow the system to check whether a value being entered in a column falls within the column's domain.

For example, you might want to prohibit any entries in the *advance* column that are greater than $100,000. Or you can make sure that a zip code column, which has been assigned a character datatype, consists only of the numbers zero through nine. If a user attempts to make an entry that violates a rule, the system rejects the data modification command.

Some systems consider defaults and rules an application-by-application decision, and do not support them through SQL. Transact-SQL centralizes them in the database, and provides SQL syntax for defining them. Either way, you should include them in your design sketch. These issues are discussed in detail in Chapter 10.

Defining the Tables in the Sample Database.   Now you are ready to write CREATE TABLE statements—to begin putting the sample database on line. First, create the *titles* table, with columns for the book's identification number, its name, its category, the publisher's identification number, the retail price of the book, the advance paid to the author(s), sales for the year to date, the contract status (has one been signed or not?), a description of the book, and the publication date.

If the names of the datatypes your system supplies are the same as the ones used in this statement, type exactly what you see here. If not, substitute the datatype definition that seems most similar.

```
create table titles
(title_id char(6) not null,
title varchar(80) not null,
type char(12) null,
pub_id char(4) null,
price money null,
advance money null,
ytd_sales int null,
contract bit not null,
```

```
notes varchar(200) null,
pubdate datetime null)
```

The *contract* column is defined here as not null because Transact-SQL's *bit* datatype (designed for two-valued data, such as "yes/no," "on/off," or "1/0") does not allow null values. If your system does not supply a *bit* datatype, or if you prefer to assign the column null status, you may create it as a character column. Such a column could allow nulls.

Notice that on this system, you can explicitly specify NULL or NOT NULL for each column. Other systems may not provide null/not null status indicators, or may assume null status if you don't indicate it in the CREATE TABLE statement.

Here are the CREATE TABLE statements for the eight remaining tables in the *bookbiz* database. The CREATE statements are also contained in Appendix D. In order to be able conveniently to install or re-install *bookbiz* at will, type these CREATE statements into an operating system file. Don't forget to put a terminator (usually the keyword "GO" or a semicolon—consult your reference manuals) between statements if your system requires it.

```
create table authors
(au_id char(11) not null,
au_lname varchar(40) not null,
au_fname varchar(20) not null,
phone char(12) null,
address varchar(40) null,
city varchar(20) null,
state char(2) null,
zip char(5) null)

create table publishers
(pub_id char(4) not null,
pub_name varchar(40) null,
address varchar(40) null,
city varchar(20) null,
state char(2) null)

create table roysched
(title_id char(6) not null,
lorange int null,
hirange int null,
royalty int null)
```

```
create table titleauthors
(au_id char(11) not null,
title_id char(6) not null,
au_ord tinyint null,
royaltyshare int null)

create table editors
(ed_id char(11) not null,
ed_lname varchar(40) not null,
ed_fname varchar(20) not null,
ed_pos varchar(12) null,
phone char(12) null,
address varchar(40) null,
city varchar(20) null,
state char(2) null,
zip char(5) null)

create table titleditors
(ed_id char(11) not null,
title_id char(6) not null,
ed_ord tinyint null)

create table sales
(sonum int not null,
stor_id char(4) not null,
ponum varchar(20) not null,
date datetime null)

create table salesdetails
(sonum int not null,
qty_ordered smallint not null,
qty_shipped smallint null,
title_id char(6) not null,
date_shipped datetime null)
```

Changing Table Definitions

After you've designed and created your database and worked with it for a while, you may find that it isn't quite right or that the requirements of your application have changed. Some systems allow you to change the

structure of a table (even after it has data in it) with a command such as
ALTER TABLE. Syntax may include keywords to add and drop columns,
and (much less common) to change a column's name, datatype, length, or
null status.

For example, to add a column to the *authors* table, your system might
allow you to type something like:

```
alter table authors
add birth_date datetime null
```

Usually, columns added with the ALTER TABLE statement must allow
nulls. That's because when the new column is added to all the existing
rows, it must contain some value, and "null" (unknown) is the obvious
choice.

Many relational systems don't provide commands for making structural
changes besides the addition of columns—for removing columns, renaming columns, or changing a column's datatype or null status. But often
there's a way around such limitations. If you can't physically drop a
column, for example, you can create a view that excludes it, and do all
your data retrieval and modification commands through that view. You
can also use a view to create the illusion of a permanent change in :

- The name of a column, simply by giving the column a new heading
  in the SELECT clause of the CREATE VIEW statement
- The datatype of a column, assuming your system has some sort of
  data conversion function

Another possible work-around for restructuring is to create a new table
with the structure you want, dump the data from the old table into an
operating system file, and then reload it into the new table. In some systems, you can use a command (often called something like SELECT
INTO) to pull data from one table into a new table that may have a different structure. See Chapter 9 for details.

CREATING INDEXES

In a relational database management system, an index is a mechanism for
boosting performance. Just as an index in a book helps you quickly find
the pages you want to read, an index on a column speeds data retrieval.

When you're looking for a particular subject in a book, you don't want to read every page to find the topic of interest. Similarly, when you're searching for a given piece of data, an index can serve as a logical pointer to its physical location.

There are several important differences, however, between an index in a book and an index in a relational database management system. The reader of a book decides whether or not to consult the index. The user of a relational database management system decides only whether or not to create an index. The system itself decides whether or not to use the index for each query the user submits. Except for the CREATE INDEX and DROP INDEX commands, indexes are transparent to database management system users because SQL includes no syntax for referring to an index in a query.

While each edition of a book and its index are printed once, the data in a relational system and its indexes may change frequently. Each time the data in a table is modified, one or more of the table's indexes may have to change to reflect those modifications. Again, users have nothing to do with keeping the indexes up to date; the system handles this task on its own.

One more characteristic that distinguishes indexes on database tables from most book indexes is that it's very common for a table to have more than one index, just as some books are indexed by subject and by author. It's also possible for a table (and for a book) to have no index at all.

This chapter explains the syntax of the CREATE INDEX and DROP INDEX statements, describes the varieties of indexes typically available in relational systems, and gives some pointers about how to decide which columns to index. Chapter 10 discusses in more detail what database indexes actually look like, and how they affect performance.

The CREATE INDEX Statement

Most systems have a command with syntax similar to this:

```
CREATE [UNIQUE] INDEX index_name
ON table_name (column_name)
```

The column and table name specify the column you want indexed and the table that contains it.

To create an index on the *au_id* column of the *authors* table, the command is:

```
create index auidind
on authors(au_id)
```

It's a good idea to plan and create your indexes when you create your table. However, SQL also allows you to create indexes after there's data in a table.

Most systems also allow **composite indexes** (indexes involving more than one column) and **unique indexes** (indexes that prevent duplication of data). Another indexing option provided in some systems is a **clustered index** (one that is sorted not only logically but physically). Check your system's reference manuals to see which type of indexes are allowed.

Composite Indexes. Composite indexes are used when two or more columns are best searched as a unit because of their logical relationship. For example, the *authors* table has a composite index on *au_fname* and *au_lname*.

The syntax for creating a composite index must specify all the columns in it. A command to create a composite index on the *authors* table might look something like this:

```
create index au_name_ind
on authors(au_lname, au_fname)
```

In most SQL dialects that support composite indexes, the columns don't have to be in the same order as the columns in the CREATE TABLE statement. For example, the order of *au_lname* and *au_fname* could be reversed in the preceding index creation statement.

Unique Indexes. A unique index is one in which no two rows are permitted to have the same index value. The system checks for duplicate values when the index is created (if data already exists), and each time data is added. Unique indexes are usually created on the primary key column(s) in order to enforce their function as unique identifiers of the row.

Specifying a unique index makes sense only when uniqueness is a characteristic of the data itself. For example, you would not want a unique index on a *last_name* column since there is likely to be more than one *Smith* or *Wong* in tables of even a few hundred rows. On the other hand, a unique index on a column holding social security numbers would be a good idea. Uniqueness is a characteristic of the data—each person has a different social security number. Furthermore, a unique index serves as an integrity check. A duplicate social security number reflects some kind of error in data entry or on the part of the government.

SQL implementations that support unique indexes must have some way of enforcing that uniqueness. Usually, the system guarantees uniqueness by rejecting commands that would:

* Create a unique index on existing data that includes duplicate values
* Change data on which there is a unique index in such a way that duplicates would be introduced

Usually, you can use the UNIQUE keyword on composite indexes as well as on single-column indexes.

Clustered Indexes. Some relational database management systems offer you the choice of a clustered or nonclustered index. When a clustered index is created, it means that the system will sort and re-sort the rows of a table on an ongoing basis, so that their physical order on the database device is always the same as their logical (indexed) order.

Since a clustered index controls the physical location of data, there can be only one clustered index per table. It is often created on the primary key.

With a nonclustered index, the physical order of the rows is not the same as their indexed order. Each of the nonclustered indexes on a table can provide access to the data in a different sorted order.

Finding data using a clustered index is almost always faster than using a nonclustered index. A clustered index is especially advantageous when many rows with contiguous **key values** (indexed values) are being retrieved—that is, on columns that are often searched for ranges of values. Once the row with the first key value is found, rows with subsequent indexed values are guaranteed to be physically adjacent, and no further accesses are necessary. However, the presence of a clustered index may slow down data modification statements, since the system must take the time to rejuggle the index when key values are changed.

How, What, and Why to Index

Indexes speed the retrieval of data. An index on a column can often make the difference between a nearly immediate response to a query and a long wait.

So why not index every column? The most significant reason is that building and maintaining an index takes time and storage space on the database device.

A second reason is that inserting, deleting, or updating data in indexed columns takes a little longer than in unindexed columns, because of the time it takes the system to maintain the index when key values are changed. But this cost is usually outweighed by the extent to which indexes improve retrieval performance.

In general, it's usually appropriate to put indexes on columns you frequently use in retrievals, especially primary key columns and columns used in joins and sorts. Here are some more precise guidelines:

- The column or columns that store the table's primary key should almost always be indexed, especially if the primary key is frequently joined to columns in other tables. A unique index on the primary key prevents duplicates and guarantees that every value in the primary key column will in fact *uniquely* identify the row.
- A column that is often accessed in sorted order probably should be indexed so that the system can take advantage of the indexed order.
- Columns that are regularly used in joins should be indexed, since the system can perform the join faster if the columns are in sorted order.
- A column that is often searched for ranges of values might be a good choice for indexing if your system provides clustered indexes. Once the row with the first value in the range is found, rows with subsequent values are guaranteed to be physically adjacent. A clustered index does not offer as much of an advantage for searches on single values.

These are some cases where indexes are not useful:

- Columns that are seldom or never referenced in queries don't benefit from indexes, since the system rarely has to search for rows on the basis of values in these columns.
- Columns that can have only two or three values (*e.g.*, male, female, unknown) gain no real advantage from being indexed.

When the system searches an unindexed column, it does so by looking at the rows one by one. The length of time it takes to perform this kind of scan is directly proportional to the number of rows in the table.

DELETING DATABASES AND DATABASE OBJECTS

Now that you know how to create databases, tables, and indexes, you may need to know how to get rid of them. All real-life SQL dialects provide statements for removing databases and their objects. Usually, the SQL keyword is DROP. (Strangely enough, not until its 1988 draft did the ISO-ANSI standard include such a command.)

In most implementations, removing a database or a database object deletes both the structure and any data associated with it. For that reason, most systems allow you to issue a DROP command only if you own the object or have special permission to delete it.

Removing a Database

The syntax of the DROP DATABASE command is usually something like:

```
DROP DATABASE database_name
```

The DROP DATABASE command is very dangerous, since removing a database usually obliterates all of its contents.

Removing a Table

The command to remove a table from a database is DROP TABLE. In most SQL dialects, its syntax is:

```
DROP TABLE table_name
```

When you issue this command, you remove the specified table from the database, together with its contents. Depending on how your system handles permissions, you may need to be the table owner or system administrator in order to drop it.

If you want to keep the table structure but remove all of its data, use the DELETE command (more about it later in this chapter).

Removing an Index

There are two situations in which you might want to drop an index:

- You or someone else has created an index on a column, but the index is not used for most or all queries.
- You are about to issue a large number of data modification statements that will change key values. Since the system may have to do a lot of work to keep the index up to date, it might be more efficient to drop the index and then re-create it (with the CREATE INDEX statement) after changing the data. It may still take some time to rebuild the index later, but you may prefer to postpone the lag time, rather than to endure a degradation in the system's performance during the data modifications.

In most systems, the command to remove an index has syntax something like this:

```
DROP INDEX table_name.index_name
```

When you issue this command the system removes the specified index from the database. To drop the index *auidind* in the *authors* table, the command is:

```
drop index authors.auidind
```

ADDING, CHANGING, AND REMOVING DATA

Once you've designed and created a database, its tables, and (optionally) its indexes, you'll want to put data into the tables and start to work—adding, changing, and removing data as necessary. You've got the structure. Now you need some contents.

SQL provides three basic commands for changing data, collectively called **data modification** statements. The INSERT statement adds new rows to the database. The UPDATE statement changes existing rows in the database. The DELETE statement removes rows from the database.

This section discusses the SQL data modification commands. The next section gives samples of the INSERT statements that load the sample data from the *bookbiz* database.

Another method of adding data to a table is to load it from an operating system file with some kind of bulk copy or bulk insert command. This method is especially appropriate when you are transferring data that was used with one database management system to another system.

Many relational database systems also have a **form system** (like a paper form with blanks where you can type data) for data modification. This is often more convenient than a data modification statement because it gives you a context in which to work. However, all data modification actions in a relational database system are based on SQL commands, so it's a good idea to look at their syntax even if you don't plan to use them.

Data modification statements are not necessarily available to everyone. The database owner and the owners of database objects can use the GRANT and REVOKE commands to decide which users are allowed to issue which data modification statements.

You can modify (INSERT, UPDATE, or DELETE) data in only one table per statement. However, in some systems, the modifications you make can be based on data in other tables, even those in other databases. You can actually pull values from one table into another, using a SQL SELECT statement within a data modification command. Instructions on this variation on data modification are given later in this chapter.

The data modification statements work on views as well as on tables, with some restrictions. See Chapter 9 for details.

Adding New Rows

The INSERT statement allows you to add rows to the database in two ways: with the VALUES keyword or with a SELECT statement. The first INSERT syntax we'll explain uses the VALUES keyword.

The VALUES keyword specifies data values for some or all of the columns in a new row. A generalized version of the syntax for the INSERT command using the VALUES keyword is:

```
INSERT INTO table_name [(insert_column_list)]
VALUES (constant1, constant2, ...)
```

This INSERT statement adds a new row to the table, giving a value for every column in the row:

```
SQL:
insert into publishers
values ('1622', 'Jardin, Inc.', '5 5th Ave.', 'Camden', 'NJ')
```

Notice that you have to type the data values in the same order as the column names in the original CREATE TABLE statement (*i.e.*, first the ID number, then the name, the address, the city, and finally the state). The VALUES data is surrounded by parentheses. Most systems require single or double quotes around character and date data, and commas to separate the values.

Use a separate INSERT statement for each row you add.

Inserting Data into Some Columns.   When you add data in some, but not all, of the columns in a row, you need to specify those columns. For example, adding data in only two columns (say *pub_id* and *pub_name*) requires a command like this:

```
SQL:

insert into publishers (pub_id, pub_name)
values ('1756', 'HealthText')
```

The order in which you list the column names has no effect on the INSERT statement as long as the order in which you list the data values matches it. The following example (which reverses the order of *pub_name* and *pub_id*) has exactly the same effect as the previous example:

```
SQL:

insert into publishers (pub_name, pub_id)
values('HealthText', '1756')
```

Both INSERT statements put "1756" in the identification number column and "HealthText" in the publisher name column. What happened in the *address*, *city*, and *state* columns? The following SELECT statement shows the row that was added to *publishers*:

```
SQL:

select pub_id, pub_name, address, city, state
from publishers
where pub_name = 'HealthText'
```

```
Results:

pub_id      pub_name              address     city     state
---------   -----------------     ---------   -------  -------
1756        HealthText            NULL        NULL     NULL
```

The system enters null values in the *address*, *city*, and *state* columns because there wasn't any value for these columns in the INSERT statement, and the *publishers* table allows null values in these columns. If your system doesn't permit null values, you'll probably see some default such as blanks or zeros in those columns.

If you had defined *city* and *state* as not null in the CREATE TABLE statement, the insert wouldn't have worked, because columns that don't permit null values won't accept a non-entry. Here's what happens with Transact-SQL when you try an INSERT statement that doesn't specify a value for the *pub_id* column, which was assigned not null status when the *publishers* table was created:

SQL:
```
insert into publishers (pub_name, address, city, state)
values('Tweedledum Books', '1 23rd St.', 'New York', 'NY')
```

Results:
```
Msg 233, Level 16, State 2
The column pub_id in table publishers may not be null.
```

SELECT in an INSERT Statement

You can use a SELECT statement in an INSERT statement to get values from one or more other tables. A simple version of the syntax for the INSERT command using a SELECT statement is:

```
INSERT INTO table_name [(insert_column_list)]
SELECT column_list
   FROM table_list
   WHERE search_conditions
```

SELECT in an INSERT statement lets you pull data from all or some of the columns from one table into another. If you insert values for a subset of the columns, you can use UPDATE at another time to add the values for the other columns.

When you insert rows from one table into another, the two tables must have compatible structures—that is, the matching columns must be the same datatypes, or datatypes between which the system automatically converts.

If all the columns of the two tables are compatible in the same order that they appeared in their CREATE TABLE statements, you don't need to specify column names in either table. Suppose a table called *newauthors* contains some rows of author information in the same format as *authors*. To add to *authors* all the rows in *newauthors*, type a command like this:

SQL:
```
insert into authors
select au_id, au_lname, au_fname, phone, address, city, state, zip
from newauthors
```

If the columns in the two tables (the one you're inserting into and the one you're getting data from) are not in the same order in their respective CREATE TABLE statements, you can use either the INSERT or the SELECT clause to re-order the columns so that they match.

For example, say the CREATE TABLE statement for the *authors* table contains the columns *au_id, au_fname, au_lname,* and *address* in that order, while *newauthors* contains *au_id address, au_lname,* and *au_fname*. You'd have to make the column sequence match in the INSERT statement. You could do this by listing the columns of *authors* in the INSERT clause:

SQL:
```
insert into authors (au_id, address, au_lname, au_fname)
select * from newauthors
```

You could also do it by listing the columns of *newauthors* in the SELECT clause:

SQL:
```
insert into authors
select au_id, au_fname, au_lname, address
   from newauthors
```

If the column sequence in the two tables fails to match, the system cannot complete the INSERT operation, or completes it incorrectly, putting data in the wrong columns. For example, you might get truncated address data in the *au_lname* column, probably not what you wanted.

Expressions.   One of the beneficial side effects of using a SELECT statement inside an INSERT statement is that it allows you to include **expressions** (strings of characters, mathematical calculations, and functions, alone or in combination with columns or each other) to change the data that you're pulling in. (See the chapters on SELECT for a full range of possibilities.)

Here's an example of a SELECT clause with an expression involving a column and a mathematical computation: imagine that one of the publishing subsidiaries has purchased a series of books from another publishing company that conveniently uses a table with exactly the same structure as the *titles* table. The newly purchased books are in a table named *Books*, and you want to load this data into *titles*. However, the company from which the books were purchased underpriced its wares, and you want to increase the price of all the new books by 50%. A statement to increase the prices and insert the rows from *Books* into *titles* looks like this:

```
SQL:
insert into titles
select title_id, title, type, pub_id, price*1.5
    advance, royalty, ytd_sales, contract, notes, pubdate
    from Books
```

Inserting Data into Some Columns.   You can use the SELECT statement to add data to some, but not all, of the columns in a row just as you do with the VALUES clause. Simply specify the columns to which you want to add data in the INSERT clause.

For example, if there are books in the *titles* table that do not yet have contracts and hence do not have entries in the *titleauthors* table, you might try to use this statement to pull their *title_id* numbers out of the *titles* table and insert them into the *titleauthors* table as place-holders:

```
SQL:
insert into titleauthors (au_id)
select title_id
    from titles
    where contract = 0
```

However, this statement is not legal, because a value is required for the *au_id* column of *titleauthors* (the table definition doesn't permit nulls and there is no default value). You can put in *xxxxxx* as a **dummy value** for *au_id* like this, using it as a constant:

```
SQL:
insert into titleauthors (title_id, au_id)
select title_id, "xxxxxx"
  from titles
  where contract = 0
```

The *titleauthors* table now contains two new rows with entries for the *title_id* column, dummy entries for the *au_id* column, and null values for the other two columns.

Most versions of SQL forbid listing the INSERT table in the FROM clause:

```
SQL:
insert into test
select *
from test
```

Transact-SQL is one system that allows it.

CHANGING EXISTING DATA: UPDATE

While the INSERT statement adds new rows to a table, the UPDATE statement changes existing rows. Use it to change values in single rows, groups of rows, or all the rows in a table.

The UPDATE statement specifies the row or rows you want to change, and the new data. The new data can be a constant or expression that you specify, or it can be data pulled from other tables.

Here's a simplified version of the UPDATE syntax for updating specified rows with an expression:

```
UPDATE table_name
SET column_name = expression
[WHERE search_conditions]
```

The UPDATE Statement

The UPDATE keyword is followed by the name of a table or view. As in all the data modification statements, you can change the data in only one table or view at a time.

If an update statement violates an integrity constraint (one of the values being added is the wrong datatype, for example) the system does not perform the update, and usually displays an error message. See Chapter 8 for restrictions on updating views.

The SET Clause

The SET clause specifies the column(s) and the changed value(s). The WHERE clause determines which row or rows will be updated. Note that if you don't have a WHERE clause, you'll update the specified columns of *all* the rows with the values in the SET clause.

For example, here's what the *publishers* table looks like:

```
SQL:
select *
from publishers
```

```
Results:
pub_id  pub_name                address        city         state
-------  ---------------------   -----------    -----------  --------
0736    New Age Books           1 1st St       Boston       MA
0877    Binnet & Hardley        2 2nd Ave.     Washington   DC
1389    Algodata Infosystems    3 3rd Dr.      Berkeley     CA
1622    Jardin, Inc.            5 5th Ave.     Camden       NJ
1756    HealthText              NULL           NULL         NULL
```

(5 rows affected)

If all the publishing houses in the *publishers* table move their head offices to Atlanta, Georgia, this is how you update the table:

```
SQL:
update publishers
set city = "Atlanta", state = "GA"
```

Here's what the table looks like now:

SQL:
```
select *
from publishers
```

Results:
```
pub_id   pub_name                address        city          state
-------  ----------------------  ------------   ------------  --------
0736     New Age Books           1 1st St       Atlanta       GA
0877     Binnet & Hardley        2 2nd Ave.     Atlanta       GA
1389     Algodata Infosystems    3 3rd Dr.      Atlanta       GA
1622     Jardin, Inc.            5 5th Ave.     Atlanta       GA
1756     HealthText              NULL           Atlanta       GA

(5 rows affected)
```

In the same way, you can change the names of all the publishers to "ZIPP!" with this statement:

SQL:
```
update publishers
set pub_name = "ZIPP!"
```

Now the table looks like this:

SQL:
```
select *
from publishers
```

Results:
```
pub_id   pub_name                address        city          state
-------  ----------------------  ------------   ------------  --------
0736     ZIPP!                   1 1st St       Atlanta       GA
0877     ZIPP!                   2 2nd Ave.     Atlanta       GA
1389     ZIPP!                   3 3rd Dr.      Atlanta       GA
1622     ZIPP!                   5 5th Ave.     Atlanta       GA
1756     ZIPP!                   NULL           Atlanta       GA

(5 rows affected)
```

You can also use computed column values in an update. To double all the prices in the *titles* table, use this statement:

```
SQL:
update titles
set price = price * 2
```

Since there is no WHERE clause, the change in prices is applied to every row in the table.

The WHERE Clause

The WHERE clause in an UPDATE statement specifies which rows to change. (It is similar to the WHERE clause in a SELECT statement, which is discussed thoroughly in Chapters 4, 5, 6, 7, and 8.) For example, in the unlikely event that northern California becomes a new state called Pacifica (abbreviated PC), and the people of Oakland vote to change the name of their city to something exciting (like Big Bad Bay City), here is how you can update the *authors* table for all former Oakland residents whose addresses are now out of date:

```
SQL:
update authors
set state = "PC", city = "Big Bad Bay City"
where state = "CA" and city = "Oakland"
```

Here's the new look of the *authors* table:

```
SQL:
select au_fname, au_lname, city, state
from authors
```

```
Results:
au_fname          au_lname          city                  state
---------------   ---------------   -------------------   -----
Johnson           White             Menlo Park            CA
Marjorie          Green             Big Bad Bay City      PC
Cheryl            Carson            Berkeley              CA
Michael           O'Leary           San Jose              CA
```

Dick	Straight	Big Bad Bay City	PC
Meander	Smith	Lawrence	KS
Abraham	Bennet	Berkeley	CA
Ann	Dull	Palo Alto	CA
Burt	Gringlesby	Covelo	CA
Chastity	Locksley	San Francisco	CA
Morningstar	Greene	Nashville	TN
Reginald	Blotchet-Halls	Corvallis	OR
Akiko	Yokomoto	Walnut Creek	CA
Innes	del Castillo	Ann Arbor	MI
Michel	DeFrance	Gary	IN
Dirk	Stringer	Big Bad Bay City	PC
Stearns	MacFeather	Big Bad Bay City	PC
Livia	Karsen	Big Bad Bay City	PC
Sylvia	Panteley	Rockville	MD
Sheryl	Hunter	Palo Alto	CA
Heather	McBadden	Vacaville	CA
Anne	Ringer	Salt Lake City	UT
Albert	Ringer	Salt Lake City	UT

```
(23 rows affected)
```

The WHERE clause of an UPDATE statement can also contain a subquery that refers to one or more other tables. For information on subqueries, see Chapter 7.

REMOVING DATA: DELETE

It's just as important to be able to remove rows as it is to be able to add or change them. Like INSERT and UPDATE, DELETE works for single-row operations as well as multiple-row operations. Also like the other data modification statements, you can delete rows based on data in other tables.

DELETE syntax looks like this:

```
DELETE FROM table_name
WHERE search_conditions
```

The WHERE clause specifies which rows to remove. If you decide to remove one row from *publishers*—the row added for publisher identification number 1622—type:

```
SQL:
delete from publishers
where pub_id = "1622"
```

Note that once you delete the row that describes this publisher, you can no longer find the books the company publishes by joining the *publishers* and *titles* tables on publisher identification numbers.

If there is no WHERE clause in the DELETE statement, *all* rows in the table are removed.

LOADING SOME SAMPLE DATA

Now you've learned what you need to know in order to create the sample database, *bookbiz*, and to load data into it. This section gives an INSERT statement for the first row of each main table. Appendix D collects all the information you need about *bookbiz*:

- An entity-relationship diagram
- A display of all the data in each table, along with information about each column's datatype, null status, and index (if any)
- CREATE statements for each of the objects in *bookbiz*
- Data modification statements for adding each sample row in the database

Here are INSERT statements that add one row of sample data into six of the tables in *bookbiz*, along with SELECT statements that display the new row:

```
authors table:

SQL:
insert authors
values('409-56-7008', 'Bennet', 'Abraham',
'415 658-9932', '6223 Bateman St.', 'Berkeley', 'CA', '94705')
```

SQL:

```
select *
from authors
where au_id = '409-56-7008'
```

Results:

```
au_id              au_lname  au_fname    phone
   address              city        state  zip
---------------  ----------  -----------  -------------
409-56-7008      Bennet      Abraham      415 658-9932
   6223 Bateman St.    Berkeley     CA     94705
```

(1 row affected)

titles table:

SQL:

```
insert titles
values ('PC8888', 'Secrets of Silicon Valley',
'popular_comp', '1389', $20.00, $8000.00, 4095, 1,
"Muckraking reporting by two courageous women on
the world's largest computer hardware and
software manufacturers.", '06/12/85')
```

SQL:

```
select *
from titles
where title_id = 'PC8888'
```

Results:

```
title_id  title                              type
   pub_id     price    advance    ytd_sales  contract
   notes
   pubdate
- - - - - - - - - - - - - - - - - - - - - - - - - - - - - - - - - - - - -
PC8888    Secrets of Silicon Valley          popular_comp
   1389       20.00   8,000.00   4095        1
   Muckraking reporting by two courageous women on the world's
   largest computer hardware and software manufacturers.
   Jun 12 1985 12:00AM
```

(1 row affected)

titleauthors table:

SQL:
```
insert titleauthors
values('409-56-7008', 'BU1032', 1, .60)
```

SQL:
```
select *
from titleauthors
where au_id = '409-56-7008'
  and title_id = 'BU1032'
```

Results:

au_id	title_id	au_ord	royaltyshare
409-56-7008	BU1032	1	0.600000

(1 row affected)

publishers table:

SQL:
```
insert publishers
values('0736', 'New Age Books', '1 1st St',
'Boston', 'MA')
```

SQL:
```
select *
from publishers
where pub_id = "0736"
```

Results:

pub_id	pub_name	address	city	state
0736	New Age Books	1 1st St	Boston	MA

(1 row affected)

editors table:

SQL:

```
insert editors
values ("321-55-8906","DeLongue","Martinella","project",
"415 843-2222","3000 6th St.","Berkeley","CA","94710")
```

SQL:

```
select *
from editors
where ed_id = "321-55-8906"
```

Results:

```
ed_id           ed_lname    ed_fname      ed_pos      phone
  address         city                    state     zip
---------------------------------------------------------------
321-55-8906    DeLongue   Martinella    project     415 843-2222
  3000 6th St.    Berkeley                CA        94710
```

(1 row affected)

titleditors table:

SQL:

```
insert titleditors
values ("826-11-9034", "BU2075", 2)
```

SQL:

```
select *
from titleditors
where ed_id = "826-11-9034"
  and title_id = "BU2075"
```

Results:

```
ed_id          title_id  ed_ord
------------   --------  ------
826-11-9034   BU2075        2
```

(1 row affected)

Saving SQL Statements in Operating System Files

Instead of submitting the CREATE statements and data modification statements to SQL interactively, we recommend that you type them into operating system files and save them under appropriate names for repeated use. This will save lots of time and frustration when you want to re-create the sample database—either because something's gone wrong, or simply because you or someone else wants to start over with a fresh copy of the database.

Check your system's reference manuals to find out how to feed statements in an operating system file to SQL. You may have to add terminators between statements and/or include statements like USE DATABASE at the beginning of each file.

In a production environment, maintaining files like these is crucial to smooth operation. It's wise to get into the practice of saving in operating system files *all* SQL statements that affect the structure of a database, including:

- CREATE statements that have been changed to reflect any ALTER statements executed during the life of the database
- Statements used to generate reports
- GRANT and REVOKE statements
- Other administrative set-up commands that may be provided in your implementation of SQL, such as statements that add users or initialize database devices

Beginning Data Retrieval

If you've executed all these CREATE TABLE and data modification commands, you've got yourself an on-line sample database with which you can practice the examples in the rest of this book. The next chapters discuss how to retrieve data with the SELECT statement.

Chapter 4

Selecting Data from the Database

AMONG THE SELECT?

In many ways, the SELECT statement is the real heart of SQL. It lets you find and view your data in a variety of ways. You use it to answer questions based on your data—how many, where, what kind of, even what if. Once you become comfortable with its sometimes dauntingly complex syntax, you'll be amazed at what the SELECT statement can do.

Since SELECT is so important, five chapters focus on it. This one starts out with the bare bones: the SELECT, FROM, and WHERE clauses, search conditions and expressions. Chapter 5 delves into some SELECT refinements—ORDER BY, the DISTINCT keyword, and aggregates. Chapter 6 covers the GROUP BY clause, the HAVING clause, and the issues related to making reports from grouped data. This chapter also summarizes the issues regarding null values in database management. Chapter 7 introduces multiple-table queries with a comprehensive discussion of joining tables. Chapter 8 moves on to **nested queries**, also known as subqueries.

Queries in this chapter use single tables so that you can focus on manipulating the syntax in a simple environment.

SELECT Syntax

The most complicated SELECT statement begins with this skeleton:

```
SELECT list_of_columns
FROM table[s]
[WHERE search_conditions]
```

The SELECT list identifies the *columns* you want to retrieve. The table list specifies the *tables* those columns are in. The WHERE clause qualifies the *rows*—it chooses the ones you want to see. Both the SELECT and WHERE clauses can include calculations, constants, and other expressions. Artful combinations of the SELECT, FROM, and WHERE clauses produce meaningful answers to your questions and keep you from drowning in a sea of data.

You can think of the SELECT and WHERE clauses as X and Y axes on a matrix. For example:

```
Select Address
From Personnel
Where Name = "Richard Roe"
```

Figure 4–1: Selecting Data from the Personnel Table

The data you get from the SELECT statement in Figure 4–1 is at the intersection of the SELECT and WHERE clauses (here *row2, column2*). Let's look at a SELECT statement a little closer to real life, with one of the sample tables, *authors*.

The *authors* table stores information about authors: their id numbers, names, addresses, and phone numbers. If you want to know just the names of authors who live in California (not their addresses and phone numbers), you use the select list and the WHERE clause to limit the data that the SELECT statement returns.

Here's a query that uses the SELECT clause's select list to limit the columns you see. It shows just first and last name for each author, ignoring id number, address, and phone.

SQL:

```
select au_lname, au_fname
from authors
```

Results:

au_lname	au_fname
White	Johnson
Green	Marjorie
Carson	Cheryl
O'Leary	Michael
Straight	Dick
Smith	Meander
Bennet	Abraham
Dull	Ann
Gringlesby	Burt
Locksley	Chastity
Greene	Morningstar
Blotchet-Halls	Reginald
Yokomoto	Akiko
del Castillo	Innes
DeFrance	Michel
Stringer	Dirk
MacFeather	Stearns
Karsen	Livia
Panteley	Sylvia
Hunter	Sheryl
McBadden	Heather
Ringer	Anne
Ringer	Albert

(23 rows affected)

Notice that this display still doesn't provide exactly what you want, since it lists all authors regardless of the state they live in. You need to refine the data retrieval statement further with the WHERE clause.

SQL:

```
select au_lname, au_fname
from authors
where state = "CA"
```

```
Results

au_lname                        au_fname
------------------------------  --------------------
White                           Johnson
Green                           Marjorie
Carson                          Cheryl
O'Leary                         Michael
Straight                        Dick
Bennet                          Abraham
Dull                            Ann
Gringlesby                      Burt
Locksley                        Chastity
Yokomoto                        Akiko
Stringer                        Dirk
MacFeather                      Stearns
Karsen                          Livia
Hunter                          Sheryl
McBadden                        Heather

(15 rows affected)
```

Now you're looking at just the names of authors having a California address. The rows for the eight authors living elsewhere are not included in the display.

In practice, SELECT syntax can be either simpler or more complex than the example shown above. It can be simpler in that the SELECT and (usually) FROM clauses are the only required ones in a SELECT statement. The WHERE clause (and all other clauses) are optional. On the other hand, the full syntax of the SELECT statement includes all of these phrases and keywords:

```
SELECT [ALL | DISTINCT] select_list
  FROM {table_name | view_name}
    [,{table_name | view_name}]...
  [WHERE search_conditions]
  [GROUP BY column_name [, column_name]...]
    [HAVING search_conditions]
  [ORDER BY {column_name | select_list_number} [ASC | DESC]
     [,{column_name | select_list_number} [ASC | DESC]]...]
```

Although SQL is a free-form language, you do have to keep the clauses in a SELECT statement in syntactical order (*i.e.*, a GROUP BY clause must come before an ORDER BY clause). Otherwise, you'll get syntax errors.

You may also need to qualify the names of database objects (according to the customs of your SQL dialect) if there is any ambiguity about which object you mean. For example, if there are several columns called *notes* in a database, you may have to specify which *notes* column you're talking about by including the database name, the table or view name, and the owner name—something like this:

```
database.owner.table_name.notes

database.owner.view_name.notes
```

The examples in this chapter involve queries on a single table, so qualification is not an important issue here. Qualifiers are also omitted in most books, articles, and reference manuals on SQL because the short forms make the SELECT statements more readable. However, it's never wrong to include them.

CHOOSING COLUMNS: THE SELECT LIST

The first clause of the SELECT statement—the one that begins with the keyword SELECT—is required in all SELECT statements. The keywords ALL and DISTINCT, which specify whether duplicate rows are to be included in the results, are optional. DISTINCT and ALL are discussed in the next chapter.

The **select list** specifies the column or columns that are to be included in the results. It can consist of one or more column names, or of an asterisk, which is shorthand for all the columns. You can also use **expressions**—constants, column names, functions, or any combination of the above connected by arithmetic operators and parentheses. Here are some examples of expressions:

```
ytd_sales * price

price * 1.2

(12000 - 500) / 13

avg(advance)
```

Make sure to separate each element in a select list from the following element with a comma.

Choosing All Columns: SELECT *

The asterisk (*) has a special meaning in the select list. It stands for *all the column names* in *all the tables* in the table list. The columns are displayed in the order in which they appeared in the CREATE TABLE statement(s).

Most people read a SELECT * statement as "select star." Use it to save typing time (and cut down on typing errors) when you want to see all the columns in a table.

The general syntax for selecting all the columns in a table is:

```
SELECT *
FROM table_list
```

Because SELECT * finds all the columns currently in a table, changes in the structure of a table (adding, removing, or renaming columns) automatically modify the results of a SELECT *. Listing the columns individually gives you more precise control over the results, but SELECT * saves typing (and the frustration of typographical errors). SELECT * is most useful for tables with few columns, since displays of many columns can be confusing. It also comes in handy when you want to get a quick look at a table's structure (what columns it has, in what order).

The following statement retrieves all columns in the *publishers* table and displays them in the order in which they were defined when the *publishers* table was created. Since no WHERE clause is included, this statement retrieves every row.

```
SQL:
select *
from publishers

Results:
pub_id pub_name              address     city         state
------ --------------------- ----------- ------------ -----
0736   New Age Books         1 1st St    Boston       MA
0877   Binnet & Hardley      2 2nd Ave.  Washington   DC
```

```
    1389   Algodata Infosystems 3 3rd Dr.    Berkeley    CA

(3 rows affected)
```

You get exactly the same results by listing all the column names in the table in order after the SELECT keyword:

SQL:

```
select pub_id, pub_name, address, city, state
from publishers
```

An asterisk in the select list of a multiple-table query will cause SQL to display all the columns in all the tables in the table list. Some systems also let you use both an asterisk and column names in the select list. This is most useful in multiple-table queries, when you qualify the asterisk with a table name. Here's a data retrieval statement that finds *publishers* information for each *title_id* in the *titles* table. You see all the columns from the *publishers* table and only one column from the *titles* table.

SQL:

```
select title_id, publishers.*
from titles, publishers
where titles.pub_id=publishers.pub_id
```

Results:

title_id	pub_id	pub_name	address	city	state
BU2075	0736	New Age Books	1 1st St	Boston	MA
PS1372	0736	New Age Books	1 1st St	Boston	MA
PS2091	0736	New Age Books	1 1st St	Boston	MA
PS2106	0736	New Age Books	1 1st St	Boston	MA
PS3333	0736	New Age Books	1 1st St	Boston	MA
PS7777	0736	New Age Books	1 1st St	Boston	MA
MC2222	0877	Binnet & Hardley	2 2nd Ave.	Washington	DC
MC3021	0877	Binnet & Hardley	2 2nd Ave.	Washington	DC
MC3026	0877	Binnet & Hardley	2 2nd Ave.	Washington	DC
TC3218	0877	Binnet & Hardley	2 2nd Ave.	Washington	DC
TC4203	0877	Binnet & Hardley	2 2nd Ave.	Washington	DC
TC7777	0877	Binnet & Hardley	2 2nd Ave.	Washington	DC

```
BU1032   1389   Algodata Infosystems   3 3rd Dr.   Berkeley   CA
BU1111   1389   Algodata Infosystems   3 3rd Dr.   Berkeley   CA
BU7832   1389   Algodata Infosystems   3 3rd Dr.   Berkeley   CA
PC1035   1389   Algodata Infosystems   3 3rd Dr.   Berkeley   CA
PC8888   1389   Algodata Infosystems   3 3rd Dr.   Berkeley   CA
PC9999   1389   Algodata Infosystems   3 3rd Dr.   Berkeley   CA
```

(18 rows affected)

If you didn't use the qualified *, you'd have to write the query this way:

SQL:
```
select title_id, publishers.pub_id, pub_name, address, city, state
from titles, publishers
where titles.pub_id=publishers.pub_id
```

(Chapter 7 explains the intricacies of the join operation. Don't worry about the syntax for this query now.)

Choosing Specific Columns

To select a subset of the columns in a table, as some of the previous examples have demonstrated, simply list the columns you want to see in the select list:

```
SELECT column_name[, column_name]...
FROM table_name
```

Separate each column name from the following column name with a comma.

Rearranging Result Columns.   The order in which columns appear in a display is completely up to you: use the select list to order them in any way that makes sense.

Here are two examples. Both of them find and display the publisher names and identification numbers from all three of the rows in the *publishers* table. The first one prints *pub_id* first, followed by *pub_name*.

The second reverses that order. The information is exactly the same; only the organization changes.

SQL:

```
select pub_id, pub_name
from publishers
```

Results:

```
pub_id    pub_name
------    ---------------
0736      New Age Books
0877      Binnet & Hardley
1389      Algodata Infosystems
```

(3 rows affected)

SQL:

```
select pub_name, pub_id
from publishers
```

Results:

```
pub_name                    pub_id
--------------------        ------
New Age Books               0736
Binnet & Hardley            0877
Algodata Infosystems        1389
```

(3 rows affected)

Expressions: More than Column Names

The SELECT statements you've seen so far show exactly what's stored in a table. This is useful, but often not useful enough. SQL lets you add to and manipulate these results to make them easier to read or to do "what if" queries. You can also use strings of characters, mathematical calculations, and functions provided by your system in the select list, with or without column names.

Renaming Columns and Naming Expressions. When the results of a query are displayed, each column has a default heading, its name as defined in the database. Column names in databases are often cryptic (so they'll be easy to type) or have no meaning to users unfamiliar with departmental acronyms, nicknames, or project jargon.

Many systems allow you to solve this problem and specify column headings to make query results easier to read and understand. To get the heading you want, simply type `column_name column_heading` in the select list in place of the column name. (Some systems allow an alternate syntax like `column_heading = column_name`.)

For example, to change *pub_name* to *Publisher*, try one of the following statements:

```
SQL:
select pub_name Publisher, pub_id
from publishers
```

```
SQL:
select Publisher = pub_name, pub_id
from publishers
```

The results now show a new column heading:

```
Results:
Publisher                                      pub_id
---------------------------------------------- ------
New Age Books                                  0736
Binnet & Hardley                               0877
Algodata Infosystems                           1389

(3 rows affected)
```

A column heading is usually not limited to the size of the current column. The *pub_id* column, for example, can take a column heading longer than its defined length of four characters. Look what happens in the display when you change the column heading to a string such as "Identification#."

```
SQL:
select Publisher=pub_name, Identification#=pub_id
from publishers
```

```
Results:
Publisher                                          Identification#
-------------------------------------------------  ---------------
New Age Books                                       0736
Binnet & Hardley                                    0877
Algodata Infosystems                               1389

(3 rows affected)
```

In most systems, the display size stretches to accommodate the longer heading; if you use a smaller heading, however, it doesn't shrink.

Most SQL dialects that allow you to add column headings have some restrictions (check your reference guide for details). Ordinarily, you can't put quotes around or spaces in a column heading: "Identification #" (with a blank between the word and the pound sign) probably won't work.

You can use the same technique to create headings for columns based on strings, calculations, and other expressions: *New_price, Double_Advance*, and so on:

```
select title, Double_Advance=advance * 2
from titles
```

Character Strings in Query Results.   Sometimes a little text can make query results easier to understand. That's where **strings** (of characters) come in handy.

Let's say you want a listing of publishers with something like "The publisher's name is" in front of each item. All you have to do is insert the string in the correct position in the select list. Be sure to enclose the entire string in single or double quotes so your system can tell it's not a column name, and separate it from other elements in the select list with commas.

Follow your system's rules for protecting embedded apostrophes and quotes if any appear in the string. Here, double quotes do the trick. If you try the query with single quotes, you'll get different results, because the apostrophe will be interpreted as a close quote.

```
SQL:
select "The publisher's name is", Publisher = pub_name
from publishers
```

```
Results:
                                  Publisher
------------------------          ---------------
The publisher's name is           New Age Books
The publisher's name is           Binnet & Hardley
The publisher's name is           Algodata Infosystems

(3 rows affected)
```

The constants create a new column in the display only—what you see doesn't affect anything that's physically in the database.

You could also break each word in the string into a separate field, like this:

```
SQL:
select "The", "publisher's", "name", "is", pub_name
from publishers
```

```
Results:
                               pub_name
--- ----------- ---- -- ---------------------------------
The publisher's name is New Age Books
The publisher's name is Binnet & Hardley
The publisher's name is Algodata Infosystems

(3 rows affected)
```

This technique makes it easy to combine columns and text. Here's an example of doing just that:

```
SQL:
select "The name for publisher #", pub_id, "is", pub_name
from publishers
```

```
Results:
                               pub_id   pub_name
------------------------ ------ -- -----------------------
The name for publisher # 0736   is New Age Books
The name for publisher # 0877   is Binnet & Hardley
The name for publisher # 1389   is Algodata Infosystems

(3 rows affected)
```

Computations with Constants.   The select list is the place that you indicate computations you want to perform on numeric data or constants. Here are the available arithmetic operators:

Symbol	Operation
+	addition
–	subtraction
/	division
*	multiplication

The arithmetic operators—addition, subtraction, division, and multiplication—can be used on any numeric column. (Some systems add **modulo**, represented as %. A modulo is the whole number remainder after division of one whole number by another. For example, 21 % 9 = 3, because 21 divided by 9 equals 2, with a remainder of 3.)

Certain arithmetic operations can also be performed on date columns, if your system provides date functions.

You can use all of these operators in the select list with column names and numeric constants in any combination. For example, to see what a projected sales increase of 100% for all the books in the *titles* table looks like, type this:

```
SQL:
select title_id, ytd_sales, ytd_sales * 2
from titles
```

Here are the results:

```
Results:
title_id ytd_sales
-------- ----------- -----------
  BU1032        4095        8190
  BU1111        3876        7752
  BU2075       18722       37444
  BU7832        4095        8190
  MC2222        2032        4064
  MC3021       22246       44492
  MC3026        NULL        NULL
  PC1035        8780       17560
  PC8888        4095        8190
  PC9999        NULL        NULL
```

```
PS1372                 375                 750
PS2091                2045                4090
PS2106                 111                 222
PS3333                4072                8144
PS7777                3336                6672
TC3218                 375                 750
TC4203               15096               30192
TC7777                4095                8190
```

```
(18 rows affected)
```

Notice the NULL values in the *ytd_sales* column and the computed column. When you perform any arithmetic operation on a null value, the result is NULL.

If your system allows it, you can give the computed column a heading (say *Projected_Sales*) by typing:

SQL:
```
select title_id, ytd_sales, ytd_sales * 2 Projected_Sales
from titles
```

For a fancier display yet, try adding character strings such as "Current sales =" and "Projected sales are" to the SELECT statement.

Sometimes, as in the previous example, you'll want both the original data and the computed data in your results. But you don't have to include the column on which the computation takes place in the select list. To see just the computed values, type:

SQL:
```
select title_id, ytd_sales * 2
from titles
```

Results:
```
title_id
-------- -----------
BU1032               8190
BU1111               7752
BU2075              37444
BU7832               8190
MC2222               4064
```

```
MC3021          44492
MC3026          NULL
PC1035          17560
PC8888           8190
PC9999          NULL
PS1372            750
PS2091           4090
PS2106            222
PS3333           8144
PS7777           6672
TC3218            750
TC4203          30192
TC7777           8190

(18 rows affected)
```

Computations with Column Names.   You can also use arithmetic operators for computations on the data in two or more columns, with no constants involved. Here's an example:

SQL:
```
select title_id, ytd_sales * price
from titles
```

Results:
```
title_id
-------- ---------------------------
BU1032           81,859.05
BU1111           46,318.20
BU2075           55,978.78
BU7832           81,859.05
MC2222           40,619.68
MC3021           66,515.54
MC3026               NULL
PC1035          201,501.00
PC8888           81,900.00
PC9999               NULL
PS1372            8,096.25
PS2091           22,392.75
PS2106              777.00
```

```
PS3333                    81,399.28
PS7777                    26,654.64
TC3218                     7,856.25
TC4203                   180,397.20
TC7777                    61,384.05
```

(18 rows affected)

Finally, you can compute new values on the basis of columns from more than one table. (The chapters on joining and subqueries give information on how to work with multiple-table queries, so check them for syntax details.)

Arithmetic Operator Precedence.   When there is more than one arithmetic operator in an expression, the system follows rules that determine the order in which the operations are carried out. According to commonly used precedence rules, multiplication and division are calculated first, followed by subtraction and addition. When more than one arithmetic operator in an expression has the same level of precedence, the order of execution is left to right. Expressions within parentheses take precedence over all other operations. Figure 4–2 illustrates the precedence hierarchy:

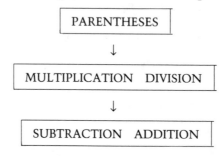

Figure 4-2. Precedence Hierarchy for Arithmetic Operators

Here's an example. The following SELECT statement subtracts the advance on each book from the gross revenues realized on its sales (*price* multiplied by *ytd_sales*). The product of *ytd_sales* and *price* is calculated first because the operator is multiplication.

SQL:

```
select title_id, ytd_sales * price - advance
from titles
```

To avoid misunderstandings, use parentheses. The query below has the same meaning and gives the same results as the previous one, but some may find it easier to understand:

```
SQL:
select title_id, (ytd_sales * price) - advance
from titles

Results:
title_id
-------- -------------------------
BU1032                 76,859.05
BU1111                 41,318.20
BU2075                 45,853.78
BU7832                 76,859.05
MC2222                 40,619.68
MC3021                 51,515.54
MC3026                      NULL
PC1035                194,501.00
PC8888                 73,900.00
PC9999                      NULL
PS1372                  1,096.25
PS2091                 20,117.75
PS2106                 -5,223.00
PS3333                 79,399.28
PS7777                 22,654.64
TC3218                    856.25
TC4203                176,397.20
TC7777                 53,384.05

(18 rows affected)
```

Another important use of parentheses is changing the order of execution—calculations inside parentheses are handled first. If parentheses are nested (one set of parentheses inside another), the most deeply nested calculation has precedence. For example, the result and meaning of the query shown above can be changed if you use parentheses to force evaluation of the subtraction before the multiplication:

SQL:

```
select title_id, ytd_sales * (price - advance)
from titles
```

Results:

```
title_id
-------- -------------------------
BU1032           -20,393,140.95
BU1111           -19,333,681.80
BU2075          -189,504,271.22
BU7832           -20,393,140.95
MC2222               40,619.68
MC3021          -333,623,484.46
MC3026                    NULL
PC1035           -61,258,499.00
PC8888           -32,678,100.00
PC9999                    NULL
PS1372            -2,616,903.75
PS2091            -4,629,982.25
PS2106              -665,223.00
PS3333            -8,062,600.72
PS7777           -13,317,345.36
TC3218            -2,617,143.75
TC4203           -60,203,602.80
TC7777           -32,698,615.95
```

```
(18 rows affected)
```

SPECIFYING TABLES: THE TABLE LIST

The **table list** names the table(s) and/or the view(s) that contain columns included in the select list and in the WHERE clause. Separate table names in the table list with commas. The FROM syntax looks like this:

```
SELECT select_list
FROM [qualifier]{table_name | view_name}
   [,[qualifier]{table_name | view_name}
```

The full naming syntax for tables and views, with qualifying database and owner names, is always permitted in the table list. It's only necessary, however, when there might be some confusion about the name.

In many SQL dialects, you can give table names **aliases** to save typing. Assign an alias in the table list by giving the alias after the table name, like this:

```
SQL:
select p.pub_id, p.pub_name
from publishers p
```

The *p* in front of each of the column names in the select list acts as a substitute for the full table name (*publishers*). This query is equivalent:

```
SQL:
select publishers.pub_id, publishers.pub_name
from publishers
```

Since only one table is involved in these queries, there is no ambiguity about which *pub_id* column you're referencing, so using the table name—either its alias or full name—as a qualifier is optional. Aliases are really useful only in multiple-table queries, where you need to qualify columns from different tables. You'll see examples of their use in the chapters on joins and subqueries.

SELECTING ROWS: THE WHERE CLAUSE

The WHERE clause is the part of the SELECT statement that specifies the search conditions. These conditions determine exactly which rows are retrieved. The general format is:

```
SELECT select_list
FROM table_list
WHERE search_conditions
```

When you run a SELECT statement with a WHERE clause, your system searches for the rows in the table that meet your conditions (also called **qualifications**).

SQL provides a variety of operators and keywords for expressing the search conditions, including these:

- Comparison operators (=, <, >, etc.)

  ```
  where advance * 2 > ytd_sales * price
  ```

- Combinations or logical negations of conditions (AND, OR, NOT)

  ```
  where advance < 5000 or ytd_sales between
  2000 and 2500
  ```

- Ranges (BETWEEN and NOT BETWEEN)

  ```
  where ytd_sales between 4095 and 12000
  ```

- Lists (IN, NOT IN)

  ```
  where state in ("CA", "IN", "MD")
  ```

- Unknown values (IS NULL and IS NOT NULL)

  ```
  where advance is null
  ```

- Character matches (LIKE and NOT LIKE)

  ```
  where phone not like "415%"
  ```

Each of these keywords and operators is explained and illustrated in this chapter.

In addition, the WHERE clause can include join conditions (see Chapter 7) and subqueries (see Chapter 8).

Comparison Operators

You often want to look at values in relation to one another, to find out which is "larger" or "smaller," or "lower" in the alphabet sort, or "equal" to some other database value or to a constant. SQL provides a set of comparison operators for these purposes. In most dialects, the comparison operators are:

Operator	Meaning
=	equal to
>	greater than
<	less than
>=	greater than or equal to
<=	less than or equal to
!=	not equal to (or)
< >	not equal to

The operators are used in the syntax:

```
WHERE expression comparison_operator expression
```

An expression can be a constant, column name, function, subquery, or any combination of them connected by arithmetic operators.

In contexts other than SQL, the comparison operators are usually used with numeric values. In SQL, they are also used with *char* and *varchar* data (< means earlier in the dictionary order and > means later) and with dates (< means earlier in chronological order and > means later). When you use character and date values in a SQL statement, be sure to put single or double quotes around them.

The order in which upper and lower case characters and special characters are evaluated depends on the character sorting sequence of the computer you are using. On ASCII machines, for example, lower case letters are considered greater than upper case letters, and upper case letters are greater than numbers.

In most systems, trailing blanks are ignored for the purposes of comparison. So, for example, "Dirk" would be considered the same as "Dirk " by the system.

The following SELECT statements and their results should give you a good sense of how the comparison operators are used. The first query finds the books that cost more than fifteen dollars:

```
SQL:
select title, price
from titles
where price > $15.00

Results:
title                                             price
------------------------------------------------- -----
The Busy Executive's Database Guide               19.99
Straight Talk About Computers                     19.99
Silicon Valley Gastronomic Treats                 19.99
```

```
But Is It User Friendly?                    22.95
Secrets of Silicon Valley                   20.00
Computer Phobic and Non-Phobic
    Individuals: Behavior Variations        21.59
Prolonged Data Deprivation:
    Four Case Studies                       19.99
Onions, Leeks, and Garlic: Cooking
    Secrets of the Mediterranean            20.95

(8 rows affected)
```

The next SELECT statement finds the authors whose last names follow McBadden's in the alphabet:

SQL:

```
select au_lname, au_fname
from authors
where au_lname >"McBadden"
```

Results:

```
au_lname                                    au_fname
------------------------------------------- -------------
White                                       Johnson
O'Leary                                     Michael
Straight                                    Dick
Smith                                       Meander
Yokomoto                                    Akiko
del Castillo                                Innes
Stringer                                    Dirk
Panteley                                    Sylvia
Ringer                                      Anne
Ringer                                      Albert

(10 rows affected)
```

The next query displays hypothetical information—it doubles the price of all books for which advances over $10,000 were paid, and displays the title identification numbers and doubled prices:

SQL:

```
select title_id, price * 2
from titles
where advance > $10000
```

Results:

```
title_id
-------- ------------------------
BU2075                      5.98
MC3021                      5.98
```

(2 rows affected)

Here's a query that finds the telephone numbers of authors that don't live in California, using the not equal comparison operator: (In different versions of SQL, the not equal operator can be != or < > .)

SQL:

```
select au_id, phone
from authors
where state != "CA"
```

Results:

```
au_id        phone
----------- ------------
341-22-1782 913 843-0462
527-72-3246 615 297-2723
648-92-1872 503 745-6402
712-45-1867 615 996-8275
722-51-5454 219 547-9982
807-91-6654 301 946-8853
899-46-2035 801 826-0752
998-72-3567 801 826-0752
```

(8 rows affected)

Connecting Conditions with Logical Operators

Use the *logical operators* AND, OR, and NOT when you're dealing with more than one condition in a WHERE clause. The logical operators are also called **Boolean operators**.

AND joins two or more conditions and returns results only when all of the conditions are true. For example, the query below will find only the rows in which the author's last name is Ringer and the author's first name is Anne. It will not find the row for Albert Ringer.

```
select *
from authors
where au_lname = 'Ringer'
and au_fname = 'Anne'
```

This example finds business books with a price higher than $10.00 and for which an advance of less than $20,000 was paid:

SQL:

```
select title, type, price, advance
from titles
where type = "business"
  and price > $10.00
  and advance < $20000
```

Results:

title			
type		price	advance
The Busy Executive's Database Guide			
business		19.99	5,000.00
Cooking with Computers: Surreptitious Balance Sheets			
business		11.95	5,000.00
Straight Talk About Computers			
business		19.99	5,000.00

```
(3 rows affected)
```

OR also connects two or more conditions, but it returns results when any of the conditions is true. The following query searches for rows containing Anne or Ann in the *au_fname* column.

SQL:

```
select au_id, au_lname, au_fname
from authors
```

```
where au_fname = 'Anne'
   or au_fname = 'Ann'
```

Results:

au_id	au_lname	au_fname
427-17-2319	Dull	Ann
899-46-2035	Ringer	Anne

(2 rows affected)

The following query searches for books with a price higher than $20 *or* an advance less than $5,000.

SQL:
```
select title, type, price, advance
from titles
where price > $20.00
   or advance < $5000
```

Results:

title type	price	advance
Silicon Valley Gastronomic Treats mod_cook	19.99	0.00
But Is It User Friendly? popular_comp	22.95	7,000.00
Computer Phobic and Non-Phobic Individuals: Behavior Variations psychology	21.59	7,000.00
Is Anger the Enemy? psychology	10.95	2,275.00
Prolonged Data Deprivation: Four Case Studies psychology	19.99	2,000.00
Emotional Security: A New Algorithm psychology	7.99	4,000.00
Onions, Leeks, and Garlic: Cooking Secrets of the Mediterranean trad_cook	20.95	7,000.00
Fifty Years in Buckingham Palace Kitchens trad_cook	11.95	4,000.00

(8 rows affected)

One more example using OR will demonstrate a potential for confusion. Let's say you want to find all the business books, as well as any books with a price higher than $10, as well as any with an advance less than $20,000. The English phrasing of this problem suggests the use of the operator AND, but the logical meaning dictates the use of OR because you want to find all the books in all three categories, not just books that meet all three characteristics at once. Here's the SQL statement that finds what you're looking for:

SQL:

```
select title, type, price, advance
from titles
where type = "business"
  or price > $10.00
  or advance < $20000
```

Results:

```
title
  type                                        price                advance
------------------------------- ---------------------- -----------
The Busy Executive's Database Guide
  business                                   19.99                 5,000.00
Cooking with Computers: Surreptitious Balance Sheets
  business                                   11.95                 5,000.00
You Can Combat Computer Stress!
  business                                    2.99                10,125.00
Straight Talk About Computers
  business                                   19.99                 5,000.00
Silicon Valley Gastronomic Treats
  mod_cook                                   19.99                     0.00
The Gourmet Microwave
  mod_cook                                    2.99                15,000.00
But Is It User Friendly?
  popular_comp                               22.95                 7,000.00
Secrets of Silicon Valley
  popular_comp                               20.00                 8,000.00
Computer Phobic and Non-Phobic Individuals: Behavior Variations
  psychology                                 21.59                 7,000.00
Is Anger the Enemy?
  psychology                                 10.95                 2,275.00
```

```
Life Without Fear
    psychology                  7.00                    6,000.00
Prolonged Data Deprivation: Four Case Studies
    psychology                 19.99                    2,000.00
Emotional Security: A New Algorithm
    psychology                  7.99                    4,000.00
Onions, Leeks, and Garlic: Cooking Secrets of the Mediterranean
    trad_cook                  20.95                    7,000.00
Fifty Years in Buckingham Palace Kitchens
    trad_cook                  11.95                    4,000.00
Sushi, Anyone?
    trad_cook                  14.99                    8,000.00
```

(16 rows affected)

Compare this query, and its results, to the earlier example that is identical except for the use of AND instead of OR.

The logical operator NOT negates an expression. When you use it with comparison operators, put it before the expression rather than before the comparison operator. The two queries below are equivalent:

SQL:

```
select au_lname, au_fname
from authors
where state != "CA"
```

SQL:

```
select au_lname, au_fname, state
from authors
where not state = "CA"
```

Here are the results:

```
Results:

au_lname                au_fname                state
----------------        --------------------    -----

Smith                   Meander                 KS
Greene                  Morningstar             TN
Blotchet-Halls          Reginald                OR
del Castillo            Innes                   MI
```

```
DeFrance          Michel              IN
Panteley          Sylvia              MD
Ringer            Anne                UT
Ringer            Albert              UT
```

(8 rows affected)

Logical Operator Precedence.   Like the arithmetic operators, logical operators are handled according to precedence rules. When both kinds of operators occur in the same statement, arithmetic operators are handled before logical operators. When more than one logical operator is used in a statement, NOT is evaluated first, then AND, and finally OR. Figure 4–3 shows the hierarchy:

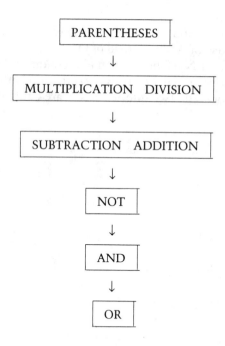

Figure 4–3. Precedence Hierarchy for Logical Operators

Some examples will clarify the situation. The following query finds all the business books in the *titles* table, no matter what their advances are, as well as all psychology books that have an advance greater than $5500. The advance condition pertains to psychology books and not to business books because the AND is handled before the OR.

```
SQL:
select title_id, type, advance
from titles
where type = "business"
   or type = "psychology"
   and advance > 5500
```

```
Results:
title_id   type         advance
--------   ----------   ----------
BU1032     business      5,000.00
BU1111     business      5,000.00
BU2075     business     10,125.00
BU7832     business      5,000.00
PS1372     psychology    7,000.00
PS2106     psychology    6,000.00

(6 rows affected)
```

The results include three business books with advances less than $5500 because the query was evaluated according to the precedence rules: first, all psychology books with advances greater than $5500 were found; then, all business books were found.

You can change the meaning of the previous query by adding parentheses to force evaluation of the OR first. With parentheses added, the query finds all business and psychology books that have advances over $5500:

```
SQL:
select title_id, type, advance
from titles
where (type = "business"
   or type = "psychology")
   and advance > 5500
```

```
Results:

title_id  type          advance
--------  ----------    ---------
BU2075    business      10,125.00
PS1372    psychology     7,000.00
PS2106    psychology     6,000.00

(3 rows affected)
```

The parentheses cause SQL to find all business and psychology books, and from among those to find those with advances greater than $5500.

Here's a query that includes arithmetic operators, comparison operators, and logical operators. It searches for books that are not bringing in enough money to offset their advances. Specifically, the query searches for any books with gross revenues (that is, *ytd_sales* times *price*) less than twice the advance paid to the author(s). The user who constructed this query has tacked on another condition—he or she wants to include in the results only books published before October 15, 1985, on the grounds that those books have had long enough to establish a sales pattern. The last condition is connected with the logical operator AND; according to the rules of precedence it is evaluated after the arithmetic operations.

```
SQL:
select title_id, type, price, advance, ytd_sales
from titles
where price * ytd_sales <  2 * advance
and pubdate < "10/15/85"
```

```
Results:

title_id  type          price      advance        ytd_sales
--------- ------------  ---------  ------------   ----------
PS2106    psychology    7.00       6,000.00       111

(1 row affected)
```

Ranges (BETWEEN and NOT BETWEEN)

Another common search condition is a range. There are two ways to specify ranges:

- With the comparison operators > and <
- With the keyword BETWEEN

Use BETWEEN to specify an **inclusive range**, in which you search for the lower value and the upper value as well as the values they bracket. For example, to find all the books with sales between (and including) 4,095 and 12,000, you could write this query:

```
SQL:
select title_id, ytd_sales
from titles
where ytd_sales between 4095 and 12000
```

```
Results:
title_id  ytd_sales
------    ---------
BU1032    4095
BU7832    4095
PC1035    8780
PC8888    4095
TC7777    4095

(5 rows affected)
```

Notice that books with sales of 4,095 are included in the results. If there were any with sales of 12,000, they would be included too. In this way, the BETWEEN range is different than the greater-than less than (> <) range. The same query using the greater-than and less-than operators returns different results, because the range is not inclusive:

```
SQL:
select title_id, ytd_sales
from titles
where ytd_sales > 4095 and ytd_sales < 12000
```

```
Results:
title_id  ytd_sales
------    -------
PC1035    8780

(1 row affected)
```

The phrase NOT BETWEEN finds all the rows that are not inside the range. To find all the books with sales outside the 4,095 to 12,000 range, type:

SQL:

```
select title_id, ytd_sales
from titles
where ytd_sales not between 4095 and 12000
```

Results:

```
title_id      ytd_sales
--------      --------
BU1111           3876
BU2075          18722
MC2222           2032
MC3021          22246
PS1372            375
PS2091           2045
PS2106            111
PS3333           4072
PS7777           3336
TC3218            375
TC4203          15096
```

```
(11 rows affected)
```

You can accomplish the the same results with comparison operators, but notice in this query that you use OR between the two *ytd_sales* comparisons, rather than AND.

SQL:

```
select title_id, ytd_sales
from titles
where ytd_sales < 4095 or ytd_sales > 12000
```

Results:

```
title_id    ytd_sales
--------    -----------
BU1111          3876
BU2075         18722
```

```
MC2222              2032
MC3021             22246
PS1372              375
PS2091              2045
PS2106              111
PS3333              4072
PS7777              3336
TC3218              375
TC4203             15096
```

```
(11 rows affected)
```

This is another case where it's easy to get confused because of the way the question can be phrased in English. You might well ask to see all books whose sales are less than 4,095 *and* all books whose sales are greater than 12,000. The logical meaning, however, calls for the use of the Boolean operator OR. If you substitute AND, you'll get no results at all, since no book can have sales that are simultaneously less than 4,095 and greater than 12,000.

Lists (IN and NOT IN)

The IN keyword allows you to select values that match any one of a list of values. For example, without IN, if you want a list of the names and states of all the authors who live in California, Indiana, or Maryland, you can type this query:

SQL:
```
select au_lname, state
from authors
where state = 'CA' or state = 'IN' or state = 'MD'
```

However, you get the same results with less typing if you use IN. The items following the IN keyword must be separated by commas and enclosed in parentheses.

SQL:
```
select au_lname, state
from authors
where state in ('CA', 'IN', 'MD')
```

This is what results from either query:

```
Results:
au_lname            state
- - - - - - - - - - - - -    - - - - -
White               CA
Green               CA
Carson              CA
O'Leary             CA
Straight            CA
Bennet              CA
Dull                CA
Gringlesby          CA
Locksley            CA
Yokomoto            CA
DeFrance            IN
Stringer            CA
MacFeather          CA
Karsen              CA
Panteley            MD
Hunter              CA
McBadden            CA

(17 rows affected)
```

The more items in the list, the greater the savings in typing by using IN rather than specifying each condition separately.

Perhaps the most important use for the IN keyword is in nested queries, also referred to as subqueries. For a full discussion of subqueries, see Chapter 8. However, the example below gives some idea of what you can do with nested queries and the IN keyword.

Suppose you want to know the names of the authors who receive less than 50% of the total royalties on the books they co-author. The *authors* table gives author names and the *titleauthors* table gives royalty information. By putting the two together using IN (but without listing the two tables in the same table list) you can extract the information you need.

The query below translates as: "Find all the *au_id*s in the *titleauthors* table in which the authors make less than 50% of the royalty on any one book. Then select from the *authors* table all the author names with *au_id*s that match the results from the *titleauthors* query."

SQL:
```
select au_lname, au_fname
from authors
where au_id in
  (select au_id
   from titleauthors
   where royaltyshare <.50)
```

Results:

au_lname	au_fname
Green	Marjorie
O'Leary	Michael
O'Leary	Michael
Gringlesby	Burt
Yokomoto	Akiko
MacFeather	Stearns
Ringer	Anne

```
(7 rows affected)
```

The seven authors' royalty shares are less than 50%.

NOT IN finds the authors that do not match the items in the list. The following query finds the names of authors who do not make less than 50% of the royalties on at least one book.

SQL:
```
select au_lname, au_fname
from authors
where au_id not in
  (select au_id
   from titleauthors
   where royaltyshare <.50)
```

Results:

au_lname	au_fname
White	Johnson
Carson	Cheryl

```
Straight          Dick
Smith             Meander
Bennet            Abraham
Dull              Ann
Locksley          Chastity
Greene            Morningstar
Blotchet-Halls    Reginald
del Castillo      Innes
DeFrance          Michel
Stringer          Dirk
Karsen            Livia
Panteley          Sylvia
Hunter            Sheryl
McBadden          Heather
Ringer            Albert

(17 rows affected)
```

Selecting NULL Values

From Chapter 1, you may recall that NULL is a placeholder for unknown information. It does not mean zero or blank.

To clarify this NULL-zero difference, take a look at the listing below showing title number, book category, and advance amount for books belonging to one particular publisher.

SQL:
```
select title, advance
from titles
where pub_id = "0877"
```

Results:
```
title                                             advance
------------------------------------------------- ----------
Silicon Valley Gastronomic Treats                       0.00
The Gourmet Microwave                              15,000.00
The Psychology of Computer Cooking                      NULL
Onions, Leeks, and Garlic: Cooking
    Secrets of the Mediterranean                    7,000.00
```

```
Fifty Years in Buckingham Palace Kitchens        4,000.00
Sushi, Anyone?                                    8,000.00
```

```
(6 rows affected)
```

A cursory perusal shows that one book (*Silicon Valley Gastronomic Treats*) has an advance of $0.00, probably due to extremely poor negotiating skills on the author's part. This author will receive no money until the royalties start coming in. Another book (*The Psychology of Computer Cooking*) has a NULL advance—perhaps the author and the publisher are still working out the details of their deal, or perhaps the data entry clerk hasn't made the entry yet. Eventually, in this case, an amount will be known and recorded. Maybe it will be zero, maybe millions, maybe a couple of thousand dollars. The point is that right now the data does not disclose what the advance for this book is, so the advance value in the table is NULL.

What happens in the case of comparisons involving NULLs? Since a NULL represents the unknown, it doesn't match anything, even another NULL. For example, a query that finds all the title identification numbers and advances for books with moderate advances (under $5,000) will not find the row for MC3026, *The Psychology of Computer Cooking*.

```
SQL:
select title_id, advance
from titles
where advance < $5000
```

```
Results:
title_id  advance
--------  ----------
MC2222          0.00
PS2091      2,275.00
PS3333      2,000.00
PS7777      4,000.00
TC4203      4,000.00
```

```
(5 rows affected)
```

Neither will a query for all books with an advance over $5,000:

```
SQL:
select title_id, advance
from titles
where advance > $5000

Results:
title_id  advance
--------  ----------
BU2075    10,125.00
MC3021    15,000.00
PC1035     7,000.00
PC8888     8,000.00
PS1372     7,000.00
PS2106     6,000.00
TC3218     7,000.00
TC7777     8,000.00

(8 rows affected)
```

NULL is neither above nor below (nor equal to) $5,000 because NULL is unknown. But don't despair! You can retrieve rows on the basis of their NULL/NOT NULL status with a special pattern:

```
WHERE column_name IS [NOT] NULL
```

Use it to find the row for MC3026 like this:

```
SQL:
select title_id, advance
from titles
where advance is null

Results:
title_id  advance
--------  ----------
MC3026        NULL
PC9999        NULL
```

You can use the same pattern in combination with other comparison operators. Here's how a query for books with an advance under $5,000 *or* a null advance would look:

```
SQL:

select title_id, advance
from titles
where advance < $5000
  or advance is null
```

```
Results:

title_id    advance
--------    ----------
MC2222          0.00
MC3026          NULL
PC9999          NULL
PS2091      2,275.00
PS3333      2,000.00
PS7777      4,000.00
TC4203      4,000.00

(7 rows affected)
```

Matching Character Strings: LIKE

Some problems can't be solved with comparisons. Here are a few examples:

- "His name begins with 'Mc' or 'Mac'—I can't remember the rest."
- "We need a list of all the 415 area code phone numbers."
- "I forget the name of the book, but it has a mention of exercise in the notes."
- "Well, it's Carson, or maybe Karsen—something like that."
- "His first name is 'Dirk' or 'Dick'. Four letters, starts with a 'D' and ends with a 'k'."

In each of these cases, you know a pattern embedded somewhere in a column, and you need to use it to retrieve all or part of the row. The LIKE keyword is designed to solve this problem. You can use it with character fields (and on some systems, with date fields). It doesn't work with numeric fields defined as integer, money, and decimal or float. The syntax is:

```
WHERE column_name [NOT] LIKE "pattern"
```

The pattern must be enclosed in quotes and include one or more **wild-cards** (symbols that take the place of missing letters or strings in the pattern).

ISO-ANSI SQL provides two wildcard characters for use with LIKE:

Wildcard	Meaning
%	any string of zero or more characters
_	any single character

Many systems offer variations (* instead of %, for example) or additions (notations for single characters that fall within a range or set, for example). Check your system's reference guide to see what's available.

Here are answers to the questions posed above and the queries that generated them. First, the search for Scottish surnames:

```
SQL:
select au_lname, city
from authors
where au_lname like "Mc%" or au_lname like "Mac%"
```

```
Results:
au_lname                                    city
----------------------------------------    -----------
MacFeather                                  Oakland
McBadden                                    Vacaville
```

```
(2 rows affected)
```

The LIKE pattern instructs the system to search for a name that begins with "Mc" and is followed by a string of any number of characters (%) or that begins with "Mac" and is followed by any number of characters. Notice that the wildcard is inside the quotes.

Now the 415 area code list:

```
SQL:
select au_lname, phone
from authors
where phone like "415%"
```

Results:

au_lname	phone
Green	415 986-7020
Carson	415 548-7723
Straight	415 834-2919
Bennet	415 658-9932
Dull	415 836-7128
Locksley	415 585-4620
Yokomoto	415 935-4228
Stringer	415 843-2991
MacFeather	415 354-7128
Karsen	415 534-9219
Hunter	415 836-7128

(11 rows affected)

Here again, you're looking for some known initial characters followed by a string of unknown characters.

The book with "exercise" somewhere in its notes is a little more tricky. You don't know if it's at the beginning or end of the column, and you don't know whether or not the first letter of the word is capitalized. You can cover all these possibilities by leaving the first letter out of the pattern and using the same "string of zero or more characters" wildcard at the beginning and end of the pattern.

SQL:

```
select title_id, notes
from titles
where notes like "%xercise%"
```

Results:

title_id	notes
PS2106	New exercise, meditation, and nutritional techniques that can reduce the shock of daily interactions. Popular audience. Sample menus included, exercise video available separately.

(1 row affected)

When you know the number of characters missing, you can use the single-character wildcard, the underbar (_). Here the first letter is either "K" or "C" and the next to the last is either "e" or "o".

```
SQL:
select au_lname, city
from authors
where au_lname like "_ars_n"
```

```
Results:
au_lname                                    city
------------------------------------- --------------------
Carson                                      Berkeley
Karsen                                      Oakland

(2 rows affected)
```

The next example is similar to the one above. It looks for four-letter first names starting with "D" and ending with "k."

```
SQL:
select au_lname, au_fname, city
from authors
where au_fname like "D__k"
```

```
Results:
au_lname                     au_fname              city
--------------------------- --------------------- --------------
Straight                     Dick                  Oakland
Stringer                     Dirk                  Oakland

(2 rows affected)
```

You can also use NOT LIKE with wildcards. To find all the phone numbers in the *authors* table that do *not* have 415 as the area code, you could use either of these queries (they are equivalent):

```
SQL:
select phone
from authors
where phone not like '415%'
```

```
SQL:
select phone
from authors
where not phone like '415%'
```

Wildcard characters are almost always used together with the LIKE key-word. Without LIKE, wildcard characters are interpreted literally and represent exactly their own values. The query below finds any phone numbers that consist of the four characters "415%" only. It will not find phone numbers that start with 415:

```
SQL:
select phone
from authors
where phone = '415%'
```

What if you want to search for a value that contains one of the wildcard characters? For example, what if the database included a book called *The 27% Solution*? You can search for the wildcards themselves with **escape characters** that strip wildcards of their magic meaning and convert them to ordinary characters.

Different SQL dialects use different escape characters. Here are some examples of LIKE with escaped and unescaped wildcard character searches, based on Transact-SQL.

Symbol	Meaning
LIKE "27%"	27 followed by any string of 0 or more characters
LIKE "27[%]"	27%
LIKE "_n"	an, in, on, etc.
LIKE "[_]n"	_n

Using pattern matching can have an adverse affect on retrieval speed. See the chapter on performance for more information.

Refining Selection Results

The next chapter covers some refinements on selection: ordering results with ORDER BY, eliminating duplicates in results with DISTINCT, and aggregate functions.

Chapter 5

Sorting Data and Other Selection Techniques

A NEW BATCH OF SELECT STATEMENT CLAUSES

Now that you're familiar with the fundamentals of the SELECT statement—SELECT, FROM, and WHERE—it's time to go on to some additional features. These include ORDER BY (for sorting query results), DISTINCT (for eliminating duplicate rows), and **aggregate functions** (for calculating group totals, sums, minimums, maximums, and counts). The next chapter covers GROUP BY (for creating groups), aggregate functions with groups, and HAVING (for putting conditions on groups).

SORTING QUERY RESULTS: ORDER BY

The ORDER BY clause can make your results more readable. It allows you to sort by any column or expression in the select list. Each sort can be in ascending or descending order.

For example, let's say you want a listing of prices, title identification numbers, and publisher numbers from the *titles* table. You might write a query like this:

SQL:
```
select price, title_id, pub_id
from titles
```

```
Results:
price                   title_id pub_id
----------------------- -------- ------
                  19.99 BU1032   1389
                  11.95 BU1111   1389
                   2.99 BU2075   0736
                  19.99 BU7832   1389
                  19.99 MC2222   0877
                   2.99 MC3021   0877
                   NULL MC3026   0877
                  22.95 PC1035   1389
                  20.00 PC8888   1389
                   NULL PC9999   1389
                  21.59 PS1372   0877
                  10.95 PS2091   0736
                   7.00 PS2106   0736
                  19.99 PS3333   0736
                   7.99 PS7777   0736
                  20.95 TC3218   0877
                  11.95 TC4203   0877
                  14.99 TC7777   0877

(18 rows affected)
```

The information you asked for is all there but it's a little hard to see what you've got because there is no meaningful order in the results. Books are listed in *title_id* order—that's where the clustered index is—but in this particular case, that organization doesn't help you understand the results. The information would probably be more useful if it were arranged by price. This is how you'd do it:

```
SQL:
select price, title_id, pub_id
from titles
order by price
```

```
Results:
price                   title_id pub_id
----------------------- -------- ------
                   NULL MC3026   0877
                   NULL PC9999   1389
                   2.99 BU2075   0736
                   2.99 MC3021   0877
```

```
 7.00 PS2106    0736
 7.99 PS7777    0736
10.95 PS2091    0736
11.95 BU1111    1389
11.95 TC4203    0877
14.99 TC7777    0877
19.99 BU1032    1389
19.99 BU7832    1389
19.99 MC2222    0877
19.99 PS3333    0736
20.00 PC8888    1389
20.95 TC3218    0877
21.59 PS1372    0877
22.95 PC1035    1389
```

```
(18 rows affected)
```

Now the rows are listed in price order.

ORDER BY Syntax

The 1986 ISO-ANSI standard doesn't include an ORDER BY clause (except in the context of the DECLARE CURSOR in embedded SQL). In most systems, the general syntax for ORDER BY looks something like this:

```
SELECT select_list
FROM table_list
[WHERE conditions]
[ORDER BY expression [ASC | DESC] [, expression [ASC | DESC] [, ...]]]
```

Most (but not all) systems require that each sort element appear in the select list, and most allow nested sorts. Check your reference manuals for details on precisely how your system handles this useful clause.

Sorts Within Sorts

Now that you have the results sorted by price, you might also want to make sure that books within each each price category by the same publisher are grouped together. Adding *pub_id* to the ORDER BY list is the way to do it:

```
SQL:
select price, title_id, pub_id
from titles
order by price, pub_id
```

```
Results:
price                       title_id pub_id
--------------------------- -------- ------
                 NULL MC3026    0877
                 NULL PC9999    1389
                 2.99 BU2075    0736
                 2.99 MC3021    0877
                 7.00 PS2106    0736
                 7.99 PS7777    0736
                10.95 PS2091    0736
                11.95 TC4203    0877
                11.95 BU1111    1389
                14.99 TC7777    0877
                19.99 PS3333    0736
                19.99 MC2222    0877
                19.99 BU1032    1389
                19.99 BU7832    1389
                20.00 PC8888    1389
                20.95 TC3218    0877
                21.59 PS1372    0877
                22.95 PC1035    1389

(18 rows affected)
```

When you use more than one column in the ORDER BY clause, sorts are **nested** (*i.e.*, ordered by *price* first and then by *pub_id* within each price category).

You can have as many levels of sorts as you like. Many systems require that each sort element appears in the select list, but they don't usually insist on ORDER BY columns and expressions being in the same sequence as SELECT columns and expressions. If you change the example to order first by *pub_id*, and then by *price*, here's what you'd see:

```
SQL:
select price, title_id, pub_id
from titles
order by pub_id, price
```

Results:

price	title_id	pub_id
2.99	BU2075	0736
7.00	PS2106	0736
7.99	PS7777	0736
10.95	PS2091	0736
19.99	PS3333	0736
21.59	PS1372	0736
NULL	MC3026	0877
2.99	MC3021	0877
11.95	TC4203	0877
14.99	TC7777	0877
19.99	MC2222	0877
20.95	TC3218	0877
NULL	PC9999	1389
11.95	BU1111	1389
19.99	BU1032	1389
19.99	BU7832	1389
20.00	PC8888	1389
22.95	PC1035	1389

```
(18 rows affected)
```

The columns are listed in the same order as in the previous results (*price* first, *title_id* second, and *pub_id* third), but the rows are arranged differently: first you see all the rows with 0736, then all those with 0877, and finally those with 1389 as the publisher identification number.

Sort Up, Sort Down

You can specify a direction—low to high or high to low—for each individual sort by using the ascending (ASC) or descending (DESC) keyword immediately after the sort item. In some systems, ascending is the default, assumed to be in effect unless you type DESC. If this is how your

DBMS works, you don't really need to use ASC except to make the direction of the sort unavoidably explicit to others who read the query.

Here's how you'd get prices to display in descending order:

```
SQL:
select price, title_id, pub_id
from titles
order by price desc, pub_id
```

```
Results:
price                     title_id pub_id
------------------------- -------- ------
                    22.95 PC1035   1389
                    21.59 PS1372   0736
                    20.95 TC3218   0877
                    20.00 PC8888   1389
                    19.99 PS3333   0736
                    19.99 MC2222   0877
                    19.99 BU1032   1389
                    19.99 BU7832   1389
                    14.99 TC7777   0877
                    11.95 TC4203   0877
                    11.95 BU1111   1389
                    10.95 PS2091   0736
                     7.99 PS7777   0736
                     7.00 PS2106   0736
                     2.99 BU2075   0736
                     2.99 MC3021   0877
                     NULL MC3026   0877
                     NULL PC9999   1389

(18 rows affected)
```

Notice that *pub_id*s are still in ascending order within each price category. You could change the direction of the *pub_id* sort like this:

```
SQL:
select price, title_id, pub_id
from titles
order by price desc, pub_id desc
```

Results:

price	title_id	pub_id
22.95	PC1035	1389
21.59	PS1372	0736
20.95	TC3218	0877
20.00	PC8888	1389
19.99	BU1032	1389
19.99	BU7832	1389
19.99	MC2222	0877
19.99	PS3333	0736
14.99	TC7777	0877
11.95	BU1111	1389
11.95	TC4203	0877
10.95	PS2091	0736
7.99	PS7777	0736
7.00	PS2106	0736
2.99	MC3021	0877
2.99	BU2075	0736
NULL	PC9999	1389
NULL	MC3026	0877

(18 rows affected)

What about Expressions?

What if you want to sort by an expression in the select list, and your system doesn't allow expressions to have column headings? How are you going to name the expression you're using in the ORDER BY clause? SQL allows you to use the expression's *position* in the select list (represented with a number) as the order element.

Here's an example of the kind of query that could cause a problem for sorting, with `price * ytd_sales` an expression in the select list:

SQL:
```
select pub_id, price * ytd_sales, price, title_id
from titles
```

Results:

pub_id	price		title_id
1389	81,859.05	19.99	BU1032
1389	46,318.20	11.95	BU1111
0736	55,978.78	2.99	BU2075
1389	81,859.05	19.99	BU7832
0877	40,619.68	19.99	MC2222
0877	66,515.54	2.99	MC3021
0877	NULL	NULL	MC3026
1389	201,501.00	22.95	PC1035
1389	81,900.00	20.00	PC8888
1389	NULL	NULL	PC9999
0877	8,096.25	21.59	PS1372
0736	22,392.75	10.95	PS2091
0736	777.00	7.00	PS2106
0736	81,399.28	19.99	PS3333
0736	26,654.64	7.99	PS7777
0877	7,856.25	20.95	TC3218
0877	180,397.20	11.95	TC4203
0877	61,384.05	14.99	TC7777

```
(18 rows affected)
```

Let's say you want to see these results sorted by publisher and then by income (`price * ytd_sales`). Since income is an expression, you can't use a simple column name. Instead, use the number "2," because the expression is the second element in the select list. (When counting select list items, start with "1" and move from left to right. Signed numbers are not allowed and don't make sense anyway).

SQL:
```
select pub_id, price * ytd_sales, price, title_id
from titles
order by pub_id, 2
```

Results:

pub_id	price		title_id
0736	777.00	7.00	PS2106
0736	8,096.25	21.59	PS1372
0736	22,392.75	10.95	PS2091

0736	26,654.64	7.99 PS7777
0736	55,978.78	2.99 BU2075
0736	81,399.28	19.99 PS3333
0877	NULL	NULL MC3026
0877	7,856.25	20.95 TC3218
0877	40,619.68	19.99 MC2222
0877	61,384.05	14.99 TC7777
0877	66,515.54	2.99 MC3021
0877	180,397.20	11.95 TC4203
1389	NULL	NULL PC9999
1389	46,318.20	11.95 BU1111
1389	81,859.05	19.99 BU1032
1389	81,859.05	19.99 BU7832
1389	81,900.00	20.00 PC8888
1389	201,501.00	22.95 PC1035

```
(18 rows affected)
```

You can use numbers to represent columns as well as expressions, and freely mix the two styles (positional numbers and column headings) as the spirit moves. ASC and DESC work with numbers just as they do with column headings. Here's an example showing sorting on the *pub_id* column by name in ascending order and then the *price* column by number in descending order:

SQL:
```
select pub_id, price * ytd_sales, price, title_id
from titles
order by pub_id, 3 desc
```

Results:

pub_id	price	title_id
0736	8,096.25	21.59 PS1372
0736	81,399.28	19.99 PS3333
0736	22,392.75	10.95 PS2091
0736	26,654.64	7.99 PS7777
0736	777.00	7.00 PS2106
0736	55,978.78	2.99 BU2075
0877	7,856.25	20.95 TC3218
0877	40,619.68	19.99 MC2222

0877	61,384.05	14.99	TC7777
0877	180,397.20	11.95	TC4203
0877	66,515.54	2.99	MC3021
0877	NULL	NULL	MC3026
1389	201,501.00	22.95	PC1035
1389	81,900.00	20.00	PC8888
1389	81,859.05	19.99	BU1032
1389	81,859.05	19.99	BU7832
1389	46,318.20	11.95	BU1111
1389	NULL	NULL	PC9999

(18 rows affected)

One thing to watch out for with numbered ORDER BY items is modifications to the select list. The order of your results may well change dramatically when you add columns to or subtract columns from the select list.

If your system lets you give select list expressions column headings, you may be able to sort by them. In this example, which returns the same results as the previous one, price * ytd_sales is named *income*, and the ORDER BY clause makes use of the heading, rather than the select list number.

```
SQL:
select pub_id, price * ytd_sales income, price, title_id
from titles
order by pub_id, income desc
```

How Do You Sort NULLs?

Not all systems order NULLs the same way. The 1986 ISO-ANSI standard specifies that when NULLs are sorted, they should be either greater than or less than all non-NULL values. Which you get depends on your implementation. In the system used to run these examples, NULL is less than all non-NULL values.

ELIMINATING DUPLICATE ROWS: DISTINCT AND ALL

The DISTINCT and ALL keywords in the select list let you specify what to do with duplicate rows in your results. ALL returns all qualified rows. DISTINCT returns only those that are unique.

For example, if you search for all the author identification codes in the *titleauthors* table using ALL, you'll find these rows:

```
SQL:
select all au_id
from titleauthors
```

```
Results:
au_id
-----------
172-32-1176
213-46-8915
213-46-8915
238-95-7766
267-41-2394
267-41-2394
274-80-9391
409-56-7008
427-17-2319
472-27-2349
486-29-1786
486-29-1786
648-92-1872
672-71-3249
712-45-1867
722-51-5454
724-80-9391
724-80-9391
756-30-7391
807-91-6654
846-92-7186
899-46-2035
899-46-2035
```

```
998 - 72 - 3567
998 - 72 - 3567

(25 rows affected)
```

Looking at the results, you'll see that there are some duplicate listings. You can eliminate them, and see only the unique *au_id*s, with DISTINCT.

SQL:

```
select distinct au_id
from titleauthors
```

Results:

```
au_id
- - - - - - - - - - -
172 - 32 - 1176
213 - 46 - 8915
238 - 95 - 7766
267 - 41 - 2394
274 - 80 - 9391
409 - 56 - 7008
427 - 17 - 2319
472 - 27 - 2349
486 - 29 - 1786
648 - 92 - 1872
672 - 71 - 3249
712 - 45 - 1867
722 - 51 - 5454
724 - 80 - 9391
756 - 30 - 7391
807 - 91 - 6654
846 - 92 - 7186
899 - 46 - 2035
998 - 72 - 3567

(19 rows affected)
```

Six rows from the first display are not in the second—they are duplicates.

DISTINCT Syntax

Some implementations of SQL use the keyword ALL to explicitly ask for all rows. In other implementations (like Transact-SQL), ALL is the default unless you explicitly specify DISTINCT. Here's what the basic syntax looks like:

```
SELECT [DISTINCT | ALL] select_list
```

Notice that you use DISTINCT or ALL only once in a select list and that it must be the first word in the select list. The example below will give you a syntax error:

```
SQL (illegal):
select state, distinct city
from authors
```

In other words, you can't select all the states but only the unique cities.

Make Distinctions

When there is more than one item in the select list, DISTINCT finds the rows where the combination of items is unique.

Here's an example that should make it clear. First, take a look at the listing of *pub_id*s and *type*s in the *titles* table.

```
SQL:
select pub_id, type
from titles
order by pub_id

Results:
pub_id type
------ ------------
0736   business
0736   psychology
0736   psychology
0736   psychology
0736   psychology
0736   psychology
```

```
0877    NULL
0877    mod_cook
0877    mod_cook
0877    trad_cook
0877    trad_cook
0877    trad_cook
1389    business
1389    business
1389    business
1389    popular_comp
1389    popular_comp
1389    popular_comp

(18 rows affected)
```

There are 18 rows. Notice that there is some repetition. (The ORDER BY is there only to make the display easy to read.) If you query for distinct publisher numbers, you'll get just three rows:

SQL:
```
select distinct pub_id
from titles
order by pub_id
```

Results:
```
pub_id
------
0736
0877
1389

(3 rows affected)
```

If you query for distinct types, you'll get six rows:

SQL:
```
select distinct type
from titles
order by type
```

```
Results:
type
- - - - - - - - - - -
NULL
business
mod_cook
popular_comp
psychology
trad_cook

(6 rows affected)
```

However, if you query for distinct combinations of publisher and type, you'll get seven rows:

```
SQL:
select distinct pub_id, type
from titles
order by pub_id
```

```
Results:
pub_id type
- - - - - - - - - - - - - - - -
0736    business
0736    psychology
0877    NULL
0877    mod_cook
0877    trad_cook
1389    business
1389    popular_comp

(7 rows affected)
```

The display above represents all the unique publisher-type combinations in the table. Publisher number 0736 has two types, publisher number 0877 has two types (and a NULL), and publisher number 1389 has two types, giving a total of seven rows. The DISTINCT applies to the select list as a whole, not to individual columns. In fact, if you use DISTINCT twice in a select list, you'll probably get an error message.

Are NULLs Distinct?   Although NULL values are by definition unknown and never equal to each other, DISTINCT treats each NULL in a particular column as a duplicate of all other nulls values in that column. If publisher number 0877 had more than one book with a NULL type, and you ran a query with DISTINCT to retrieve the two columns, you'd still see the publisher/NULL combination listed only once.

DISTINCT *.   If your system allows DISTINCT *, compare the results of two queries like these:

```
SQL:
select distinct *
from titles
```

```
SQL:
select *
from titles
```

Most likely, you'll get exactly the same results from each query, because each row in a table should be unique. If you don't, you should take another look at the database design. Why is there more than one row with a given set of values in a table? How can you retrieve a particular row if it is precisely the same as one or more other rows?

DISTINCT and Non-Select-list ORDER BY.   In most SQL dialects, every element in the ORDER BY clause must appear in the select list. In systems that allow more flexibility (non-select-list elements in the ORDER BY clause) you can run queries with DISTINCT in the select list and a non-select-list ORDER BY element.

With Transact-SQL, for example, sorting by a column not in the select list has the same effect as including that column in the DISTINCT select list: it increases the number of rows displayed. Take a look at this query:

```
SQL:
select distinct pub_id
from titles
order by type
```

Since there are only three publishers in the database, you'd probably expect three rows in the results. However, this is what you get:

```
Results:
pub_id
------
0877
0736
1389
0877
1389
0736
0877

(7 rows affected)
```

Why are there seven rows in the results? The clue is in the ORDER BY clause, where *type* stars: you get the same number of rows when you turn the query around, searching for distinct types but sorting by publishers.

```
SQL:
select distinct type
from titles
order by pub_id

Results:
type
------------
business
psychology
NULL
mod_cook
trad_cook
business
popular_comp

(7 rows affected)
```

Now it's clear where the seven rows come from. Transact-SQL handles the query as if it were a request for all possible unique combinations of the items in the DISTINCT select list and the non-select-list ORDER BY items. There are, in fact, seven unique combinations of *pub_id* and *type*.

If your system allows non-select-list elements in the ORDER BY clause, run a few experimental queries to see how it handles this kind of situation.

AGGREGATE FUNCTIONS

Aggregates are functions you can use to get summary values. You apply aggregates to *sets* of rows: to all the rows in a table, to just those rows specified by a WHERE clause, or to groups of rows set up in the GROUP BY clause (discussed in the next chapter). No matter how you structure the **sets**, you get *a single value for each set of rows*.

Take a look at the difference in the results of these two queries: the first finds each individual yearly sale value in the titles table (one sale listing per row), the second calculates the total yearly sales for all books in the *titles* table (one total sale listing per set, and the table is the set).

```
SQL:
select ytd_sales
from titles

Results:
ytd_sales
-----------
       4095
       3876
      18722
       4095
       2032
      22246
       NULL
       8780
       4095
       NULL
        375
       2045
        111
       4072
       3336
        375
      15096
       4095

(18 rows affected)
```

```
SQL:
select sum(ytd_sales)
from titles

Results:

 - - - - - - - - - - -
       97446

(1 row affected)
```

The first returns results for each qualified row in the table. The second summarizes all the qualified rows into one row. Notice that there is no column heading for the aggregate column. If your system allows you to specify column headings for expressions, you can use a query like this to make the results easier to read:

```
SQL:
select sum(ytd_sales) Total
from titles

Results:
       Total
 - - - - - - - - - - -
       97446

(1 row affected)
```

Most dialects of SQL do not allow you to mix row-by-row results and set results. The select list must be pure, either all columns and expressions (row values) or all aggregates (set values). The only exception is for grouping columns—columns on which you base groups when you use a GROUP BY clause. (GROUP BY and aggregates will be covered in Chapter 6.)

Here's a query that's usually not allowed, because it mixes a row value with a set value:

```
SQL:
select price, sum(price)
from titles
```

The problem is that *price* returns a value for each row, while *sum(price)* returns a value for each set (here, the table as a whole). Unless your system was designed to handle this kind of query, it will find the two results incompatible and give you a syntax error.

If your system doesn't reject the query, it will probably give results like these (produced by Transact-SQL):

```
Results:
price
------------------------------    -------------------------------
                    19.99                         236.26
                    11.95                         236.26
                     2.99                         236.26
                    19.99                         236.26
                    19.99                         236.26
                     2.99                         236.26
                     NULL                         236.26
                    22.95                         236.26
                    20.00                         236.26
                     NULL                         236.26
                    21.59                         236.26
                    10.95                         236.26
                     7.00                         236.26
                    19.99                         236.26
                     7.99                         236.26
                    20.95                         236.26
                    11.95                         236.26
                    14.99                         236.26

(18 rows affected)
```

The unlabeled column on the right shows the grand total of all the prices in the table, while the column on the left shows the price for each row. Notice that the total price is the same in each row: this is because there is only one value for the sum, and it's based on the set (here the table as a whole), not the row.

To get summary and row results on most systems, you have to run two queries.

Aggregate Syntax

Since aggregates are functions, they always take an **argument**. The argument is an expression, and it is enclosed in parentheses.

The general syntax of the aggregate functions is:

```
aggregate_function ([DISTINCT] expression)
```

Here's a list of all the aggregate functions:

Aggregate Function	Result
SUM([DISTINCT] expression)	the total of (distinct) values in the numeric expression
AVG([DISTINCT] expression)	the average of (distinct) values in the numeric expression
COUNT([DISTINCT] expression)	the number of (distinct) non-null values in the expression
COUNT(*)	the number of selected rows
MAX(expression)	the highest value in the expression
MIN(expression)	the lowest value in the expression

You can use DISTINCT with any aggregate except COUNT(*). However, note that DISTINCT gives you no advantage with MIN and MAX, because the minimum distinct price is the same as the minimum price.

The expression used in the general syntax statement is often a column name, but it can also be a constant, a function, or any combination of column names, constants, and functions connected by arithmetic (and in some systems by bit-wise) operators.

For example, with this statement, you can find what the average price of all books would be if the prices were doubled:

```
SQL:
select avg(price * 2)
from titles
```

Results:

```
- - - - - - - - - - - - -
            29.53
```

(1 row affected)

COUNT and COUNT(*). The apparent similarity of COUNT and COUNT(*) can lead to confusion. However, the two are really not the same. COUNT takes an argument (a column name or an expression) and discovers all non-NULL occurrences of that argument, while COUNT(*) counts all rows, whether or not any particular column contains a null value. This example lets you compare the two:

SQL:

```
select count(price), count(*)
from titles
```

Results:

```
- - - - - - - - - - -  - - - - - - - - - - -
          16            18
```

(1 row affected)

The results produced by the two functions are different because two rows in the *titles* table have NULL in the *price* column. If you used a column with no nulls instead, you'd get the same results from count() and count(*):

SQL:

```
select count(title_id), count(*)
from titles
```

Results:

```
- - - - - - - - - - -  - - - - - - - - - - -
          18            18
```

(1 row affected)

The difference in function between the two counts can be useful for tracking NULL values in particular columns.

Aggregates and Datatypes.   You can use SUM and AVG with numeric columns only. MIN, MAX, COUNT, and COUNT(*) work with all types of data.

For example, you can use MIN (minimum) to find the lowest value—the one closest to the beginning of the alphabet—in a *char* column:

```
SQL:
select min(au_lname)
from authors

Results:

--------------------------
Bennet

(1 row affected)
```

Of course, there is no meaning in the sum or average of all author last names.

DISTINCT Aggregates.   You can use DISTINCT with SUM, AVG, COUNT, MIN, and MAX (it goes inside the parentheses and before the argument). As noted earlier, DISTINCT doesn't change the results with MIN and MAX.

DISTINCT eliminates duplicate values before calculating the sum, average, or count. Here's an example:

```
SQL:
select count(price)
from titles

Results:

-----------
         16

(1 row affected)

SQL:
select count(distinct price)
from titles
```

Results:

```
-----------
          11
```

(1 row affected)

The first query finds out how many non-NULL prices there are in the *titles* table. The second calculates the number of different non-NULL prices. Apparently there is some overlap—five books have the same price.

Some systems specify that when you use DISTINCT, the argument can't be an arithmetic expression; it must be a column name only. However, other systems are more lenient. Check your reference manual to find out what you can do. You might want to see if you can run both of these queries, or only the first:

SQL:
```
select count(price * 2)
from titles
```

Results:

```
-----------
          16
```

(1 row affected)

SQL:
```
select count(distinct price * 2)
from titles
```

Results:

```
-----------
          11
```

(1 row affected)

The first query doubles all the prices and counts the total number of prices. The second does the same arithmetic, but counts only the

unique prices. Systems that do not allow calculated columns with DIS-
TINCT will rule the second query illegal.

DISTINCT does not work at all with COUNT(*). This is because
COUNT(*) always returns one and only one row. DISTINCT has no
meaning here.

Generally speaking, you can use DISTINCT no more than once in a
select list. This is because, when no aggregates are involved, DISTINCT
applies to the select list as a whole, and not to individual columns in the
select list. But limiting DISTINCT to once per select list can cause some
special problems when you use aggregates. For example, consider comparing the results of two aggregate operations. If you take the count and the
sum of the *price* column, you'll get these results:

```
SQL:
select count(price), sum(price)
from titles

Results:

- - - - - - - - - - -     - - - - - - - - - - - - - - - - - - - - - - - -
          16                              236.26

(1 row affected)
```

It's easy to see that the average price is $236.26 divided by sixteen.

If you use DISTINCT with just one of the two columns, the results
may not be so useful:

```
SQL:
select count(price), sum(distinct price)
from titles

Results:

- - - - - - - - - - -     - - - - - - - - - - - - - - - - - - - - - - - -
          16                              161.35

(1 row affected)
```

The difference in this and the previous sum value indicates that there are
duplicate prices, and that they have not been included in this sum calculation. However, they still show up in the count column. Dividing the

distinct sum by the count will not give an accurate value for average price. Putting DISTINCT on the count rather than the sum also gives incorrect data for calculating an average price.

```
SQL:
select count(distinct price), sum(price)
from titles

Results:

----------- -------------------------
         11                    236.26

(1 row affected)
```

It's clear that what you need here is either no DISTINCT or two DISTINCTs. Because of this requirement, some systems make an exception to the DISTINCT-only-once rule to allow you to use DISTINCT as many times as you like, as long as it is part of an aggregate, like this:

```
SQL:
select count(distinct price), sum(distinct price)
from titles

Results:

----------- -------------------------
         11                    161.35

(1 row affected)
```

Check your reference manual to see if your system allows multiple DISTINCTs when you have multiple aggregates.

Note that DISTINCT in the select list and DISTINCT as part of an aggregate do not give the same results:

```
SQL:
select count(au_id)
from titleauthors
```

Results:

```
-----------
        25

(1 row affected)
```

SQL:
```
select count(distinct au_id)
from titleauthors
```

Results:

```
-----------
        19

(1 row affected)
```

SQL:
```
select distinct count(au_id)
from titleauthors
```

Results:

```
-----------
        25

(1 row affected)
```

The first query finds all the author identification numbers in the table. The second counts the unique numbers only. Applying a DISTINCT to the select list as a whole, rather than in the aggregate, gives the same result as the first query. This is because the aggregate does its work first, returning one row, and then DISTINCT cheerfully eliminates any duplicates of this row. Since there is only one row of results, there are by definition no duplicates.

Aggregates and WHERE.   You can use aggregate functions in a select list, as in the previous examples, or in the HAVING clause of a SELECT statement. (More about this in Chapter 6.)

You can't use aggregate functions in a WHERE clause. If you do, you'll get a syntax error. However, you can use a WHERE clause to restrict the rows used in the aggregate calculation. Here's a statement that finds the average advance and total year-to-date sales for all the rows in the *titles* table.

SQL:
```
select avg(advance), sum(ytd_sales)
from titles
```

Results:

```
------------------------ -----------
           5,962.50           97446
```

(1 row affected)

To see the same figures for business books only, you could write this query:

SQL:
```
select avg(advance), sum(ytd_sales)
from titles
where type = "business"
```

Results:

```
------------------------ -----------
           6,281.25           30788
```

(1 row affected)

Apparently, business writers do a little better than the average writer.

How do the aggregates and the WHERE clause interact? The WHERE clause does its job first, finding all business books. Then the functions perform their calculations on the retrieved rows.

Null Values and the Aggregate Functions. If there are any null values in the column on which the aggregate function is operating, they are ignored for the purposes of the function.

For example, if you ask for the COUNT of advances in the *titles* table, your answer is not the same as if you ask for the COUNT of title names, because of the NULL values in the *advance* column:

```
SQL:
select count(advance)
from titles

Results:

------------
            16

(1 row affected)

SQL:
select count(title)
from titles

Results:

------------
            18

(1 row affected)
```

The exception to this rule is COUNT(*), which counts each row, whether or not a column value is NULL.

If no rows meet the query conditions, COUNT returns zero. The other functions all return NULL. Here are examples (there is no "poetry" type in the *titles* table):

```
SQL:
select count(distinct title)
from titles
where type = "poetry"

Results:

------------
           0

(1 row affected)
```

```
SQL:
select avg(advance)
from titles
where type = "poetry"

Results:

- - - - - - - - - - - - -
            NULL

(1 row affected)
```

Scalar and Vector Aggregates.   When an aggregate function returns a single value, as in all the examples so far, it is called a **scalar aggregate**.

CREATING REPORTS FROM DATA

Chapter 6 explores the GROUP BY clause and the use of aggregate functions with groups to return an array of values (one per group). Aggregates used in this way are called **vector aggregates**. The HAVING clause, closely bound to GROUP BY and vector aggregates, is also explored. Finally, NULL is taken apart and put back together one last time.

Chapter 6

Grouping Data and Reporting From It

GROUPING

The previous chapter discussed some SELECT features: the DISTINCT keyword and the ORDER BY clause. It also introduced the aggregate functions. There, aggregates were used only with the table as a whole—but that's just a small part of the aggregate story. In real life, aggregate functions are most frequently used in combination with the GROUP BY clause.

This chapter focuses on GROUP BY, which returns groups of rows, and on the HAVING clause, which puts conditions on GROUP BY results much as WHERE qualifies individual rows. The chapter concludes with a recapitulation of nulls in all their glory.

THE GROUP BY CLAUSE

The GROUP BY clause is intimately connected to aggregates. In fact, GROUP BY doesn't really have much use without aggregate functions. GROUP BY divides a table into sets, while aggregate functions produce summary values for each set. These values are called vector aggregates. (Recall that a scalar aggregate is a single value produced by an aggregate function.)

GROUP BY Syntax

Here's what GROUP BY looks like in the context of a SELECT statement:

```
SELECT select_list
FROM table_list
[WHERE conditions]
GROUP BY group_by_list
```

In most SQL dialects, every item in the GROUP BY list must be a column name (not an expression) and must also appear in the select list. In other words, GROUP BY items must be equivalent to or a subset of select list items—you can make groups only out of things you select. (You can have groups within groups.)

Here is an example with a single entry in the GROUP BY clause:

SQL:
```
select pub_id, count(type)
from titles
group by pub_id
```

Results:
```
pub_id
------ -----------
0736               6
0877               5
1389               6

(3 rows affected)
```

You can include the grouping column (*pub_id*) as well as the aggregate in the select list. All the rows that make up the first group have 0736 in the *pub_id* column, all those in the second have 0877, and all those in the third have 1389. The COUNT generates a single value (the number of types) for each group. Both items in the select list (the publishers and the COUNT) are single-valued per set—there is only one publisher and one type total for each group.

Groups within Groups.   Just as you can sort by multiple items, so can you form groups within groups. Separate the grouping elements with commas and go from large groups to progressively smaller ones.

SQL:
```
select pub_id, type, count(type)
```

```
from titles
group by pub_id, type
```

Results:

```
pub_id type
------ ------------ -----------
0736   business              1
0736   psychology            5
0877   NULL                  0
0877   mod_cook              2
0877   trad_cook             3
1389   business              3
1389   popular_comp          3
```

```
(7 rows affected)
```

This example is much the same as the previous one, but it uses nested groups. Essentially, you are first dividing the rows in the table by publisher. Then you are separating the rows in each publisher group by type, ending up with seven groups, or sets. Once you have the sets established, you apply the aggregate to each, and come up with a number that reveals how many books belong to each type within each publisher.

Restrictions.   GROUP BY looks straightforward, but it's caused its share of headaches for SQL users.

Here, for example, is a query that seems reasonable but won't work on most systems:

SQL:

```
select pub_id, type, count(type)
from titles
group by pub_id
```

Since the table is divided into sets by publisher (group by pub_id) and there are three publishers, the query must return no more than three rows, and each select list item must have a single value for the set. Unfortunately, there is more than one type per publisher, so most systems find the query impossible to answer. You could solve this problem by adding *type* to the GROUP BY clause, as shown in the example just before this one.

Another limitation in most SQL implementations concerns expressions. Generally, you can put only vanilla column names in the GROUP BY clause. Aggregate expressions and column headings are too exotic and will get you nothing but syntax errors unless you have a system which allows these variations:

```
SQL:

select pub_id, sum(price)
from titles
group by pub_id, sum(price)
```

```
SQL:

select pub_id, sum(price) total
from titles
group by pub_id, total
```

Don't confuse GROUP BY syntax conventions with those for ORDER BY. The nesting syntax is similar, but with ORDER BY, you can refer to select list items by positional number. This won't work with GROUP BY.

How about multiple summary values for multiple levels of grouping? Let's say you're sorting by *pub_id* and *type*. You want to see the total number of books for each publisher, and the total number of books for each type of book the publisher carries. You might think something like this would do the trick:

```
SQL:

select pub_id, count(title_id), type, count(title_id)
from titles
group by pub_id, type
```

When you look at the results, however, it's clear you're on the wrong track:

```
Results:
pub_id             type
------ ----------- ----------- -----------
   0736            1 business            1
   0736            5 psychology          5
   0877            1 NULL                1
   0877            2 mod_cook            2
```

```
0877              3 trad_cook          3
1389              3 business           3
1389              3 popular_comp       3
```

```
(7 rows affected)
```

The number of books is the same for publisher and for type, and the results don't make much sense in light of what you are trying to get. What you're seeing (in two columns) is the number of books for each publisher/type combination, since that is the bottom level of the group. To get the results you want, you need to run two queries: the first one grouped by publisher (to give the publisher totals) and the second grouped by publisher and then by type within each publisher (to give the publisher/type totals).

SQL:
```
select pub_id, count(title_id)
from titles
group by pub_id
```

The results of the first query make it clear that each publisher has six books.

Results:
```
pub_id
------ -----------
0736              6
0877              6
1389              6
```

```
(3 rows affected)
```

The results of the second query show the total number of books for each publisher/type combination.

SQL:
```
select pub_id, type, count(title_id)
from titles
group by pub_id, type
```

```
Results:
pub_id type
------ ------------ -----------
0736   business              1
0736   psychology            5
0877   NULL                  1
0877   mod_cook              2
0877   trad_cook             3
1389   business              3
1389   popular_comp          3

(7 rows affected)
```

If you group by type alone, you'll get different results for this data:

```
SQL:
select type, count(title_id)
from titles
group by type

Results:
type
------------ -----------
NULL                  1
business              4
mod_cook              2
popular_comp          3
psychology            5
trad_cook             3

(6 rows affected)
```

In this last set of results, there are four books in the business category. However, two publishers sell this type of book—one has a single business book and the other has three. The query results don't show how many are in each publisher/type combination.

Since the need to see multiple levels of summary values is so pervasive, many database vendors provide a report generator of some type. However, the report generator usually is an application program rather than a part of

SQL because report results with multiple levels of summary values are not able to be represented as relational tables.

Transact-SQL does provide an extension that represents a SQL-based approach to the problem. Here's an example:

```
SQL (extension):
select pub_id, type, title_id
from titles
order by pub_id, type
compute count(title_id) by pub_id, type
compute count(title_id) by pub_id
```

```
Results:
pub_id type          title_id
------ ------------  ----------
0736   business      BU2075
                     count
                     ----------
                               1


pub_id type          title_id
------ ------------  ----------
0736   psychology    PS1372
0736   psychology    PS2091
0736   psychology    PS2106
0736   psychology    PS3333
0736   psychology    PS7777
                     count
                     ----------
                               5

                     count
                     ----------
                               6


pub_id type          title_id
------ ------------  ----------
0877   NULL          MC3026
                     count
                     ----------
                               1
```

```
pub_id type               title_id
------ ------------        -----------
0877   mod_cook            MC2222
0877   mod_cook            MC3021
                           count
                           -----------
                                     2

pub_id type               title_id
------ ------------        -----------
0877   trad_cook           TC3218
0877   trad_cook           TC4203
0877   trad_cook           TC7777
                           count
                           -----------
                                     3
                           count
                           -----------
                                     6

pub_id type               title_id
------ ------------        -----------
1389   business            BU1032
1389   business            BU1111
1389   business            BU7832
                           count
                           -----------
                                     3

pub_id type               title_id
------ ------------        -----------
1389   popular_comp PC1035
1389   popular_comp PC8888
1389   popular_comp PC9999
                           count
                           -----------
                                     3
                           count
                           -----------
                                     6

(28 rows affected)
```

This report shows row values, sub-group totals, and group totals in one set of results. Note that these results, unlike the results of other SQL queries, are not a relation, and cannot be further manipulated by other SQL statements.

Nulls and Groups.   Since nulls represent "the great unknown," there is no way to know whether one null is equal to any other null. Each unknown value may or may not be different from another. However, if the grouping column contains more than one null, all of them are put into a single group.

The *type* column in the *titles* table contains a null. Here's an example that groups the rows by the *type* column and counts the number of rows in each group:

```
SQL:
select type, count(*)
from titles
group by type

Results:
type
------------ -----------
NULL                  1
business              4
mod_cook              2
popular_comp          3
psychology            5
trad_cook             3

(6 rows affected)
```

Notice that there is one row that has a NULL type. If you used `count(type)` instead of `count(*)` in the query, you'd get 0 instead of 1 in the second column:

```
SQL:
select type, count(type)
from titles
group by type
```

Results:
```
type
-----------  -----------
NULL                    0
business                4
mod_cook                2
popular_comp            3
psychology              5
trad_cook               3
```

(6 rows affected)

Why is there still a NULL group, even though it has a count of zero? While count(*) finds all rows in a group, independent of the value in any particular column, count() works with a specified column and tallies only the non-nulls for that column. GROUP BY registers the existence of a type called NULL and forms a group for it. Count(type) duly calculates how many items are in the group. It finds only a NULL, which it doesn't include in the total, and hence records zero.

What happens if there's more than one NULL in a grouping column (like *advance*)? Here's a query that answers the question:

SQL:
```
select advance, count(*)
from titles
group by advance
```

Results:
```
advance
-------------------------  -----------
                    NULL             2
                    0.00             1
                2,000.00             1
                2,275.00             1
                4,000.00             2
                5,000.00             3
                6,000.00             1
                7,000.00             3
                8,000.00             2
```

```
          10,125.00              1
          15,000.00              1
```

```
(11 rows affected)
```

Two books have null advances. Both of them are grouped under NULL advance. Note that, as expected, zero advance forms a separate group because zero is not the same as null.

GROUP BY without Aggregates. Used without aggregates, GROUP BY is similar to DISTINCT. It divides a table into groups and returns one row for each group. Remember, whenever you use GROUP BY, each item in the select list has to produce a single value per set. Here are some examples to make the relationship to DISTINCT clearer. First, a listing of all the publishers in the *titles* table:

SQL:

```
select pub_id
from titles
```

Results:

```
pub_id
------
1389
1389
0736
1389
0877
0877
0877
1389
1389
1389
0877
0736
0736
0736
0736
0877
0877
0877
```

```
(18 rows affected)
```

Next, a listing of all the publishers grouped by publisher:

SQL:
```
select pub_id
from titles
group by pub_id
```

Results:
```
pub_id
------
0736
0877
1389


(3 rows affected)
```

The results are exactly the same as if you had selected all the unique publishers.

A listing of book types grouped by *type* is precisely the same as what you'd get from the query `"select distinct type"`:

SQL:
```
select type
from titles
group by type
```

Results:
```
type
------------
NULL
business
mod_cook
popular_comp
psychology
trad_cook


(6 rows affected)
```

GROUP BY with Aggregates.   The last chapter discussed basic aggregate syntax without GROUP BY and this one has covered GROUP BY syntax.

Now we can put the two together. The fact is, GROUP BY and aggregates were made for each other. GROUP BY creates the sets, and aggregates calculate per-set values. The two together can give you some very useful information.

Let's examine some typical queries. This statement finds the average advance and sum of year-to-date sales for *each type of book*:

```
SQL:
select type, avg(advance), sum(ytd_sales)
from titles
group by type
```

```
Results:
type
------------  ----------   ----------
NULL          NULL         NULL
business      6,281.25     30788
mod_cook      7,500.00     24278
popular_comp  7,500.00     12875
psychology    4,255.00      9939
trad_cook     6,333.33     19566

(6 rows affected)
```

The summary values produced by SELECT statements with GROUP BY and aggregates appear as new columns in the results.

Here's a query looking for relationships between price categories and average advance:

```
SQL:
select price, avg(advance)
from titles
group by price
```

```
Results:
price
------------------------  ------------------------
              NULL                    NULL
              2.99                    12,562.50
              7.00                     6,000.00
```

```
      7.99                    4,000.00
     10.95                    2,275.00
     11.95                    4,500.00
     14.99                    8,000.00
     19.99                    3,000.00
     20.00                    8,000.00
     20.95                    7,000.00
     21.59                    7,000.00
     22.95                    7,000.00
```

(12 rows affected)

GROUP BY with WHERE.   You've seen that when there's no grouping and aggregates are working on the table as a whole, you can use the WHERE clause to specify which rows participate in the aggregate calculations. The same is true when you have groups.

The WHERE clause acts first to find the rows you want. Then the GROUP BY clause divides these favored few (or many) into groups. Rows that WHERE doesn't select don't make it into any groups. Here's an example:

SQL:

```
select type, avg (price)
from titles
where advance > 5000
group by type
```

Results:

```
type
- - - - - - - - - - -  - - - - - - - - - - - - - - - - - - - - - - -
business                     2.99
mod_cook                     2.99
popular_comp                21.48
psychology                  14.30
trad_cook                   17.97
```

(5 rows affected)

Now, the same query without the WHERE clause:

SQL:

```
select type, avg (price)
from titles
group by type
```

Results:

```
type
------------   --------------------------
NULL                           NULL
business                      13.73
mod_cook                      11.49
popular_comp                  21.48
psychology                    13.50
trad_cook                     15.96
```

(6 rows affected)

It returns an extra row (one with a NULL type and NULL average price) and different average price values for all but the popular computing type. The extra row is easy to explain—since the WHERE clause looked for rows with advances greater than $5,000, it didn't include any rows with NULL advances. The row with a NULL type has a NULL advance, so the first set of results, based on groups formed after the WHERE clause eliminated unqualified rows, does not include a group with a NULL type.

If you look at results from a query for *type*, *price*, and *advance*, and then apply the WHERE clause manually by marking with an asterisk the rows in each group that have an advance greater than $5,000, you'll see how the results of the first query (the one with both WHERE and GROUP BY) were generated:

SQL:

```
select type, price, advance
from titles
```

Results:

type	price	advance
business	19.99	5,000.00
business	11.95	5,000.00
business	2.99	10,125.00*
business	19.99	5,000.00

mod_cook	19.99	0.00
mod_cook	2.99	15,000.00*
NULL	NULL	NULL
popular_comp	22.95	7,000.00*
popular_comp	20.00	8,000.00*
popular_comp	NULL	NULL
psychology	21.59	7,000.00*
psychology	10.95	2,275.00
psychology	7.00	6,000.00*
psychology	19.99	2,000.00
psychology	7.99	4,000.00
trad_cook	20.95	7,000.00*
trad_cook	11.95	4,000.00
trad_cook	14.99	8,000.00*

(18 rows affected)

Only the rows with advances greater than $5,000 are included in the groups that give rise to the query results. Since there's just one row in the *business* group, for example, with a qualifying advance, the average price is the same as the price in that row. In the *popular_comp* group, on the other hand, two rows meet the WHERE conditions, and the average is halfway between the two.

Notice that the column in the WHERE clause doesn't have to have anything to do with the select list or the grouping list.

Orderly Groups

GROUP BY divides rows into sets, but it doesn't necessarily put those sets in any order. If you want your results sorted in some particular way, use ORDER BY. Remember that the sequence of clauses in SELECT statements is fixed, and ORDER BY always goes after GROUP BY.

For example, to find the average price for books of each type with advances over $5,000 and order the results by average price, the statement is:

```
SQL:
select type, avg (price)
from titles
where advance >5000
group by type
order by 2

Results:
type
type
------------ -------------------------
business                        2.99
mod_cook                        2.99
psychology                     14.30
trad_cook                      17.97
popular_comp                   21.48

(5 rows affected)
```

THE HAVING CLAUSE

In its most common usage, the HAVING clause is a WHERE clause for groups. Just as WHERE limits rows, HAVING limits groups. Most of the time, you use HAVING with GROUP BY.

When there are aggregates in the select list of a query, WHERE clause conditions apply to the aggregates, while HAVING conditions apply to the query as a whole, after you've calculated the aggregates and set up the groups. One way to keep this difference in mind is to recall the order of the clauses in the SELECT statement. Remember that WHERE comes after FROM, and HAVING comes after GROUP BY. An example at the end of this section explores WHERE and HAVING interactions in some detail.

In terms of allowed elements, HAVING search conditions are identical to WHERE search conditions, with one exception: WHERE search conditions cannot include aggregates, while HAVING search conditions often do. In most systems, each element in the HAVING clause must also appear in the select list. WHERE, of course, does not have this limitation. You can put as many conditions as you want in a HAVING clause.

Garden-Variety HAVING

Here's the standard use of HAVING: GROUP BY divides the rows into sets (by type) and HAVING puts a condition on the sets eliminating those sets that include only one book:

SQL:

```
select type, count(*)
from titles
group by type
having count(*) > 1
```

Results:

```
type
- - - - - - - - - - - - - - - - - - - - - -
business            4
mod_cook            2
popular_comp        3
psychology          5
trad_cook           3

(5 rows affected)
```

Notice that you couldn't simply substitute WHERE for HAVING in this query, since WHERE does not allow aggregates.

Here's an example of a HAVING clause without aggregates. It groups the *titles* table by type and eliminates those types that do not have "p" as the first letter:

SQL:

```
select type
from titles
group by type
having type like 'p%'
```

Results:

```
type
- - - - - - - - - - - -
popular_comp
psychology

(2 rows affected)
```

When you want more than one condition included in the HAVING clause, you can combine them with AND, OR, or NOT. For example, to group the *titles* table by publisher, and to include only those groups of publishers with identification numbers greater than 0800, who have paid more than $15,000 in total advances and whose books average less than $20 in price, the statement is:

```
SQL:
select pub_id, sum(advance), avg(price)
from titles
group by pub_id
having sum(advance) > 15000
  and avg(price) < 20
  and pub_id > "0800"
```

```
Results:
pub_id
------ ---------------- ----------------
0877            34,000.00           14.17
1389            30,000.00           18.98
(2 rows affected)
```

The following statement illustrates the use of GROUP BY, HAVING, WHERE, and ORDER BY clauses in one SELECT statement. It produces the same groups and summary values as the previous example, but does so after eliminating the titles with prices under $5. It also orders the results by *pub_id*.

```
SQL:
select pub_id, sum(advance), avg(price)
from titles
where price >=5
group by pub_id
having sum(advance) > 15000
  and avg(price) < 20
  and pub_id > "0800"
order by pub_id
```

```
Results:
pub_id
------  ------------------------   ------------------------
0877                19,000.00                        16.97
1389                30,000.00                        18.98

(2 rows affected)
```

HAVING and WHERE

Although WHERE and HAVING look the same, it's important to remember the difference in their basic functions. For example, in the query just above, you'd get quite different results if you put the >=$5 qualification in the HAVING clause instead of the WHERE:

SQL:
```
select pub_id, sum(advance), avg(price)
from titles
group by pub_id
having sum(advance) > 15000
  and avg(price) < 20
  and pub_id > "0800"
  and price >=5
order by pub_id
```

Results:
```
pub_id
------  ------------------------   ------------------------
0877                34,000.00                        14.17
1389                30,000.00                        18.98

(2 rows affected)
```

The reason for this is that WHERE eliminates rows before grouping but HAVING goes to work after grouping. (Many systems limit HAVING clause conditions to elements found in the select list. If yours is in this camp, the `price >=5` qualifier will not be legal because there is no unaggregated *price* in the select list.)

Here's a somewhat less complex query pair to puzzle over while figuring out the interaction of the two clauses.

SQL:
```
select pub_id, type, count(advance)
from titles
where advance >10000
group by pub_id, type
```

Results:
```
pub_id type
------ ------------ -----------
0736   business              1
0877   mod_cook              1

(2 rows affected)
```

SQL:
```
select pub_id, type, count(advance)
from titles
group by pub_id, type
having advance >10000
```

Results:
```
pub_id type
------ ------------ -----------
0736   business              1
0877   mod_cook              2

(2 rows affected)
```

The first query, using WHERE as the qualifier, finds two groups, each with one book. The second, using HAVING, also finds two groups, but one of the groups has two books. Why is this?

In essence, WHERE looks at all the rows and keeps only those with advances greater than $10,000 (the ones marked in the conceptual table below with stars on the right).

```
pub_id type          advance
------ ------------ -------------------------
1389   business                     5,000.00
```

```
1389    business                          5,000.00
0736    business                         10,125.00  ***
1389    business                          5,000.00
0877    mod_cook                              0.00
0877    mod_cook                         15,000.00  ***
0877    NULL                                  NULL
1389    popular_comp                      7,000.00
1389    popular_comp                      8,000.00
1389    popular_comp                          NULL
0736    psychology                        7,000.00
0736    psychology                        2,275.00
0736    psychology                        6,000.00
0736    psychology                        2,000.00
0736    psychology                        4,000.00
0877    trad_cook                         7,000.00
0877    trad_cook                         4,000.00
0877    trad_cook                         8,000.00
```
(18 rows affected)

Then, WHERE functions finished, it releases the two rows for grouping and aggregate calculation. Clearly there are two groups, each containing one book. Hence, the results.

HAVING, of course, pertains to the query as a whole, not to individual rows. That's why its results are a little different. The query using HAVING processes grouping and aggregate values first. The first step finds the groups.

```
pub_id type
------ ------------ -----------
0736    business           1
0736    psychology         5
0877    NULL               1
0877    mod_cook           2
0877    trad_cook          3
1389    business           3
1389    popular_comp       3
```
(7 rows affected)

Then, groups determined, the HAVING condition is applied: which groups contain one or more rows with advances over $10,000? Two groups qualify, the first group (0736-business) publishes one business title; the second group (0877-mod_cook) publishes two modern cooking titles.

While WHERE eliminates rows first and then groups the date, HAVING groups first and then eliminates rows. If you paraphrased the two queries, the first would be something like "Show me, for all books with advances over $10,000, the number of advances paid per type within each publisher." The second might be closer to "Show me the number of advances paid per type within each publisher for each type that includes books receiving over $10,000 in advances."

Again, if your system restricts the HAVING clause to elements in the select list, you won't be able to run this kind of query at all (*advance* does not appear in the select list except as an aggregate) and the whole question is not relevant.

MORE ON NULLS

Nulls and the quirks connected with them have come up several times in this chapter and in earlier chapters. In this section, we'll pull all those bits and pieces together and go into more detail about the conceptual problems of nulls, with the goal of helping you avoid some of the mistakes often produced by misunderstandings about nulls.

The first point to consider, though it is hardly reassuring, is that even the experts consider nulls a pesky problem. Chris Date, for example, has been wrestling with nulls for years. In a 1986 paper ("Null Values in Database Management," *Relational Database: Selected Writings*, 313), he argues that nulls should be done away with altogether. The problem of nulls, he says, "is generally not well understood, and...any attempt to incorporate support for null values into an implemented system should be considered premature at this time."

Date is not suggesting that we should forego any way of representing missing or unknown data. He is well aware that in the real world, incomplete information abounds.

Actually, there are a number of different kinds of incomplete information. Date offers several examples of data that may never be known: entries such as "date of birth unknown" in historical records, "to be announced" instead of a speaker's name in a meeting agenda, or "present whereabouts unknown" in a police blotter may remain in a database forever. Sometimes, a value that isn't known now will be determined later, as in the *price* and *advance* columns of the *titles* table in our sample database. Other data is missing in the sense that it is inapplicable. The attribute does not apply to the entity in question. Data for the "assessed value of house" will never make sense for a renter, for example. In today's database products, nulls are used to represent both missing and inapplicable values.

There are other wrinkles, too. Sometimes you don't know precisely what a value is, but you know something about what it's not. You might not know a person's exact birth date, for example, but you know it was between 1860 and 1880. Or negotiations with an author might have already gotten far enough along so that it's clear the advance is going to be larger than $10,000. These kinds of unknown pieces of information are called **distinguished nulls**—their values are not precisely known, but some things about them are clear.

Some types of computer programs—statistical packages, for example—support many kinds of distinguished nulls. In RDBMS's, however, distinguished nulls are very problematic in terms both of definition and implementation. To date, no system we know of supports them.

Some RDBMS's have refrained from implementing nulls altogether—because it's too much trouble to support them. Date suggests an alternative to the SQL concept of nulls, which we'll consider briefly later in this section. But most of today's database management systems use nulls much as we've described them here. Let's summarize what we've said about nulls in earlier chapters.

Nulls and Database Design

In systems that support nulls, you can specify whether a column allows nulls when you create a table. Setting up columns that can accept nulls means that the database system can automatically handle these two situations:

- You're adding a new row to a table, but don't have the information to be entered in some of the fields. The database system automatically marks these positions as nulls.
- You're restructuring a table by adding a new column to it. What gets entered in that new column in all the existing rows? Again, the database system automatically marks nulls.

Comparisons Involving Nulls

We pointed out in Chapter 3 that since nulls represent the unknown, a null can't possibly be known to match any other value, even another null. (Of course, you can't be sure that a null doesn't match any other value, either.)

For example, the advance for the book called *Net Etiquette* is represented as null. Does this mean that it is larger than $5,000? Smaller than $5,000? Is it larger or smaller than with the advance for *The Psychology of Computer Cooking*, also represented as null?

Based on the definition of null as unknown, of course, the answer to all these questions is unknown. You might also say that the answer is "maybe." That's what we mean when we say that null implies **three-valued logic** instead of the more intuitively understandable two-valued logic. With nulls, the possibilities are never just true and false; they're true, false, and maybe.

The counter-intuitive nature of three-valued logic often leads to confusion. Consider the unsuspecting user who asks for a listing of all titles with advances greater than $5,000, and gets a list of eight titles. The user then asks for the titles with advances less than $5,000, and gets five. Finally, he or she determines that there are three titles with advances of exactly $5,000. The user then concludes that there are sixteen titles in all, forgetting that the titles with unknown advances are not reported by any of the queries. This is because, of course, the database system interpreted the first question as, "Give me all titles *known* to have advances greater than $5,000."

Here are a few other likely sources of confusion. If you sort the books by advance, all those with null advances are shown at the beginning or the end of the report, depending on how your system sorts nulls. This implies pretty strongly both that these advances are less than (or more than) any of the others, and that all the nulls are equal to each other, since they are shown together.

Similarly (as far as confusion potential goes), when you select distinct values, all the nulls are eliminated except one. This suggests that the nulls in question are equal to each other!

One aspect of the problem of nulls is simply remembering that they may exist. For example, suppose you want to notify all the authors whose royalty payments for the year totaled less than $600 that they need not report this amount to the IRS. Those whose payments are unknown wouldn't show up in your report unless you specifically search for them with an operator such as IS NULL.

Nulls and Computations

The really sticky problems associated with nulls become apparent when you try to figure out what to do with those unknown values when you operate on them.

It's easy enough to see that when you perform an arithmetic operation on an unknown value, the result can only be unknown. You can double all the advances, for example, and the advance for *Net Etiquette* is still null. You can subtract it from the advance for *The Psychology of Computer Cooking*, and you certainly can't say that the answer is zero: it is still null.

But what if you want to find the average of all advances? Here's what you'd do:

```
SQL:

select avg(advance) from titles

Results:

-------------------------
              5,962.50

(1 row affected)
```

Let's check up on SQL, by querying it for the sum of all the advances, and then for the number of books:

```
SQL:

select sum(advance) from titles

select count(*) from titles

Results:

-------------------------
            95,400.00

(1 row affected)

-----------
        18

(1 row affected)
```

Don't reach for your calculator. What you'll find is that 95,400 / 18 does not give the answer that SQL did. The reason for the discrepancy is that SQL throws out the two null advances in the sum, and in the count that it does for the purposes of calculating the average. However, the nulls are included for the purposes of count(*).

The situation is very confusing. You asked for the average of all the advances, and got a figure that looked very precise. But it cannot be precise, since the data on which it was based is itself incomplete and imprecise.

SQL does the best it can, as the rules for nulls and aggregates given earlier demonstrate. But it is extremely misleading in cases like the one just described.

Nulls and Groups

The 1986 ISO-ANSI standard says that in a SQL that is "level 2–compatible" with the standard, each null generates a distinct group. Level 1 compatibility, however, allows each implementor to determine whether this is true. In many dialects of SQL, all nulls are put into a single group for the purposes of GROUP BY.

Defaults as an Alternative to Nulls

One alternative to a null is a default, a dummy value entered by the database management system when the user provides no explicit value. SQL has no way to specify defaults, but most database vendors supply some mechanism for defining them, usually through a form generator or an application builder.

One of the advantages of defaults over nulls is that you can give a particular column an appropriate value, instead of having to rely on null everywhere. A good default for the *type* column might be "unknown," while one for the *date* column might be "TBD" or today's date.

But defaults create difficulties as disturbing as those associated with nulls. What happens, for example, when you enter some data through interactive SQL, which does not support defaults; some data through an application that does support defaults; and some through a completely different application? You'll wind up with some data with defaults and some...well, it's hard to say. Depending on which system you use and how it's set up, the columns entered through bare SQL or a different application may have nulls, may be rejected, or may have some other default.

Another problem is that each default will vary according to the datatype of the column for which it is specified. The interpretation of defaults in relational and arithmetic operations can also wreak havoc.

Most observers agree that defaults will never provide a solution to the problems associated with nulls. In fact, defaults probably create more trouble than they're worth as long as they are defined in application programs rather than being stored in and controlled by the database itself. A few of today's database management products do support defaults stored in the database, including Transact-SQL. But nulls, with all their complexities, will always be with us.

As a convenience, some database management systems allow you to assign particular display values to nulls. This can be done through an application program or as a SQL extension. For example, this query shows the types in the database, and the number of rows for each:

```
SQL:

select type, count(*)
from titles
group by type


Results:

type
------------ -----------
NULL                    1
business                4
mod_cook                2
popular_comp            3
psychology              5
trad_cook               3

(6 rows affected)
```

One of the types is unknown. Here's how you'd use a Transact-SQL function called isnull() to display a different value for the null:

```
SQL (variant):
select isnull(type, "What?"), count(*)
from titles
group by type
```

Results:

```
------------ -----------
What?                  1
business               4
mod_cook               2
popular_comp           3
psychology             5
trad_cook              3
```

(6 rows affected)

The `isnull()` function has two arguments: the name of the column, and the value to display for any nulls found in that column. You can also use the function for doing "what if" math, substituting different display values for the original nulls. Of course, the actual value in the database is not affected.

Here's a query that shows *title_id*, *advance*, and *price* for titles that have an advance less than $6,000, or a null advance:

SQL:

```
select title_id, advance, price
from titles
where advance <6000 or advance is null
order by price
```

Results:

title_id	advance	price
MC3026	NULL	NULL
PC9999	NULL	NULL
BU1111	5,000.00	11.95
TC4203	4,000.00	11.95
BU1032	5,000.00	19.99
BU7832	5,000.00	19.99
MC2222	0.00	19.99
PS7777	4,000.00	31.96

```
PS2091                    2,275.00                      43.80
PS3333                    2,000.00                      79.96
```

(10 rows affected)

Two rows show null advances and null prices. To see what the same data would look like with different values for the nulls, try something like this:

SQL (variant):
```
select title_id, isnull(advance,4000 ), isnull(price, 35.00)
from titles
where advance <6000 or advance is null
order by price
```

Results:
```
title_id
-------- ------------------------- -------------------------
BU1111                    5,000.00                      11.95
TC4203                    4,000.00                      11.95
BU1032                    5,000.00                      19.99
BU7832                    5,000.00                      19.99
MC2222                        0.00                      19.99
PS7777                    4,000.00                      31.96
MC3026                    4,000.00                      35.00
PC9999                    4,000.00                      35.00
PS2091                    2,275.00                      43.80
PS3333                    2,000.00                      79.96
```

(10 rows affected)

The values and the position of the two rows have changed. Check the manuals to see if a similar capability exists in your system.

BEGINNING MULTI-TABLE QUERIES

The next two chapters give more information about the SELECT statement. Chapter 7 focuses on joins, while Chapter 8 explores nested queries, or subqueries.

Chapter 7

Joining Tables for Comprehensive Data Analysis

WHAT IS A JOIN?

Joins complete the triad of operations that a relational query language must provide: selection, projection, and join. The join operation lets you retrieve and manipulate data from more than one table in a single SELECT statement. Joining two tables is a little like making a seam to join two pieces of material. Once you have made the seam, you can work with the whole cloth.

Though it may seem odd, there is no explicit "JOIN" verb in the SQL language. You specify joins in the WHERE clause of a SELECT statement. Like projections, which are specified in the select list of the SELECT statement, joins are expressed implicitly rather than explicitly.

You specify each join (there can be more than one in a single SELECT statement) on two tables at a time, using a column from each table as a **connecting column** or **join column**. A connecting column should have values that match or compare easily, representing the same or similar data in each of the tables participating in the join. For example, the *title_id* column in the *titles* table matches the *title_id* column in the *salesdetails* table.

Connecting columns almost always have the same datatype. The values in connecting columns are **join-compatible**: their values come from the same general class of data.

Join Syntax

A skeleton version of join syntax is:

```
SELECT select_list
FROM table_1, table_2 [,table_3 ...]
WHERE [table_1.]column  join_operator  [table2.]column
```

The FROM clause's table list must include at least two tables, and the columns specified in the WHERE clause must be join-compatible. When the join columns have identical names, you must qualify the columns with their table names in the select list and in the WHERE clause.

For example, if you wanted to know the names of the editors of *Secrets of Silicon Valley*, you'd need a join on the *ed_id* column that appears in the two tables *editors* and *titleditors*:

SQL:

```
select ed_lname, ed_fname,ed_pos
 from editors, titleditors
 where editors.ed_id = titleditors.ed_id
   and titleditors.title_id = "PC8888"
```

Results:

ed_lname	ed_fname	ed_pos
DeLongue	Martinella	project
Samuelson	Bernard	project
Kaspchek	Chistof	acquisition

```
(3 rows affected)
```

This join selects the names of editors who are connected to the *title_id* "PC8888", by joining on the *ed_id* column that appears in both the *editors* and the *titleditors* tables.

WHY JOINS ARE NECESSARY

In a database that has been designed according to the normalization rules, one table may not give you all the information you need about a particular entity. For comprehensive data analysis, you must assemble data from several of the tables you created when you normalized your database. The relational model—having led you to partition your data into several single-subject tables following the rules of normalization and good clean database design—relies on the join operation to enable you to perform *ad hoc* queries and produce comprehensible reports. Thus, the join operation is one of the key operations of the relational model.

Joins and the Relational Model

Joins are possible because of the relational model, and they are necessary because of the relational model.

Joins are possible in a relational database management system because the relational model's data independence permits you to bring data from separate tables into new and unanticipated relationships. Relationships among data values become explicit when the data is manipulated—when you *query* the database, not when you *create* it.

You need not know that data will join in advance. You can discover new relationships among data in different tables by joining the tables. For example, you could find out whether any names of an organization's board members match those of contributors to a political campaign with a query such as:

```
SQL:
select board_members.name
  from board_members, political_contributors
where board_members.name = political_contributors.name
```

Or, using the sample database, you could use a join query to find out whether any editor is also an author:

```
SQL:
select ed_lname from editors, authors
where ed_id = au_id
```

This query is a little tricky. Since an editor and an author can have the same last name, you need to join on the ID column, which uniquely identifies each of the suspects. As a row's unique identifier, a primary key is often particularly useful in join queries.

Joins are necessary because during the process of analysis that distributes data over the relational database landscape, you cleanly separate information on separate entities. You can get a comprehensive view of your data only if you can re-connect the tables. That's the whole point of joins.

A corollary of the join capability is that it gives you unlimited flexibility in adding new kinds of data to your database. You can always create a new table that contains data about a different subject. If the new table has an eligible field, you can link it to existing tables by joining.

That's how relational databases grow—if tables need to split, you can always reconstruct the rows by joining. If new tables are needed, you can always link them in to the rest of the database by joining.

For example, our *bookbiz* database might need an *invoices* table for billing stores. Such a table could link to the *sales* and *salesdetails* tables by *sonum* (sales order number), and (presumably) to a new *stores* table on the *stor_id* column.

Your database design should anticipate likely joins and build in eligible join columns, which are usually primary key or foreign key columns for their tables. Primary keys join to the corresponding foreign keys. Without join columns available as links, it will be more difficult to run queries on multiple tables.

A PRELIMINARY JOIN EXAMPLE

In the SELECT syntax, the preconditions for a join are:

- naming more than one table in the FROM list; and
- adding conditions in the WHERE clause to create the join on the connecting columns.

You can use any of the relational operators to express the relationship between the join columns, but equality is the most common (a value in the join column from one table is equal to a value in the join column from another table). For example, if an author calls to ask which editors live close to a publisher's home office, a join query can provide the answer. This query finds the names of editors who live in the same city as Algodata Infosystems:

SQL:
```
select ed_lname, ed_id, editors.city, pub_name, publishers.city
from editors, publishers
where editors.city = publishers.city
and pub_name = "Algodata Infosystems"
```

Results:

```
ed_lname                                      ed_id        city
  pub_name                                     city
-----------------------------------------  ----------  ----------
DeLongue                                      321-55-8906  Berkeley
  Algodata Infosystems                         Berkeley
Kaspchek                                      943-88-7920  Berkeley
  Algodata Infosystems                         Berkeley
```

```
(2 rows affected)
```

The join query promptly reports that two editors, DeLongue and Kaspchek, live in the same city (Berkeley) as Algodata Infosystems. This was information you didn't know before. In fact, all you had to know was the publisher's name, and the join supplied you with all that additional information. You told the system: "Join on the city, whatever that is, and tell me the editors' names, whoever they are."

Stating the join in the WHERE clause is not as intuitive as using a JOIN verb would be. How easy it would be to rephrase this query as:

SQL:

```
join editors, publishers
where ed_city = pub_city
and pub_name = "Algodata Infosystems"
display pub_name, ed_lname, ed_id, publishers.city
```

A JOIN keyword is part of the proposed ISO-ANSI standard.

Testing for Successful Joins

In relational theory, a join is the projection and restriction of the product. The product, or **Cartesian product**, is the set of all possible combinations of the rows from the two tables.

The system first examines all possible combinations of the rows from two tables, then eliminates all the rows that do not meet the conditions of the projection (columns) and restriction (selection of rows). The actual procedure that a system follows is more sophisticated, and varies from implementation to implementation. See the section on "How Joins are Processed" at the end of this chapter.

With join queries, more so than with other types of SQL queries, you should test your queries on a sample of your data to make sure that you're getting the results you really want. An insufficiently restricted join query can return results that need a good pruning before you can be sure that they are correct, or useful.

HOW TO GET A GOOD JOIN

What makes for a good join column? Ideally, a join column is a key column for its table, either a primary key or a foreign key. When a key is composite, you can join on all the columns of the key.

Since the primary key logically connects to related foreign key columns in other tables, key columns are usually ideal candidate columns on which to construct a join. Such a join is likely to be useful and logically appropriate, because the database designer planned ahead for it. Primary key-foreign key joins are based on the expectation that foreign keys will be kept consistent with their primary keys, in order to preserve the referential integrity of the database.

The designation of primary and foreign keys is part of database design, but most versions of SQL include no keywords or syntax for explicitly declaring keys—an omission that has drawn some criticism. Some systems permit explicit marking of primary and foreign keys, and can even "recommend" joins. See also the discussion of database design in Chapter 2 for more details on selecting columns for primary and foreign keys.

If a join is to have meaningful results, the columns being compared should have similar values—values drawn from the same general class of data. Such columns will have the same or similar datatypes, and the same or similar data values. In addition to considerations of type, of course, you must consider meaning. For example, you could join authors' ages (such as 25, 30, 50) to numbers in the *salesdetails* table's *qty_shipped* column, but the results would be meaningless. The columns have superficial similarities, but they are not logically related.

In most systems, columns being joined need not have the same name, though they often will. Although they need not be of identical *datatypes*, the datatypes of join columns must be **compatible**—types that the system easily converts from one type into the other. For example, the system may easily convert among any of the numeric type columns—such as *integer*, *decimal*, or *float*—and among any of the character type and date columns—such as *character*, *varchar*, or *datetime*. This implicit conversion enables easy joining of integer type columns to float type columns, or of character type columns to date type columns. Datatype-compatible join columns are, generally speaking, both character types, or both numeric types. You can specify explicit conversion with the type conversion function, as noted in Chapter 3.

Joins and Nulls

Most SQL implementations are clear about what happens when nulls are present in columns being joined. If there are nulls in the connecting columns of tables being joined, the nulls will never join because nulls represent unknown or inapplicable values (and there is no reason to believe one unknown value matches another). However, E.F.Codd lists joins on nulls, the so-called **maybe-joins**, as among the necessary features of the relational model. IBM's DB2 language supports the maybe-join, but few other SQLs do, and there is ongoing debate about how a system should deal with joins of null values. Since maybe there are joins, and maybe there aren't, the response of the typical system is to display only actual joins, and to remain silent about maybe-joins. The consequence of not supporting the maybe-join is that some needed or useful information would not appear in query results.

IMPROVING THE READABILITY OF JOIN RESULTS

When you join tables, the system compares the data in the specified fields and displays the results of the comparison as a table of the qualifying rows.

The results show a row for each successful join. Data from any of the tables is duplicated as needed. In the earlier example, joining editors and publishers by city, "Algodata Infosystems" appears twice in the results even though this publisher appears only once in the *publishers* table.

Join query results replicate data from qualifying rows as needed in order to regularize the table display. As with any query, the results of a join query display as a table without altering the database tables in any way. The join operation simply permits the system to manipulate data from multiple tables as if it were contained in a single table.

You don't have to name the join column twice in the select list, or even include it in the results at all, in order for the join to succeed. However, you may need to qualify the name of a join column with its table name in the select list or in the join specification of the WHERE clause.

The first example could be restated as:

```
SQL:
select ed_lname
from editors, publishers
where editors.city = publishers.city
and pub_name = "Algodata Infosystems"
```

```
Results:
ed_lname
-------------------------------------------

DeLongue
Kaspchek

(2 rows affected)
```

This would be the "just the facts, ma'am" version.

Choose Columns Carefully for Ad Hoc Join Queries

As with any SELECT statement, the columns you name after the SELECT keyword are the columns you want the query results to display, in their desired order.

If you use SELECT* the columns appear in their CREATE TABLE order. In a query to find the title or titles associated with sales order number 1, you might join the *salesdetails* table to *titles* on *title_id*:

```
SQL:
select *
  from titles, salesdetails
where titles.title_id = salesdetails.title_id
and sonum = 1
```

```
Results:
title_id
title
type            pub_id price                        advance
ytd_sales       contract
notes
```

```
pubdate                sonum      qty_ordered qty_shipped title_id
date_shipped
- - - - - - - - - - - - - - - - - - - - - - - - - - - - - - - - - - - - - - - - - -
PS2091
 Is Anger the Enemy?
 psychology    0736                  10.95                  2,275.00
        2045          1
```

Carefully researched study of the effects of strong emotions on the body.
Metabolic charts included.

```
 Jun 15 1985 12:00AM          1        75          75
PS2091
 Sep 15 1985 12:00AM
```

```
(1 row affected)
```

The above display shows a table that has one row and 14 columns. Since this system wraps the results in the display, each row occupies multiple horizontal lines. A join that creates a very wide row can present you with results that are hard to read. If your system has a problem displaying such results in a readable form, you should choose columns carefully for *ad hoc* queries, and use the asterisk notation with discrimination. The limitations of most terminal screens and printers dictate careful choice of columns for the display of results.

Both tables must be named in the table list in order for the system to perform the join. The FROM clause's table list sets the stage—it puts the system on alert to perform a join. The order of the tables (or views) in the list affects the results display only when you use select * to specify the select list.

The table list should name all the tables that will participate in any of the query's joins. You can specify a join on more than two tables, so long as you join tables two at a time. Two-way joins are the most common, but we give some examples of three-way joins later in this chapter. Check your reference manuals for information on the maximum number of joins allowed in a single query.

Aliases in the Table List Improve Readability

In order to make join queries easier to type and more readable, you may want to give the tables alias names (use a "range variable," as the ISO-

ANSI proposed standard puts it) in the table list. Assigning an alias to each table name is particularly helpful when you join on identically named columns, which have to be qualified with the table name each time they're used.

Here's how you could use aliases in a query to find authors who live in the same city as their publishers:

```
SQL:
select au_lname, au_fname
from authors a, publishers p
where a.city = p.city
```

```
Results:
au_lname                                          au_fname
------------------------------------------------  -----------
Carson                                            Cheryl
Bennet                                            Abraham
```

(2 rows affected)

If you wanted to display the city name, you'd also need to qualify it in the select list with one of the table name aliases (*a* or *p*). The names in the table list can be those of tables or views.

SPECIFYING JOIN CONDITIONS

A join is often based on equality, or matching values in the joining columns. Joins based on equality are indicated with the "=" comparison operator in the join part of the WHERE clause. Joins can also be constructed on other conditions: the join operator can be any one of the comparison operators, or a special operator for specifying an **outer join** (which we'll discuss later).

In addition to the equality operator, the other comparison operators that can be used to specify comparison conditions are:

>	greater than
>=	greater than or equal to
<	less than
<=	less than or equal to
!= (or <>)	not equal to

Transact-SQL also provides the operators !> and !< which are equivalent to <= and >= respectively. In relational database jargon, joins that use any of the comparison operators are collectively called **theta** joins.

Joins Based on Equality

By definition, an **equijoin** joins on matching values and displays the join's seam—the connecting column from each table that participates in the join.

This query finds titles that are connected with a particular sales order number:

```
SQL:
select title, titles.title_id, sonum, salesdetails.title_id
from titles, salesdetails
where sonum = 14
and titles.title_id = salesdetails.title_id
```

```
Results:
title
title_id       sonum    title_id
--------       -------  --------

Computer Phobic and Non-Phobic Individuals: Behavior Variations
PS1372         14       PS1372

Life Without Fear
PS2106         14       PS2106

Prolonged Data Deprivation: Four Case Studies
PS3333         14       PS3333

Emotional Security: A New Algorithm
PS7777         14       PS7777


(4 rows affected)
```

Since there's really no need to display information redundantly, you can eliminate the display of one of the connecting columns by restating the query so that it displays the join column only once. Such a display is called a **natural join**. The natural join version of the previous query is:

```
SQL:
select title, titles.title_id, sonum
from titles, salesdetails
where sonum = 14
and titles.title_id = salesdetails.title_id
```

```
Results:
title
title_id sonum
-----------------------------------------------------------------
-------- -----------
Computer Phobic and Non-Phobic Individuals: Behavior Variations
PS1372            14
Life Without Fear
PS2106            14
Prolonged Data Deprivation: Four Case Studies
PS3333            14
Emotional Security: A New Algorithm
PS7777            14

(4 rows affected)
```

Now we have a natural join, because the column *title_id* does not appear twice in the results. Some systems use the natural join display as the default display for a join, because it makes the results more readable. It doesn't matter which *title_id* column you include, but you have to qualify it in the select list with its table name.

The natural join is only one variant on the equijoin: in addition, we have all of the joins based on various kinds of inequality, and (as mentioned) the maybe-joins that compare known values to null, or unknown, values.

Joins Not Based on Equality

Joins not based on equality can be described by their comparison condition, as "less-than join", "greater-than join", and so forth. This

example of a less-than join displays orders that were shipped on a date
later than the sale:

SQL:
```
select distinct sales.sonum, sales.stor_id, sales.date,
  salesdetails.date_shipped
from sales, salesdetails
where sales.date < salesdetails.date_shipped
  and sales.sonum = salesdetails.sonum
```

Results:

sonum	stor_id	date	date_shipped
1	7066	Sep 13 1985	Sep 15 1985
2	7067	Sep 14 1985	Sep 15 1985
3	7131	Sep 14 1985	Sep 18 1985
4	7131	Sep 14 1985	Sep 18 1985
6	8042	Sep 14 1985	Sep 22 1985
7	6380	Sep 13 1985	Sep 20 1985
9	8042	Mar 11 1988	Mar 28 1988
10	7896	Oct 28 1987	Oct 29 1987
11	7896	Dec 12 1987	Jan 12 1988
12	8042	May 22 1987	May 24 1987
14	7131	May 29 1987	Jun 13 1987
15	7067	Jun 15 1987	Jun 17 1987
19	7896	Feb 21 1988	Mar 15 1988

```
(13 rows affected)
```

The following example joins the *titles* table to the *roysched* table
on the *title_id* column, then uses a ">=" join and a "<=" join to find
the appropriate *royalty* rate based on the year-to-date sales recorded
in the *ytd_sales* column from the *titles* table. Based on the total year-
to-date sales, the royalty figure shows what royalty rate is assigned to that
unit sales range in the *roysched* table. The results of this join could be
extended to help calculate an author's royalty, based on the price (or net
price) of each title. This example uses aliases for table names to make the
query easier to read.

SQL:

```
select t.title_id, t.ytd_sales, r.royalty
from titles t, roysched r
where t.title_id = r.title_id
   and t.ytd_sales >= r.lorange and t.ytd_sales <= r.hirange
```

Results:

title_id	ytd_sales	royalty
BU1032	4095	0.100000
BU1111	3876	0.100000
BU2075	18722	0.180000
BU7832	4095	0.100000
MC2222	2032	0.120000
MC3021	22246	0.200000
PC1035	8780	0.160000
PC8888	4095	0.100000
PS1372	375	0.100000
PS2091	2045	0.120000
PS2106	111	0.100000
PS3333	4072	0.100000
PS7777	3336	0.100000
TC3218	375	0.100000
TC4203	15096	0.140000
TC7777	4095	0.100000

(16 rows affected)

Joining a Table with Itself: the Self-Join

The **self-join** is another variant on the equijoin. A self-join compares values within a column of a single table. For example, you can use a self-join to find out which authors in Oakland, California have exactly the same zip code.

Since this query involves a join of the *authors* table with itself, the *authors* table appears in two roles. You must distinguish these roles by giving the *authors* table two *different* aliases—*au1* and *au2*—in the FROM clause's table list. These aliases are also used to qualify the column names in the rest of the query. Here's how you could state this query:

SQL:
```
select au1.au_fname, au1.au_lname, au1.zip
from authors au1, authors au2
where au1.city = "Oakland"
and au1.zip = au2.zip
```

Results:

au_fname	au_lname	zip
Marjorie	Green	94618
Dick	Straight	94609
Dick	Straight	94609
Dick	Straight	94609
Dirk	Stringer	94609
Dirk	Stringer	94609
Dirk	Stringer	94609
Stearns	MacFeather	94612
Livia	Karsen	94609
Livia	Karsen	94609
Livia	Karsen	94609

(11 rows affected)

These results are a bit hard to read, and don't appear to be correct. In order to clarify the situation, let's first attempt to get rid of the duplicate rows. The above results show duplicates for three of the authors: Straight, Stringer, and Karsen. To eliminate duplicate rows, use the keyword DISTINCT to modify the select list.

SQL:
```
select distinct au1.au_fname, au1.au_lname, au1.zip
from authors au1, authors au2
where au1.city = "Oakland"
and au1.zip = au2.zip
```

Results:

au_fname	au_lname	zip
Livia	Karsen	94609
Dick	Straight	94609

```
Dirk              Stringer                        94609
Marjorie          Green                           94618
Stearns           MacFeather                      94612
```

(5 rows affected)

Now the results are free from duplicates, but they show all five authors who live in Oakland, not just those who share a zip code! What's going on?

The self-join compares all the zip code values to themselves, so that each Oakland author's zip code automatically matches his or her own zip code. Therefore, all the Oaklanders appear in the results. In order to eliminate the authors that match only themselves, you need to add one more condition to the WHERE clause:

SQL:
```
select distinct au1.au_fname, au1.au_lname, au1.zip
from authors au1, authors au2
where au1.city = "Oakland"
and au1.zip = au2.zip
and au1.au_id != au2.au_id
```

Results:

au_fname	au_lname	zip
Livia	Karsen	94609
Dick	Straight	94609
Dirk	Stringer	94609

(3 rows affected)

That looks better. In the first, unrestrained example the duplicate rows for these three authors resulted from each author's match with self and with the other two qualifying authors. If you omit the DISTINCT qualifier from the above example, you would still get duplicates from each author's match with the other two qualifying authors.

SQL:
```
select au1.au_fname, au1.au_lname, au1.zip
from authors au1, authors au2
where au1.city = "Oakland"
```

```
and au1.zip = au2.zip
and au1.au_id != au2.au_id
```

au_fname	au_lname	zip
Dick	Straight	94609
Dick	Straight	94609
Dirk	Stringer	94609
Dirk	Stringer	94609
Livia	Karsen	94609
Livia	Karsen	94609

```
(6 rows affected)
```

Eliminating duplicates could be important to an analysis of the validity of the results, in cases where you really want to know "How many?" as well as "Who?".

Not-Equal Comparison in Self-Joins

The clause that eliminates the self-joins of authors with themselves in the previous example uses a not-equal join—a join with the not-equal operator. Not-equal joins are of particular value in restricting the rows returned by a self-join. A not-equal join can also be stated with the NOT keyword. The expression *NOT column_name = column_name* is equivalent to *column_name != column_name*. The previous query could be restated as:

SQL:
```
select distinct au1.au_fname, au1.au_lname, au1.zip
from authors au1, authors au2
where au1.city = "Oakland"
and au1.zip = au2.zip
and not au1.au_id = au2.au_id
```

As another example of combining a not-equal join with a self-join, the following query reports *title_id*s and *author_id*s for books that have more than one author (*i.e.*, all the rows in the *titleauthors* table where there are two or more rows with the same *title_id*, but different *au_id* numbers).

SQL:

```
select distinct t1.title_id, t1.au_id
from titleauthors t1, titleauthors t2
where t1.title_id = t2.title_id
and t1.au_id != t2.au_id
order by t1.title_id
```

Results:

```
title_id au_id
-------- -----------
BU1032    213-46-8915
BU1032    409-56-7008
BU1111    267-41-2394
BU1111    724-80-9391
MC3021    722-51-5454
MC3021    899-46-2035
PC8888    427-17-2319
PC8888    846-92-7186
PS1372    724-80-9391
PS1372    756-30-7391
PS2091    899-46-2035
PS2091    998-72-3567
TC7777    267-41-2394
TC7777    472-27-2349
TC7777    672-71-3249
```

(15 rows affected)

The != join is necessary here again in order for the results to make sense.

In some cases, the self-join is an alternative to the grouping mechanism provided by GROUP BY and HAVING. With Transact-SQL (or any version that allows both set and row elements in the SELECT clause) the results of the query just shown can be duplicated with this query using GROUP BY and HAVING:

SQL (variant):

```
select title_id, au_id
from titleauthors
group by title_id
having count (au_id) > 1
```

Joining More than Two Tables

The *titleauthors* table of our sample database offers a good example of a situation that often requires more than two tables to participate in a join. The design of the *bookbiz* database (which has been normalized) dictates that you must join three tables in order to obtain complete information about books and their authors.

For example, to find the titles of all the books of a particular type (*trad_cook*) and the names of their authors, the query is:

SQL:
```
select au_lname, au_fname, title
from authors, titles, titleauthors
where authors.au_id = titleauthors.au_id
and titles.title_id = titleauthors.title_id
and titles.type = "trad_cook"
```

Results:
```
au_lname                au_fname
          title
- - - - - - - - - - - - - - - - -   - - - - - - - - - - - - - - - - - - - - - - - - -
- - - - - - - - - - - - - - - - - - - - - - - - - - - - - - - - - - - - - - - - - - - - -
Panteley                Sylvia
     Onions, Leeks, and Garlic: Cooking Secrets of the Mediterranean
Blotchet-Halls          Reginald
     Fifty Years in Buckingham Palace Kitchens
O'Leary                 Michael
     Sushi, Anyone?
Gringlesby              Burt
     Sushi, Anyone?
Yokomoto                Akiko
     Sushi, Anyone?
```

(5 rows affected)

The database design uses *titleauthors* as an intermediate table that joins with both *authors* and *titles*. You need this three-way join in order to find out even so simple a fact as who wrote which book.

When there is more than one join condition in a statement, the join conditions are almost always connected with AND, as in the preceding examples. Connecting two join conditions with OR is rarely justified: the results are not likely to make sense because the conditions are not restrictive enough.

Outer Joins: Showing the Background

The joins we've discussed so far include only rows that satisfy the join condition in the results. Occasionally, you may want to display the rows of one table that do not satisfy the join condition. An **outer join** shows you the join rows against the background of rows that did not meet the join conditions.

An outer join typically shows you the join, plus all the rows that did not qualify from the first-named table in the join specification. Other outer join operators can display all the rows that did not qualify from the *second*-named table in the join specification, or even from both tables. The proposed ISO-ANSI standard provides language for retrieving either the LEFT (first-named) table for an outer join or the RIGHT (second-named) table. Typically, outer join operators are provided only as an extension of joins based on equality. Many systems don't provide outer join operators.

The outer join operators that Transact-SQL provides are:

    `*=`   include all rows from the first-named table

    `=*`   include all rows from the second-named table

Recall that the query for authors who live in the same city as a publisher returns two names, Abraham Bennet and Cheryl Carson.

To include all the names from the *authors* table, regardless of whether or not they qualify for the join, you would use an outer join, as follows:

```
SQL:
select au_fname, au_lname, pub_name
from authors, publishers
where authors.city *= publishers.city

Results:
au_fname      au_lname              pub_name
---------     -----------------     ---------------
Johnson       White                 NULL
Marjorie      Green                 NULL
```

```
Cheryl      Carson            Algodata Infosystems
Michael     O'Leary           NULL
Dick        Straight          NULL
Meander     Smith             NULL
Abraham     Bennet            Algodata Infosystems
Ann         Dull              NULL
Burt        Gringlesby        NULL
Chastity    Locksley          NULL
Morningstar Greene            NULL
Reginald    Blotchet-Halls    NULL
Akiko       Yokomoto          NULL
Innes       del Castillo      NULL
Michel      DeFrance          NULL
Dirk        Stringer          NULL
Stearns     MacFeather        NULL
Livia       Karsen            NULL
Sylvia      Panteley          NULL
Sheryl      Hunter            NULL
Heather     McBadden          NULL
Anne        Ringer            NULL
Albert      Ringer            NULL
```

(23 rows affected)

The outer join operator "*=" tells the system to include all the rows from the first table in the join specification (here, *authors*) in the results, whether or not there is a match on the *city* column in the *publishers* table. (The symbol for this outer join operator is the one that Transact-SQL provides; other systems may use different notation.) The outer join results show "no match" for most of the authors listed, as the results indicate with null values in the *pub_name* column.

You can specify that an outer join show non-matching rows either from the first table in the join specification (a "left" outer join), or from the second (a "right" outer join). The outer join operator "=*" includes all the rows in the second table in the join specification in the results, regardless of whether there is matching data in the first table.

Substituting the right outer join operator shows the publishers that do not co-exist in the same city with any authors, as well as the publisher that did satisfy the join condition:

```
SQL:
select au_fname, au_lname, pub_name
from authors, publishers
where authors.city =* publishers.city
```

Results:

au_fname	au_lname	pub_name
NULL	NULL	New Age Books
NULL	NULL	Binnet & Hardley
Cheryl	Carson	Algodata Infosystems
Abraham	Bennet	Algodata Infosystems

```
(4 rows affected)
```

As in any join, the results of an outer join can be restricted by other conditions in the WHERE clause. This means that you can zoom in on precisely the value or values you want to see, and use the outer join to show the rows that didn't make the cut. Let's look at the equijoin first, and then compare it to the outer join. For example, if you wanted to find out which title had sold more than 50 copies from any store, you'd use this query:

```
SQL:
select stor_id, title from sales, titles
where qty > 50
and sales.title_id = titles.title_id
```

Results:

stor_id	title
7066	Is Anger the Enemy?

```
(1 row affected)
```

To show, in addition, the titles that didn't sell more than 50 copies in any store, you'd use an outer join query:

```
SQL:
select stor_id, title from sales, titles
where qty > 50
and sales.title_id =* titles.title_id
```

Results:

```
stor_id title
------- ------------------------------------------------------------
NULL    The Busy Executive's Database Guide
NULL    Cooking with Computers: Surreptitious Balance Sheets
NULL    You Can Combat Computer Stress!
NULL    Straight Talk About Computers
NULL    Silicon Valley Gastronomic Treats
NULL    The Gourmet Microwave
NULL    The Psychology of Computer Cooking
NULL    But Is It User Friendly?
NULL    Secrets of Silicon Valley
NULL    Net Etiquette
NULL    Computer Phobic and Non-Phobic Individuals: Behavior Variations
NULL    Is Anger the Enemy?
NULL    Life Without Fear
NULL    Prolonged Data Deprivation: Four Case Studies
NULL    Emotional Security: A New Algorithm
NULL    Onions, Leeks, and Garlic: Cooking Secrets of the Mediterranean
NULL    Fifty Years in Buckingham Palace Kitchens
NULL    Sushi Anyone?
```

(18 rows affected)

Outer Joins and Null Values. If there are nulls in the columns of the tables being joined, the nulls will never match each other. And, the result of a join of NULL with any other value is NULL. Since nulls represent unknown or inapplicable values, SQL has no reason to believe one unknown value matches another.

You can detect the presence of nulls in a column from one of the tables being joined only by using an outer join. Here are two tables, each of which has a NULL in the column that will participate in the join. A left outer join displays the NULL in the first table.

```
Table 1:
a           b
----------- ------
          1 one
       NULL three
          4 join4
```

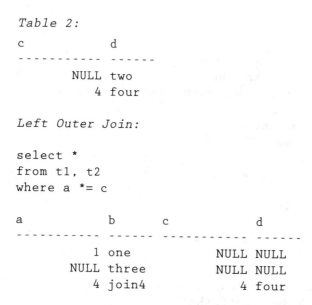

```
Table 2:

c           d
----------- ------
        NULL two
          4 four

Left Outer Join:

select *
from t1, t2
where a *= c

a           b      c           d
----------- ------ ----------- ------
          1 one            NULL NULL
       NULL three          NULL NULL
          4 join4             4 four
```

Note that the results do not make it particularly easy to distinguish a
NULL in the data column *a* from a NULL that represents a failure to join
columns *c* and *d*. When null values are present in data being joined, it is
usually preferable to omit them from the results by using a regular join.

HOW THE SYSTEM PROCESSES JOINS

It's not all that uncommon to make a mistake in a join statement that
results in an incomprehensible report. If your join results seem to contain
too many rows, and include a great many duplicate rows, you probably
need to restate your join query. The excess output—although it is not
what you intended—does reveal something about the way a relational system processes joins.

Conceptually speaking, the first step in processing a join is to form the
Cartesian product of the tables—all the possible combinations of the rows
from each of the tables. Once the system obtains the Cartesian product, it
uses the columns in the select list for the projection, and the conditions in
the WHERE clause for the selection, to eliminate the rows that do not
satisfy the join.

The Cartesian product is the matrix of all the possible combinations that could satisfy the join condition. If there is only one row in each table, there is only one possible combination. To show the product of two tables having one row each, we use data values of *a*, *b* in one table and *c*, *d* in the other, with the column names *one*, *two* in the first table and *three*, *four* in the second table:

```
one two
--- ---
a   b


three four
----- ----
c     d
```

The Cartesian product is:

```
one two three four
--- --- ----- ----
a   b   c     d
```

If you have two rows in each table, the Cartesian product is four rows (2 × 2):

```
First table:
one two
--- ---
a   b
c   d


Second table:
three four
----- ----
c     d
e     f


Cartesian product:
one two three four
--- --- ----- ----
a   b   c     d
```

```
a    b    e    f
c    d    c    d
c    d    e    f
```

(4 rows affected)

The number of rows in the Cartesian product increases geometrically in direct relation to the number of rows in the two tables. It equals the number of rows in the first table times the number of rows in the second table. As soon as you have any significant amount of data, a Cartesian product can produce an overwhelming number of rows.

All you have to do in order to create a Cartesian product right at your own terminal is to set up a two table query and omit the join condition. The query that produced the Cartesian product above was:

```
SQL:
select * from test, test2
```

The Join Clause Constrains the Cartesian Product

A valid join in the WHERE clause is essential to producing comprehensible multi-table query results. Without a valid join, precisely stated and refined, a query on two tables can produce an uncontrolled display of the whole multiplicity of possible connections between the two tables.

In the *bookbiz* database, the Cartesian product of the *publishers* table (3 rows) and the *authors* table (23 rows), shows a results display of 69 rows (3 rows x 23 rows). This result is not only excessive, but also downright misleading, since it seems to imply that every author in the database has a relationship with every publisher in the database—which is not true at all. Getting the Cartesian product represents a failure of communication between you and your system.

If you add the join to the earlier query, it properly constrains the results:

```
SQL:
select * from test, test2
where one = three
```

Results:

```
one two three four
--- --- ----- ----
c   d   c     d
```

(1 row affected)

DIVING INTO SUBQUERIES

In the next chapter we turn our attention to subqueries. Subqueries are the other method that relational systems provide for querying multiple tables. Although joins and subqueries are often interchangeable, there are some cases in which only a subquery yields the desired results.

Chapter 8

Structuring Queries with Subqueries

WHAT IS A SUBQUERY?

A **subquery** is a SELECT statement that nests inside the WHERE clause of another SELECT statement. Less often, subqueries nest inside an INSERT, UPDATE, or DELETE statement, or inside another subquery. A statement that includes a subquery operates on rows from one table based on its evaluation of the subquery's SELECT statement. (The SELECT statement can refer to the same table as the outer query, or to a different table.)

The ability to nest SQL statements is the reason that the SQL language was originally referred to as the Structured Query Language. The term "subquery" is often used to refer to an entire set of statements that includes one or more subqueries, as well as to an individual nestling. We often use the term subquery in this chapter to refer to the whole query. Each **enclosing statement**, the next level up in a subquery, is the outer level for its inner subquery.

Most subqueries are evaluated (conceptually) from the inside out. That is, the outer query takes an action based on the results of the evaluation of the inner query. In a special type of subquery, the **correlated subquery**, the outer SQL statement provides the values for the inner subquery to evaluate. We discuss correlated subqueries in a later section.

Simplified Subquery Syntax

A simplified form of the subquery syntax shows how a subquery nests in a SELECT statement:

```
SELECT [DISTINCT] select_list
FROM table_list
WHERE {expression {[NOT] IN | comparison_operator} | [NOT] EXISTS}
( SELECT [DISTINCT] subquery_select_list
  FROM table_list
  WHERE search_conditions )
```

Outer query search conditions (including joins) can also appear in the outer query WHERE clause, either before or after the inner query.

What Subqueries Do

A subquery's SELECT statement sets search conditions for a WHERE clause in several ways, among them:

- Producing an "IN" list of values for evaluation by the outer statement,
- Returning a single value for use with a comparison operator, or
- Returning a "truth" value for an existence test (testing whether or not data exists that meets the conditions).

The inner query can operate on one table and the outer on another, or the subquery can operate on the same table, like a self-join.

Why Use a Subquery

Some people find subquery syntax difficult to read, and consequently fear that subqueries are difficult to write. Indeed, many subqueries can be replaced by an equivalent join query. However, if you can't construct an equivalent join query, the only alternative will be to use a series of queries and pass the results from one query to another. This is obviously less efficient than mastering the art of the subquery.

As an example of how a subquery can save labor, consider the problem of finding "all the books that are the same price as *Straight Talk About Computers.*"

One option is to do the job in two steps. First, find the price of *Straight Talk:*

```
SQL:
select price
from titles
where title = "Straight Talk About Computers"
```

```
Results:
price
-------------
        $19.99
```

Now, use the result (the price) in a second query to find all the books that cost the same as *Straight Talk*:

```
SQL:
select title, price
from titles
where price = $19.99
```

```
Results:
title                                               price
------------------------------------------------    -----
The Busy Executive's Database Guide                 19.99
Straight Talk About Computers                       19.99
Silicon Valley Gastronomic Treats                   19.99
Prolonged Data Deprivation: Four Case Studies       19.99

(4 rows affected)
```

With a subquery you can solve the problem with a single statement:

```
SQL:
select title, price
from titles
where price =
    (select price
     from titles
     where title = "Straight Talk About Computers")
```

```
Results:

title                                          price
---------------------------------------------- ----------
The Busy Executive's Database Guide             19.99
Straight Talk About Computers                   19.99
Silicon Valley Gastronomic Treats               19.99
Prolonged Data Deprivation: Four Case Studies   19.99

(4 rows affected)
```

Subqueries can perform wonders of selection and comparison, so that one set of statements and nested subqueries can replace several non-subquery statements. This improves efficiency and could even affect performance.

Comparing Joins and Subqueries

As you develop your SQL style, you will use both joins and subqueries for your multi-table queries. Whether you use a join or a subquery can be simply a matter of individual preference: they can often be used interchangeably to solve a given problem. Some SQL users automatically reach for a subquery at every opportunity; others prefer joins. As we will demonstrate shortly, subqueries exceed the capabilities of joins for certain queries. In some cases, a subquery is the shortest route to the results you need. In other cases, it's the only way from here to there.

To clarify the difference in syntax between a join and a subquery, compare these two queries:

Join:
```
select pub_name, au_lname
from publishers, authors
where publishers.city = authors.city
```

Subquery:
```
select pub_name
from publishers
where publishers.city in
  (select city from authors)
```

The above queries (a restatement of an example from Chapter 7) both report that Algodata Infosystems is located in the same city as two of the authors.

Note that the subquery can return rows from only one table, while the join query can return results from both.

Subqueries and Self-Joins. Many statements in which the subquery and the outer query refer to the same table can be alternatively stated as self-joins. For example, you can find authors who live in the same city as Livia Karsen by using a subquery:

```
SQL:
select au_lname, au_fname, city
from authors
where city in
    (select city
     from authors
     where au_fname = "Livia"
     and au_lname = "Karsen")
```

```
Results:
au_lname              au_fname              city
---------------       ---------------       ----------
Green                 Marjorie              Oakland
Straight              Dick                  Oakland
Stringer              Dirk                  Oakland
MacFeather            Stearns               Oakland
Karsen                Livia                 Oakland
```

```
(5 rows affected)
```

Or, you can use a self-join:

```
SQL:
select au1.au_lname, au1.au_fname, au1.city
from authors au1, authors au2
where au1.city = au2.city
and au2.au_lname = "Karsen"
and au2.au_fname = "Livia"
```

SUBQUERY RULES

Subquery rules primarily concern the select list of the subquery, with some additional restrictions on functions you can specify in a subquery. Your SQL may have more or fewer restrictions, but here are some of the common ones:

- The select list of an inner subquery introduced with a comparison operator or IN can include only one expression or column name, and the subquery must return a single value. The column you name in the WHERE clause of the outer statement must be join-compatible with the column you name in the subquery select list.
- Subqueries introduced by an unmodified comparison operator (a comparison operator not followed by the keyword ANY or ALL, explained later in this chapter) cannot include GROUP BY and HAVING clauses unless you determine in advance that the grouping returns a single value. Subqueries with ANY or ALL must also return a single value, so that grouping the results is meaningless.
- The DISTINCT keyword cannot be used with subqueries that include a GROUP BY clause.
- Subqueries cannot manipulate their results internally. That is, a subquery cannot include the ORDER BY clause or the INTO keyword. The optional DISTINCT keyword may effectively order the results of a subquery, since some systems eliminate duplicates by first ordering the results.
- The select list of a subquery introduced with EXISTS almost always consists of the asterisk (*). There is no need to specify column names, since you are only testing for the existence (or non-existence) of any rows that meet the criteria. The select list rules for a subquery introduced with EXISTS are otherwise identical to those for a standard select list.

A survey of the three main types of subqueries will clarify these restrictions and the reasons for them. As we have mentioned, the three basic types of subqueries are:

1. Subqueries that operate on lists, introduced with IN, or with a comparison operator modified by ANY or ALL;

2. Subqueries that are introduced with an unmodified comparison operator, and must return a single value;
3. Subqueries that are an existence test, introduced with EXISTS.

SUBQUERIES INTRODUCED WITH IN

Subqueries introduced by the keyword IN take the general form:

Start of SELECT, INSERT, UPDATE, DELETE statement; or subquery
    WHERE [expression [NOT] IN (subquery)
[End of SELECT, INSERT, UPDATE, DELETE statement; or subquery]

The result of the inner subquery is a list of zero or more values. Once the subquery returns results, the outer query makes use of them.

This query finds the names of the publishers who have published business books:

    SQL:

    select pub_name
    from publishers
    where pub_id in
      (select pub_id
       from titles
      where type = "business")

    Results:

    pub_name

    New Age Books
    Algodata Infosystems

    (2 rows affected)

Without the DISTINCT qualifier the query would return four rows, one for each business type book in the *titles* table. You can attach the DISTINCT qualifier to either the inner or the outer selection.

Conceptually, the statement and subquery are evaluated in two steps. First, the inner query returns the identification numbers of those publishers that have published business books (1389 and 0736):

SQL:

```
select pub_id
from titles
where type = "business"
```

Results:

```
pub_id
------
1389
1389
0736
1389

(4 rows affected)
```

Second, these values are substituted into the outer query, which finds the (distinct) names that go with the identification numbers in the *publishers* table. Conceptually, the process is:

SQL:

```
select distinct pub_name
from publishers
where pub_id in ("1389", "0736")
```

Results:

```
pub_name
-----------------------------------------
New Age Books
Algodata Infosystems

(2 rows affected)
```

Another way to formulate this query using a subquery is:

SQL:

```
select distinct pub_name
from publishers
where "business" in
    (select type
     from titles
     where pub_id = publishers.pub_id)
```

Note that the expression following the WHERE keyword in the outer query can be a constant as well as a column name. Other types of expressions (for example, combinations of constants and column names) are also legal.

As with many subqueries, you could also formulate this query as a join query:

SQL:

```
select distinct pub_name
from publishers, titles
where publishers.pub_id = titles.pub_id
and type = "business"
```

With a join query, however, you also have the option of displaying the title of each business book in the results:

SQL:

```
select pub_name, title
from publishers, titles
where publishers.pub_id = titles.pub_id
and type = "business"
```

Results:

```
pub_name
    title
------------------------------------------
Algodata Infosystems
    The Busy Executive's Database Guide
Algodata Infosystems
    Cooking with Computers: Surreptitious Balance Sheets
New Age Books
    You Can Combat Computer Stress!
Algodata Infosystems
    Straight Talk About Computers

(4 rows affected)
```

This statement and the subquery versions all find publishers who have published business books. They are all equally correct and produce the same results. In cases like this one the rule is "to each according to taste."

Here's another example of a statement that you could formulate either with a subquery or with a join query. The English version of the query is, "Find the names of all second authors who live in California and receive less than 30 percent of the royalties on the books they co-author." Using a subquery the statement is:

SQL:

```
select au_lname, au_fname
from authors
where state = "CA"
and au_id in
    (select au_id
     from titleauthors
     where royaltyshare < 30
     and au_ord = 2)
```

Results:

au_lname	au_fname
MacFeather	Stearns

(1 row affected)

The inner query is evaluated producing a list of the ID's of the three co-authors who meet the qualification of living in California. The system then evaluates the outer query.

Notice that it's legal to include more than one condition in the WHERE clause of both the inner and the outer query. A subquery can even include a join—joins and subqueries are by no means mutually exclusive.

Using a join the query is expressed like this:

SQL:

```
select au_lname, au_fname
from authors, titleauthors
where state = "CA"
    and authors.au_id = titleauthors.au_id
    and royaltyshare < 30
    and au_ord = 2
```

In sum: A join can always be expressed as a subquery. A subquery can often, but not always, be expressed as a join.

SUBQUERIES INTRODUCED WITH NOT IN

Subqueries introduced with the keyword phrase NOT IN also return a list of zero or more values.

This query finds the names of the publishers who have *not* published business books (the inverse of an earlier example):

SQL:
```
select distinct pub_name
from publishers
where pub_id not in
    (select pub_id
     from titles
     where type = "business")
```

Results:
```
pub_name
------------------------------------------
Binnet & Hardley

(1 row affected)
```

The query is exactly the same as the previous one except that NOT IN is substituted for IN. However, you cannot convert this NOT IN statement to a "not equal" join. The analogous "not equal" join has a different meaning—it finds the names of publishers who have published *some* book that is not a business book.

SQL:
```
select distinct pub_name from publishers, titles
where publishers.pub_id = titles.pub_id
and type != "business"
```

Results:
```
pub_name
------------------------------------------
New Age Books
Binnet & Hardley
Algodata Infosystems

(3 rows affected)
```

To refresh your memory about interpreting the meaning of joins based on inequality, refer to Chapter 7.

Qualifying Column Names

In the earlier example, the *pub_id* column in the WHERE clause of the outer query is implicitly qualified by the table name in the outer query's FROM clause, *publishers*.

```
SQL:
select distinct pub_name
from publishers
where pub_id in
    (select pub_id
     from titles
     where type = "business")

Results:
pub_name
------------------------------------------
New Age Books
Algodata Infosystems

(2 rows affected)
```

The reference to *pub_id* in the select list of the subquery is qualified by the subquery's FROM clause—that is, by the *titles* table.

The general rule is that column names in a statement are implicitly qualified by the table referenced in the FROM clause at the same level.

Here's what the query looks like with these implicit assumptions spelled out:

```
SQL:
select distinct pub_name
from publishers
where publishers.pub_id in
    (select titles.pub_id
```

```
from titles
where type = "business")
```

It is never wrong to state the table name explicitly, and you can always override implicit assumptions about table names with explicit qualifications.

COMPARISON OPERATOR SUBQUERIES

This section discusses subqueries that are introduced with one of the comparison operators =, !=, >, >=, <, or <=. These subqueries take the general form:

```
Start of SELECT, INSERT, UPDATE, DELETE statement; or subquery

    WHERE expression comparison_operator [ANY | ALL] (subquery)

[End of SELECT, INSERT, UPDATE, DELETE statement; or subquery]
```

A subquery introduced with an **unmodified comparison operator** (a comparison operator not followed by ANY or ALL) must resolve to a single value. Ideally, in order to use a subquery introduced by an unmodified comparison operator, you must be familiar enough with your data and with the nature of the problem to know that the subquery will return exactly one value.

For example, if you suppose each publisher to be located in only one city, and you wish to find the names of authors who live in the city where Algodata Infosystems is located, you can write a SQL statement with a subquery introduced with the simple comparison operator "=":

```
SQL:
select au_lname, au_fname
from authors
where city =
    (select city
     from publishers
     where pub_name = "Algodata Infosystems")
```

Results:

```
au_lname          au_fname
--------------    --------------
Carson            Cheryl
Bennet            Abraham
```

(2 rows affected)

Aggregate Functions Guarantee a Single Value

Comparison operator subqueries often include aggregate functions because these functions are guaranteed to return a single value. For example, to find the names of all books with prices that are higher than the current minimum price:

SQL:
```
select title
from titles
where price >
    (select min(price)
     from titles)
```

Results:
```
title
-------------------------------------------------------------------
The Busy Executive's Database Guide
Cooking with Computers: Surreptitious Balance Sheets
Straight Talk About Computers
Silicon Valley Gastronomic Treats
But Is It User Friendly?
Secrets of Silicon Valley
Computer Phobic and Non-Phobic Individuals: Behavior Variations
Is Anger the Enemy?
Life Without Fear
Prolonged Data Deprivation: Four Case Studies
Emotional Security: A New Algorithm
Onions, Leeks, and Garlic: Cooking Secrets of the Mediterranean
Fifty Years in Buckingham Palace Kitchens
Sushi, Anyone?
```

(14 rows affected)

First the inner query finds the minimum price in the *titles* table, then the outer query uses this value to select qualifying titles.

GROUP BY and HAVING Must Return a Single Value

Comparison operator subqueries cannot include GROUP BY and HAVING clauses unless you know that they return a single value. For example, this query finds the books priced higher than the lowest priced book in the *trad_cook* category:

```
SQL:
select title, type
from titles
where price >
    (select min(price)
     from titles
     group by type
     having type = "trad_cook")
```

```
Results:
 title
 type
--------------------------------------------------------
 The Busy Executive's Database Guide
 business

 Straight Talk About Computers
 business

 Silicon Valley Gastronomic Treats
 mod_cook

 But Is It User Friendly?
 popular_comp

 Secrets of Silicon Valley
 popular_comp
```

```
Computer Phobic and Non-Phobic Individuals: Behavior Variations
psychology

Prolonged Data Deprivation: Four Case Studies
psychology

Onions, Leeks, and Garlic: Cooking Secrets of the Mediterranean
trad_cook

Sushi, Anyone?
trad_cook

(7 rows affected)
```

Comparison Operators Modified with ANY or ALL

A comparison operator subquery can use the keywords ALL or ANY as modifiers. Subqueries introduced with a modified comparison operator take the general form:

Start of SELECT, INSERT, UPDATE, DELETE statement; or subquery

     WHERE expression comparison_operator [ANY | ALL] (subquery)

[End of SELECT, INSERT, UPDATE, DELETE statement; or subquery]

ALL Means Greater than All Values. Using the "`>`" comparison operator as an example, "`> ALL`" means greater than every value—in other words, greater than the largest value. For example, "`> ALL (1, 2, 3)`" means greater than 3.

ANY Means Greater than Some Value. "`> ANY`" means greater than at least one value—in other words, greater than the minimum. So "`> ANY (1, 2, 3)`" means greater than 1.

    The use of ALL and ANY can be a little tricky because computers can't tolerate the ambiguity that these words sometimes have in English. (The proposed ISO-ANSI SQL standard suggests the keyword "SOME" as an alternative to "ANY" to avoid confusion.)

    For example, you might ask the question, "Which books commanded an advance greater than any book published by Algodata Infosystems?"

This question can be paraphrased to make the SQL "translation" of it more clear: "Which books commanded an advance greater than the largest advance paid by Algodata Infosystems?" The ALL keyword (*not* the ANY keyword) is what's required here:

```
SQL:
select title
from titles
where advance > all
    (select advance
     from publishers, titles
     where titles.pub_id = publishers.pub_id
     and pub_name = "Algodata Infosystems")
```

```
Results:
title
- - - - - - - - - - - - - - - - - - - - - - - - - - - - - - - - - - - - - - - - -
You Can Combat Computer Stress!
The Gourmet Microwave

(2 rows affected)
```

For each title, the inner query finds a list of advance amounts paid by Algodata. The outer query looks at the largest value in the list and determines whether the title currently being considered has commanded an even bigger advance.

If an inner subquery introduced with ALL and a comparison operator does not return any values, the entire query fails. For example:

```
SQL:
select title
from titles
where advance > all
    (select advance
     from publishers, titles
     where titles.pub_id = publishers.pub_id
     and pub_name = "Fictitious Books")
```

Results:

```
title
```

```
- - - - - - - - - - - - - - - - - - - - - - - - - - - - - - - - - - - - - - - - - - - - - - - - - -
```

```
(0 rows affected)
```

A query with ANY find values greater than "some" value of a subquery. The following query finds the titles that got an advance larger than the minimum advance amount ($5,000) paid by Algodata Infosystems.

SQL:

```sql
select distinct title, advance
from titles
where advance > any
    (select advance
     from titles, publishers
     where titles.pub_id = publishers.pub_id
     and pub_name = "Algodata Infosystems")
```

Results:

```
title
advance
```

```
- - - - - - - - - - - - - - - - - - - - - - - - - - - - - - - - - - - - - - - - - - - - - - - - - -
```

```
Sushi, Anyone?
8,000.00

Life Without Fear
6,000.00

The Gourmet Microwave
15,000.00

But Is It User Friendly?
7,000.00

Secrets of Silicon Valley
8,000.00

You Can Combat Computer Stress!
10,125.00
```

Computer Phobic and Non-Phobic Individuals: Behavior Variations
7,000.00

Onions, Leeks, and Garlic: Cooking Secrets of the Mediterranean
7,000.00

(8 rows affected)

For each title, the inner query finds a list of advance amounts paid by Algodata. The outer query looks at all the values in the list and determines whether the title currently being considered has commanded an advance larger than any of those amounts.

If the subquery does not return any values, the entire query fails.

Comparing IN, ANY, and ALL. The "=ANY" operator is exactly equivalent to IN. For example, to find authors that live in the same city as some publisher, you can use either IN or =ANY:

SQL:

```
select au_lname, au_fname
from authors
where city in
   (select city
    from publishers)
```

or

SQL:

```
select au_lname, au_fname
from authors
where city = any
   (select city
    from publishers)
```

Results:

au_lname	au_fname
Carson	Cheryl
Bennet	Abraham

(2 rows affected)

However, the "!=ANY" operator is different than NOT IN. !=ANY means "not = a *or* not = b *or* not = c." NOT IN means "not = a *and* not = b *and* not = c."

For example, say you want to find the authors who live in a city where no publisher is located. You might try this query:

SQL:

```
select distinct au_lname, au_fname
from authors
where city != any
    (select city
     from publishers)
```

The results include all 23 authors. This is because every author lives in *some* city where no publisher is located, since each author lives in one and only one city.

What's happened is that the inner query finds all the cities in which publishers are located, and then, for *each* city, the outer query finds the authors who don't live there. The DISTINCT keyword eliminates duplicates, without changing the fact that this query is essentially wrong.

Here's what happens when you substitute NOT IN in this query:

SQL:

```
select au_lname, au_fname
from authors
where city not in
    (select city
     from publishers)
```

Results:

au_lname	au_fname
del Castillo	Innes
Blotchet-Halls	Reginald
Gringlesby	Burt
DeFrance	Michel
Smith	Meander
White	Johnson
Greene	Morningstar
Green	Marjorie

```
Straight        Dick
Stringer        Dirk
MacFeather      Stearns
Karsen          Livia
Dull            Ann
Hunter          Sheryl
Panteley        Sylvia
Ringer          Anne
Ringer          Albert
Locksley        Chastity
O'Leary         Michael
McBadden        Heather
Yokomoto        Akiko
```

(21 rows affected)

These are the results you want. They include all the authors except
Cheryl Carson and Abraham Bennet, who live in Berkeley, where Algodata Infosystems is located.

You get the same results as in the previous example with the "!= ALL"
operator, which is equivalent to NOT IN:

```
select au_lname, au_fname
from authors
where city != all
   (select city
    from publishers)
```

SUBQUERIES INTRODUCED WITH EXISTS

When a subquery is introduced with the keyword EXISTS, the subquery
functions as an "existence test." The EXISTS keyword in a WHERE
clause tests for the existence or non-existence of data that meet the criteria of the subquery.

A subquery introduced with EXISTS takes this general form:

Start of SELECT, INSERT, UPDATE, DELETE statement; or subquery

WHERE [NOT] EXISTS (subquery)

[End of SELECT, INSERT, UPDATE, DELETE statement; or subquery]

To find the names of all the publishers who publish business books, the
query is:

SQL:

```
select distinct pub_name
from publishers
where exists
    (select *
     from titles
     where pub_id = publishers.pub_id
     and type = "business")
```

Results:

```
pub_name
------------------------------------------
New Age Books
Algodata Infosystems

(2 rows affected)
```

EXISTS tests for presence or absence of "the empty set" of rows. If the
subquery returns at least one row, the subquery evaluates to "true." This
means that an EXISTS phrase will succeed and a NOT EXISTS phrase will
fail. If the subquery returns the empty set (no rows), the subquery evaluates to "false." This means that a NOT EXISTS phrase will succeed and
an EXISTS phrase will fail.

In this case, the first publisher's name is Algodata Infosystems, with an
identification number of 1389. Does Algodata Infosystems pass the
existence test? That is, are there any rows in the *titles* table in which
pub_id is 1389 and *type* is business? If so, "Algodata Infosystems" should
be one of the values selected. The same process is repeated for each of the
other publisher's names.

Notice that the syntax of subqueries introduced with EXISTS differs a
bit from the syntax of other subqueries, in these ways:

- The keyword EXISTS is not preceded by a column name, constant,
  or other expression.
- The select list of a subquery introduced by EXISTS almost always
  consists of an asterisk (*). There is no real point in listing column
  names, since you are simply testing for the existence of rows that
  meet the subquery's conditions.

The EXISTS keyword is very important, because there is often no alternative, non-subquery formulation. In practice, an EXISTS subquery is always a correlated subquery. Instead of having the outer query operate on values that the inner query supplies, the outer query presents values, one by one, that the inner query tests.

You can use EXISTS to express all "list" subqueries that would use IN, ANY, or ALL. Some examples of statements using EXISTS and their equivalent alternatives follow.

Here are two queries that find titles of books published by any publisher located in a city that begins with the letter B:

```
SQL:
select title
from titles
where pub_id in
    (select pub_id
     from publishers
     where city like "B%")
```

```
Results:
title
--------------------------------------------------------
You Can Combat Computer Stress!
Is Anger the Enemy?
Life Without Fear
Prolonged Data Deprivation: Four Case Studies
Emotional Security: A New Algorithm
The Busy Executive's Database Guide
Cooking with Computers: Surreptitious Balance Sheets
Straight Talk About Computers
But Is It User Friendly?
Secrets of Silicon Valley
Net Etiquette

(11 rows affected)
```

or

```
SQL:
select title
from titles
where exists
   (select *
    from publishers
    where pub_id = titles.pub_id
    and city like "B%")
```

The second query produces the same results in a different order, since it evaluates the tables in a different order. The results show that 11 of the books in the *titles* table are published by a publisher located in either Boston or Berkeley.

NOT EXISTS Seeks the Empty Set

NOT EXISTS is the inverse of EXISTS. NOT EXISTS queries succeed when the subquery returns no rows.

For example, to find the names of publishers who do not publish business books, the query is:

```
SQL:
select pub_name
from publishers
where not exists
   (select *
    from titles
    where pub_id = publishers.pub_id
    and type = "business")

Results:
pub_name
-----------------------------------------
Binnet & Hardley

(1 row affected)
```

This query finds the titles for which there have been no sales:

```
SQL:
select title
from titles
where not exists
    (select title_id
     from salesdetails
     where title_id = titles.title_id)
```

Results:
```
title
------------------------------------------------------------
The Psychology of Computer Cooking
Net Etiquette

(2 rows affected)
```

Using EXISTS to Find Intersection and Difference

Subqueries introduced with EXISTS and NOT EXISTS can be used for two set theory operations: **intersection** and **difference**. The intersection of two sets contains all elements that belong to both of the two original sets. The difference contains the elements that belong only to the first of the two sets.

The intersection of *authors* and *publishers* over the *city* column is the set of cities in which both an author and a publisher are located:

```
SQL:
select distinct city
from authors
where exists
    (select *
     from publishers
     where authors.city = publishers.city)
```

Results:
```
city
---------------------
Berkeley

(1 row affected)
```

The difference between *authors* and *publishers* over the *city* column is the set of cities where an author lives but no publisher is located (*i.e.*, all the cities except Berkeley):

SQL:

```
select distinct city
from authors
where not exists
  (select *
   from publishers
   where authors.city = publishers.city)
```

Results:

```
city
--------------------
Gary
Covelo
Oakland
Lawrence
San Jose
Ann Arbor
Corvallis
Nashville
Palo Alto
Rockville
Vacaville
Menlo Park
Walnut Creek
San Francisco
Salt Lake City

(15 rows affected)
```

The query posed in the chapter on joins, "how do you find the names of authors who are both sole authors and co-authors?" is an example of an intersection query that is possible to answer in a single step if you use a subquery, and impossible to answer with a single join query.

Here's the subquery that finds the two authors who have been both sole authors and co-authors:

SQL:
```
select authors.au_id, au_lname, au_fname
from authors, titleauthors
where royaltyshare < 1.0
 and authors.au_id = titleauthors.au_id
 and authors.au_id in
  (select distinct authors.au_id
    from authors, titleauthors
    where titleauthors.royaltyshare = 1.0
     and authors.au_id = titleauthors.au_id)
```

Results:

au_id	au_lname	au_fname
213-46-8915	Green	Marjorie
998-72-3567	Ringer	Albert

```
(2 rows affected)
```

First the inner query selects the identification numbers of authors whose royalty share is equal to 100 percent, and then the outer query compares these IDs to its selection of authors whose royalty share is less than 100 percent. There is no equivalent join query formulation. No amount of self-joining can produce these results, since this query requires joining two different selections from the same table. The only way to solve this puzzle using a join is to create two views of a joined *authors* and *titleauthors* table, and then join the views.

SQL:
```
create view view1
as
select authors.au_id, au_lname, au_fname
from authors, titleauthors
where royaltyshare < 1.0
and authors.au_id = titleauthors.au_id

create view view2
as
select authors.au_id, au_lname, au_fname
from authors, titleauthors
```

```
where royaltyshare = 1.0
and authors.au_id = titleauthors.au_id

select view1.au_id, au_lname, au_fname
from view1, view2
where view1.au_id = view2.au_id
```

For more details on views, see Chapter 9.

CORRELATED SUBQUERIES

Many of the previous queries could be evaluated (conceptually) by executing the subquery once, and substituting the resulting value or values into the WHERE clause of the outer query. In queries that include a correlated subquery (also known as a **repeating subquery**), the subquery depends on the outer query for its values. This means that the subquery executes repeatedly, once for each row that the outer query selects.

Recall that subqueries introduced with EXISTS or NOT EXISTS will always be correlated subqueries. The inner query tests each value that the outer query presents to it. Correlated subqueries can also be introduced with IN or with comparison operators, as in the following examples.

You can find the names of all authors who earn 100% royalty on a book with this statement:

SQL:

```
select distinct au_lname, au_fname
from authors
where 1.00 in
    (select royaltyshare
     from titleauthors
     where au_id = authors.au_id)
```

Results:

au_lname	au_fname
Carson	Cheryl
Ringer	Albert
Straight	Dick
White	Johnson

```
Green              Marjorie
Panteley           Sylvia
Locksley           Chastity
del Castillo       Innes
Blotchet-Halls     Reginald
```

```
(9 rows affected)
```

Unlike most of the previous subquery examples, you cannot evaluate this statement's subquery independently. The value that the subquery needs for *authors.au_id* is a *variable*—it changes as the system examines different rows of the *authors* table.

Conceptually, that's exactly how the system processes this query:

the system tests each row of the *authors* table against the condition. Say that the system first examines the row for Cheryl Carson. The variable *authors.au_id* takes the value "238–95–7766," which the system substitutes into the inner query:

```
SQL:
select royaltyshare
from titleauthors
where au_id = "238- 95- 7766"
```

The result is 1.00, so the outer query evaluates to:

```
SQL:
select au_lname, au_fname
from authors
where 1.00 in (1.00)
```

Since this is true, the row for Cheryl Carson is included in the results. If you go through the same procedure with the row for Abraham Bennet, you will see that this row is not eligible for the results.

Correlated Subqueries on a Single Table

You can use a correlated subquery on a single table, for example to find which types of books are common to more than one publisher:

```
SQL:
select distinct t1.type
from titles t1
where t1.type in
    (select t2.type
     from titles t2
     where t1.pub_id != t2.pub_id)

Results:
type
--------------------
business

(1 row affected)
```

Aliases are required here to distinguish the two different roles in which the *titles* table appears. This nested query is equivalent to the self-join statement:

```
SQL:
select distinct t1.type
from titles t1, titles t2
where t1.type = t2.type
and t1.pub_id != t2.pub_id
```

Correlated Subqueries with Comparison Operators

To find sales where the quantity ordered is less than the average order for sales of that title, the query is:

```
SQL:
select s1.sonum, s1.title_id, s1.qty_ordered
from salesdetails s1
where qty_ordered <
    (select avg(qty_ordered)
     from salesdetails s2
     where s1.title_id = s2.title_id)
order by title_id
```

Results:

```
sonum       title_id qty_ordered
----------- -------- -----------
          8 BU1032             5
          5 MC3021            15
          2 PS2091            10
          3 PS2091            20
          7 PS2091             3
```

(5 rows affected)

The outer query selects the rows of the *salesdetails* table (that is, of *s1*,) one by one. The subquery calculates the average quantity for each order being considered for selection in the outer query. For each possible value of *s1*, the system evaluates the subquery and includes the row in the results if the quantity is less than the calculated average for that table.

In this query and in the next one, a correlated subquery mimics a GROUP BY statement. To find titles whose price is greater than the average for books of its type, the query is:

SQL:

```
select t1.type, t1.title
from titles t1
where t1.price >
    (select avg(t2.price)
     from titles t2
     where t1.type = t2.type)
```

Results:

```
type
    title
---------
    -------------------------------------------------
business
    The Busy Executive's Database Guide
business
    Straight Talk About Computers
mod_cook
    Silicon Valley Gastronomic Treats
popular_comp
    But Is It User Friendly?
```

```
psychology
    Computer Phobic and Non-Phobic Individuals: Behavior Variations
psychology
    Prolonged Data Deprivation: Four Case Studies
trad_cook
    Onions, Leeks, and Garlic: Cooking Secrets of the Mediterranean
```

```
(7 rows affected)
```

For each possible value of *t1*, the system evaluates the subquery and includes the row in the results if the price value in that row is greater than the calculated average. It is not necessary to group by type explicitly, because the self-join in the WHERE clause of the subquery effectively evaluates average prices by type.

Correlated Subqueries in a HAVING Clause

You can also use a correlated subquery in a HAVING clause. This kind of formulation will, for example, find types of books in which the maximum advance is at least twice the average advance for that type.

```
SQL:
select t1.type
from titles t1
group by t1.type
having max(t1.advance) >=all
    (select 2 * avg(t2.advance)
    from titles t2
    where t1.type = t2.type)
```

```
Results:
type
- - - - - - - - - -
mod_cook
```

```
(1 row affected)
```

In this case, the subquery is evaluated once for each group defined in the outer query—once for each type of book.

SUBQUERIES IN MULTIPLE LEVELS OF NESTING

A subquery may itself include one or more subqueries. You can nest any number of subqueries.

An example of a problem that can be solved using a statement with multiple levels of nested queries is, "Find the names of authors who have participated in writing at least one popular computing book."

SQL:

```
select au_lname, au_fname
from authors
where au_id in
    (select au_id
     from titleauthors
     where title_id in
         (select title_id
          from titles
          where type = "popular_comp") )
```

Results:

au_lname	au_fname
Carson	Cheryl
Dull	Ann
Hunter	Sheryl
Locksley	Chastity

(4 rows affected)

The innermost query returns the title ID numbers PC1035, PC8888, and PC9999. The query at the next level up is evaluated with these title ID's, and returns the author ID numbers. Finally, the outer query uses the author ID's to find the names of the authors.

You can also express this query as a join:

SQL:

```
select au_lname, au_fname
from authors, titles, titleauthors
where authors.au_id = titleauthors.au_id
and titles.title_id = titleauthors.title_id
and type = "popular_comp"
```

SUBQUERIES IN UPDATE, DELETE, AND INSERT STATEMENTS

Subqueries can nest in UPDATE, DELETE, and INSERT statements as well as in SELECT statements.

The following query doubles the price of all books published by New Age Books. The statement updates the *titles* table; its subquery references the *publishers* table.

```
SQL:
update titles
set price = price * 2
where pub_id in
    (select pub_id
     from publishers
     where pub_name = "New Age Books")
```

An equivalent UPDATE statement using a join (for systems that allow a FROM clause in UPDATE) is:

```
SQL:
update titles
set price = price * 2
from titles, publishers
where titles.pub_id = publishers.pub_id
and pub_name = "New Age Books"
```

You can remove all records of sales orders for business books with this nested select statement:

```
SQL:
delete salesdetails
where title_id in
    (select title_id
     from titles
     where type = "business")
```

An equivalent DELETE statement using a join (for systems that allow a FROM clause listing multiple tables in DELETE) is:

SQL:

```
delete salesdetails
from salesdetails, titles
where salesdetails.title_id = titles.title_id
and type = "business"
```

ON TO VIEWS

Now that you can write plain and fancy queries using functions, joins, and subqueries, you have most of the power of the SQL language at your command. The remaining issues are ones of how to customize your view of your data, and how to preserve database integrity and security.

Views, which we cover in the next chapter, are a means of naming a specific selection of data from one or more tables so that it can be treated as a **virtual table**. Views can also be used as a security mechanism.

Chapter 9

Creating and Using Views

WITH A VIEW TOWARD FLEXIBILITY

Like the join operation, the view is a hallmark of the relational model. A view creates a virtual table from a SELECT statement, and opens up a world of flexibility for data analysis and manipulation. You can think of a view as a movable frame or window, through which you can see data. This metaphor explains why people speak of looking at data or changing data "through" a view.

Previous chapters have demonstrated how to use a SELECT statement to choose rows, combine tables, rename columns, and make calculations until you've derived specific information in a specific form. Creating a view based on a SELECT statement gives you an easy way to examine and handle just the data you (or others) need—no more, no less.

Views are not separate copies of the data in the table(s) or view(s) from which they're derived. In fact, views are called virtual tables because they do not exist as independent entities in the database, as do "real" tables. (The ISO-ANSI term for a view is a **viewed table**; a native database table is a **base table**.)

The data dictionary stores the *definition* of the view—the view's SELECT statement. When a view is called by a user, the database system associates the appropriate data with it. A view presents the end result of this process, hiding all its technical underpinnings. Its beauty lies in its transparency: naive users aren't frightened by joins, crafty users aren't tempted to look at (or try to alter) data that is none of their business, and impatient users aren't slowed down by the need to type long SQL statements.

CREATING VIEWS

Here's the syntax of a view definition statement:

```
CREATE VIEW view_name [(column_name [, column_name]...)]
AS
SELECT_statement
```

This example creates a view that displays the names of authors who live in Oakland, CA and their books:

SQL:

```
create view oaklanders
as
select au_fname, au_lname, title
from authors, titles, titleauthors
where authors.au_id = titleauthors.au_id
  and titles.title_id = titleauthors.title_id
  and city = "Oakland"
```

SQL:

```
select * from oaklanders
```

Results:

au_fname	au_lname	title
Marjorie	Green	The Busy Executive's Database Guide
Marjorie	Green	You Can Combat Computer Stress!
Dick	Straight	Straight Talk About Computers
Stearns	MacFeather	Cooking with Computers: Surreptitious Balance Sheets
Stearns	MacFeather	Computer Phobic and Non-Phobic Individuals: Behavior Variations
Livia	Karsen	Computer Phobic and Non-Phobic Individuals: Behavior Variations

```
(6 rows affected)
```

When you name a view, be sure to follow your system's rules for identifiers. The first line of the CREATE VIEW statement names the view; the SELECT statement that follows defines it. As you've already seen, the SELECT statement need not be a simple selection of the rows and columns of one particular table. You can create a view using more than one table and/or other views, with a SELECT statement of almost any complexity, using projection and selection to define the columns and rows you want to include.

Dropping Views

Most versions of SQL have a command for removing views with syntax something like this:

```
DROP VIEW view_name
```

If a view depends on a table (or on another view) that has been dropped, you won't be able to use the view. However, if you create a new table (or view) with the same name to replace the dropped one, you could use the view again so long as the columns referenced in the view definition still exist. Check your system's reference manuals for details.

ADVANTAGES OF VIEWS

To clarify the advantages of using views, consider several different types of users of the *bookbiz* database. Let's say that the promotion manager needs to know which authors are connected to which books, and who has first, second, and third billing on the cover. Prices, sales, advances, royalties, and personal addresses are not of interest, but the promotion manager does need some information from each of the three tables: *titles*, *authors*, and *titleauthors*. Without a view, a query something like this might be used:

```
SQL:
select titles.title_id, au_ord, au_lname, au_fname
from authors, titles, titleauthors
where authors.au_id=titleauthors.au_id and
      titles.title_id = titleauthors.title_id
```

This query involves a lot of typing, and there are any number of places where an error might slip in. Quite a bit of knowledge of the database is required, too.

Creating a view called *books* that is based on this SELECT statement would facilitate the use of this particular set of data. Here's the statement that creates the view:

```
SQL:
create view books
as
select titles.title_id, au_ord, au_lname, au_fname
from authors, titles, titleauthors
where authors.au_id=titleauthors.au_id and
      titles.title_id = titleauthors.title_id
```

Now the promotion manager can use the view to get the same results, without thinking about joins or select lists or search conditions:

```
SQL:
select * from books

Results:
title_id   au_ord au_lname       au_fname
---------  ------ ------------   -------------------
BU1032        1   Bennet         Abraham
BU1032        2   Green          Marjorie
BU1111        1   MacFeather     Stearns
BU1111        2   O'Leary        Michael
   .
   .
   .
TC7777        1   Yokomoto       Akiko
TC7777        2   O'Leary        Michael
TC7777        3   Gringlesby     Burt

(25 rows affected)
```

A view can be used in a SQL statement just as if it were a table. For example, the promotion manager might want to order the results of the view alphabetically by author's last name, like this:

SQL:

```
select * from books
order by au_lname
```

An accountant might want to create a different view. He or she doesn't care who the first or second author is. Let's assume that all the accountant needs to know is the bottom line: to whom should checks be written, and for how much. The query involves computing how many books were sold at what price, with what percentage rate for each author:

SQL:

```
select au_lname, au_fname,
   Total_Income = sum(price * ytd_sales * royalty * royaltyshare)
from authors, titles, titleauthors, roysched
where authors.au_id=titleauthors.au_id
  and titles.title_id = titleauthors.title_id
  and titles.title_id = roysched.title_id
  and ytd_sales between lorange and hirange
group by au_lname, au_fname
```

If the accountant uses this SELECT statement to create a view named *royaltychecks*, the equivalent query is:

SQL:

```
select * from royaltychecks
```

The results (who gets a check and for how much) are:

Results:

au_lname	au_fname	Total_Income
Bennet	Abraham	4,911.54
Blotchet-Halls	Reginald	25,255.61
Carson	Cheryl	32,240.16
DeFrance	Michel	9,977.33
Dull	Ann	4,095.00
Green	Marjorie	13,350.54
Gringlesby	Burt	1,841.52
Hunter	Sheryl	4,095.00
Karsen	Livia	607.22

```
Locksley              Chastity               2,665.46
MacFeather            Stearns                2,981.50
O'Leary              Michael                3,694.25
Panteley             Sylvia                   785.63
Ringer               Albert                 1,421.27
Ringer               Anne                   4,669.34
Straight             Dick                   8,185.91
White                Johnson                8,139.93
Yokomoto             Akiko                  2,455.36
del Castillo         Innes                  4,874.36
```

```
(19 rows affected)
```

Finally, consider an executive at the parent publishing company who needs to find out how the different categories of books are doing at each subsidiary. A query something like this can be used:

```
select pub_id, type, sum(price * ytd_sales),
    avg(price), avg(ytd_sales)
from titles
group by pub_id, type
```

However, the executive may not want to bother with anything so complex. If a view named *current* existed, a much simpler statement could be used:

SQL:

```
select * from current
```

Results:

```
PUB#  TYPE            INCOME       AVG_PRICE   AVG_SALES
----  ------------    -----------  ----------  ---------
0736  business         55,978.78        2.99      18722
0736  psychology      139,319.92       13.50       1987
0877  NULL                  NULL        NULL       NULL
0877  mod_cook        107,135.22       11.49      12139
0877  trad_cook       249,637.50       15.96       6522
1389  business        210,036.30       17.31       4022
1389  popular_com     283,401.00       21.48       6437
```

```
(7 rows affected)
```

Using this view, the busy executive can quickly see which publishing lines are making money, and compare the relationship between income, average price, and average sales.

Why View?

As the previous examples demonstrate, you can use views to focus, simplify, and customize each user's perception of the database. In addition, views provide a security mechanism. Finally, they can protect users from the effects of changes in the database structure.

Focus, Simplification, Customization. Views allow the promotion manager, the accountant, and the executive in the previous examples to focus in on the particular data and tasks of interest or concern. No extraneous or distracting information gets in the way.

Working with the data is simpler, too. When favorite joins, projections, and/or selections are already defined as views, it's relatively simple to add other clauses. Constructing the entire underlying query, on the other hand, could be a daunting prospect.

Views are a good way of customizing a database, or tailoring it to suit a variety of users with dissimilar interests and skill levels. Our three users see the data in different ways, even when they're looking at the same three tables at the same time.

Security. Views provide security by hiding sensitive or irrelevant parts of the database. If permissions are set up properly, the accountant can find out how big an author's check should be, but can't look at the underlying figures or compare his or her own paycheck to a co-worker's. You can restrict the accountant's access in the database to just those views that are relevant to accounting. Using views as a security mechanism is discussed in more detail in Chapter 10.

Independence. Finally, there's the issue of independence. From time to time, you may have to modify the structure of the database. But there's no reason that users should suffer from these changes. For example, say you split the *titles* table into two new tables and drop *titles*. The new tables would look something like this:

```
titletext table:
title_id    title                                 type          notes
----------  ------------------------------------  -----------   -----
```

```
titlenumbers table:
title_id   pub_id      price      advance    ytd_sales  pub_date
---------- ---------   ---------  ---------  ---------   ---------
```

Notice that the old *titles* table can be regenerated by joining the *title_id* columns of the two new tables. To shield the changed structure of the database from users, you can create a view that is the join of the two new tables. You can even name it *titles*—and in most systems, doing so means you won't have to change any views that were based wholly or in part on the old *titles*.

Unfortunately, in some systems this kind of view provides only partial independence. Certain data modification statements on the new *titles* may not be allowed because of the restrictions on updating views that are explained later in this chapter.

HOW VIEWS WORK

What actually happens in the database when you create a view, and what happens when you use it?

Creating a view means defining it in terms of its base tables. Although the ISO-ANSI proposed standard is vague on this point, in most systems the view definition's SELECT statement is not executed when the view is created. Instead, the definition of the view is stored in the data dictionary, without any data stored in association with it. When you access data through the view, you are accessing the data that is stored in association with the underlying tables. In other words, creating a view does not generate a copy of the data, either at the time the view is defined or at the time the view is accessed.

When you query a view, it looks exactly like any other database table. You can display it and operate on it much as you can any other table, with restrictions that vary among SQL dialects. Some versions of SQL have been enhanced so that there are no restrictions at all on querying through views, and very few on updating them. (The restrictions on updating views are explained later in this chapter.)

When you modify the data you see through a view, you are actually changing the data in the underlying base tables. Conversely, when you change the data in the base tables, these changes are automatically reflected in the views derived from them.

Suppose you are interested only in books priced higher than $15 and for which an advance of more than $5,000 was paid. This straightforward SELECT statement would find the rows that qualify:

```
select *
from titles
where price > $15
   and advance > $5000
```

Now suppose you have a slew of retrieval and update operations to do on this collection of data. You could, of course, combine the conditions shown in the previous query with any command that you issue. However, for convenience, you can create a view in which just the records of interest are visible:

```
SQL:
create view hiprice
as
select *
from titles
where price > $15
   and advance > $5000
```

When SQL receives this command, it does not actually execute the SELECT statement that follows the keyword AS. Instead, it stores the SELECT statement (which is in fact the definition of the view *hiprice*) in the data dictionary.

Now, when you display or operate on *hiprice*, SQL combines your statement with the stored definition of *hiprice*. For example, you can change all the prices in *hiprice* just as you can change any other table:

```
SQL:
update hiprice
set price = price * 2
```

SQL actually finds the view definition in the data dictionary and converts this update command into the statement:

```
SQL:
update titles
set price = price * 2
```

```
where price > $15
    and advance > $5000
```

In other words, SQL knows from the view definition that the data to be updated is in *titles*. It also knows that it should increase the prices only in those rows that meet the conditions on the *price* and *advance* columns given in the view definition.

Having issued the first update statement—the update to *hiprice*—you can see its effect either through the view or in the *titles* table. Conversely, if you had created the view and then issued the second update statement, which operates directly on the base table, the changed prices would also be visible through the view.

If you update a view's underlying table in such a way that more rows qualify for the view, they become visible through the view. For example, say you increase the price of the book *You Can Combat Computer Stress* to $25.95. Since this book now meets the qualifying conditions in the view definition statement, it becomes part of the view.

Rules for Naming View Columns

Assigning alias names to a view's columns is optional. If you don't give names in the CREATE VIEW clause, the view's columns inherit their names from the columns in the underlying table(s). If you do want to choose new names, put them inside parentheses following the view name, separated by commas. (In some systems, you can also rename columns in the select list as usual.)

There are a couple of circumstances in which new names for the view's columns are required:

- One or more of the view's columns is derived from an arithmetic expression, a built-in function, or a constant
- The view would wind up with more than one column of the same name (usually because the view definition's select statement includes a join, and the columns from the joined tables have the same name).

The first circumstance can be illustrated with the CREATE VIEW statement for the view called *current* used by the executive we discussed earlier in this chapter:

```
SQL:
create view current (PUB#, TYPE, INCOME, AVG_PRICE, AVG_SALES)
as
select pub_id, type, sum(price * ytd_sales),
  avg(price), avg(ytd_sales)
from titles
group by pub_id, type
```

The computed columns in the select list don't really have names, so you must give them new names in the CREATE VIEW clause. Otherwise, you'd have no way to refer to them. When you work with the view *current*, always use the new names, like this:

```
SQL:
select PUB#, AVG_SALES
from current
```

Using the old names, such as *pub_id* or *avg(ytd_sales)*, won't work.

The second circumstance in which assigning new column names is required usually arises when there's a join in the SELECT statement and the joining columns have the same name. Even though they are qualified with different table names in the SELECT statement, you have to rename them in order to resolve the ambiguity:

```
SQL:
create view cities (Author, Authorcity, Pub, Pubcity)
as
select au_lname, authors.city, pub_name, publishers.city
from authors, publishers
where authors.city = publishers.city
```

Of course, you are free to rename columns in a view definition statement whenever it's helpful to do so. Just remember that when you rename any column in a view, you have to rename all of them: the number of column names inside the parentheses has to match the number of items in the select list.

Whether or not you rename a view column, its datatype and null status depend on how it was defined in its base table(s).

Creating Views with Joins and Subqueries

The examples shown so far include views defined with computed columns, aggregates, and joins. Views defined with joins are legal only in some dialects of SQL, as are views defined with subqueries. Here's an example of a view definition that includes three joins and a subquery. It finds the author ID, title ID, publisher, and price of each book with a price that's higher than the average of all the books' prices.

SQL:
```
create view highaverage
as
select authors.au_id, titles.title_id, pub_name, price
from authors, titleauthors, titles, publishers
where authors.au_id = titleauthors.au_id and
      titles.title_id = titleauthors.title_id and
      titles.pub_id = publishers.pub_id and
      price >
          (select avg(price)
          from titles)
```

Now that the view has been created, you can use it to display the results:

SQL:
```
select * from highaverage
```

Results:

au_id	title_id	pub_name	price
213-46-8915	BU1032	Algodata Infosystems	19.99
409-56-7008	BU1032	Algodata Infosystems	19.99
274-80-9391	BU7832	Algodata Infosystems	19.99
712-45-1867	MC2222	Binnet & Hardley	19.99
238-95-7766	PC1035	Algodata Infosystems	22.95
427-17-2319	PC8888	Algodata Infosystems	20.00
846-92-7186	PC8888	Algodata Infosystems	20.00
724-80-9391	PS1372	New Age Books	21.59
756-30-7391	PS1372	New Age Books	21.59
172-32-1176	PS3333	New Age Books	19.99
807-91-6654	TC3218	Binnet & Hardley	20.95

```
267-41-2394    TC7777    Binnet & Hardley    14.99
472-27-2349    TC7777    Binnet & Hardley    14.99
672-71-3249    TC7777    Binnet & Hardley    14.99
```

```
(14 rows affected)
```

Let's use *highaverage* to illustrate one more variety of view: a view derived from another view. Here's how to create a view that displays all the higher-than-average-priced books published by Binnet & Hardley:

```
SQL:
create view highBandH
as select *
from highaverage
where pub_name = "Binnet & Hardley"
```

Restrictions on Creating Views

In spite of the many kinds of views that can be created, there are always limits. The limits vary widely from SQL to SQL; some of the views already shown in this chapter would be illegal in certain implementations of SQL.

The reason for most of the limits is the problem of interpreting data modification statements on certain kinds of views. The view updating problem is explained and illustrated later in this chapter. Here, suffice it to say that many implementations of SQL prohibit the creation of many kinds of views because of update ramifications.

The Check Option

One of the problems with updating a view is that it is possible to change its values in such a way as to make them ineligible for the view. For example, consider a view that displays all books with prices less than $5.00. What happens if you update one of those book prices through the view, changing its price to $5.99?

To help deal with this problem, the ISO-ANSI proposed standard includes an optional clause, WITH CHECK OPTION, in the syntax of the CREATE VIEW statement. (Many commercial implementations of SQL, however, have not incorporated it.)

The WITH CHECK OPTION clause appears after the select conditions in the CREATE VIEW syntax, like this:

```
CREATE VIEW view_name [(column_name [, column_name]...)]
AS
SELECT_statement
WITH CHECK OPTION
```

The WITH CHECK OPTION clause tells SQL to reject any attempt to modify a view in a way that makes one or more of its rows ineligible for the view. In other words, if a data modification statement (UPDATE, INSERT, or DELETE) causes some rows to disappear from the view, the statement is considered illegal.

As an example, recall the view *hiprice*, which includes all titles whose price is greater than $15 and whose advance is greater than $5,000:

SQL:

```
create view hiprice
as
select title, price, advance
from titles
where price > $15
and advance > $5000
```

SQL:

```
select * from hiprice
```

Results:

```
title
  price                 advance
------------------------------------------------------------------
But Is It User Friendly?
  22.95                 7,000.00
Secrets of Silicon Valley
  20.00                 8,000.00
Computer Phobic and Non-Phobic Individuals: Behavior Variations
  21.59                 7,000.00
Onions, Leeks, and Garlic: Cooking Secrets of the Mediterranean
  20.95                 7,000.00

(4 rows affected)
```

This statement updates one of the books visible through *hiprice*, changing its price to $14.99.

```
SQL:

update hiprice
set price = $14.99
where title = "Secrets of Silicon Valley"
```

If WITH CHECK OPTION had been part of the definition of *hiprice*, the update statement would be rejected because the new price of *Secrets of Silicon Valley* would make it ineligible for the view. Since the definition of *hiprice* does not include the WITH CHECK OPTION clause, the update statement is accepted. But the next time you look at the data through *hiprice*, you'll no longer see *Secrets of Silicon Valley*.

The check option can be included only if the view being defined is otherwise updatable. Some dialects of SQL limit the availability and applicability of this option in several other ways. One common limitation is that the check option is not enforced on the "next generation" of view—that is, on a view of a view. For example, say *hiprice* is defined with the check option, and then *hiprice_business* is derived from it, with no check option included in its definition. If you change the price of a book in *hiprice_business* to less than $15, the check option is not applied, and the statement is accepted, even though this book would henceforth not be visible through either view.

In a limited way, the check option addresses the issue of data integrity. In effect, it allows you to specify rules for modifying data through views. If the conditions specified in the view definition are violated by a data modification statement, the statement is considered illegal. The ability to specify rules in a more flexible way, and to associate rules with base tables as well as with views, is provided in a few implementations of SQL, as discussed in Chapter 10.

View Resolution

The process of combining a query on a view with its stored definition and translating it into a query on the view's underlying tables is called view resolution. Several problems can arise during this process.

If any of the tables, views, or columns that underlie a view has been dropped or renamed, or if any datatype incompatibilities have been introduced by restructuring, the system won't be able to resolve the view and you won't be able to use it. Instead, SQL generates an error message.

If you add columns to a view's underlying table, the new columns may not appear in a view defined with a SELECT * clause unless you delete and redefine the view. This is because many dialects of SQL interpret and expand the asterisk shorthand at the time they create the view. In Transact-SQL, for example, the expansion of the asterisk shorthand is the only kind of interpretation that is done when a view is created, rather than when it's queried or modified. Check your system's reference manuals for details on how your implementation works.

Redefining Views

Since views can be defined in terms of other views, it's possible to wind up with a chain of views, each dependent on another. Just as an actual chain can break at any link, so can a chain of views. Any one of the views in the chain might be redefined in such a way that its dependent views no longer make sense.

As an example, three generations of views derived on the *authors* table are shown here.

```
SQL:
create view number1
as select au_lname, phone
from authors
where zip like  "94%"

SQL:
select * from number1

Results:
au_lname                                         phone
---------------------------------------------    ------------
White                                            408 496-7223
Green                                            415 986-7020
Carson                                           415 548-7723
Straight                                         415 834-2919
Bennet                                           415 658-9932
```

```
Dull                                          415  836 - 7128
Locksley                                      415  585 - 4620
Yokomoto                                      415  935 - 4228
Stringer                                      415  843 - 2991
MacFeather                                    415  354 - 7128
Karsen                                        415  534 - 9219
Hunter                                        415  836 - 7128

(12 rows affected)


SQL:
create view number2
as select au_lname, phone
from number1
where au_lname like "[M-Z]%"


SQL:
select * from number2

Results:
au_lname                                      phone
----------------------------------------      -----------
White                                         408  496 - 7223
Straight                                      415  834 - 2919
Yokomoto                                      415  935 - 4228
Stringer                                      415  843 - 2991
MacFeather                                    415  354 - 7128

(5 rows affected)


SQL:
create view number3
as select au_lname, phone
from number2
where au_lname = "MacFeather"

SQL:
select * from number3
```

```
Results:

au_lname                                             phone
---------------------------------------------------  ------------
MacFeather                                           415 354-7128

(1 row affected)
```

What would happen if you redefined view *number2* with different selection criteria (such as `au_lname, phone where zip like "947%"`). Would view *number3*, which depends on view *number2*, still be accessible? The answer is that it depends on the implementation. In some systems, view *number3* would be fine, though the data seen through it would be different. When you used a query that referenced either *number2* or *number3*, view resolution would take place as usual.

Of course, it would be possible to redefine view *number2* in such a way that view *number3* becomes impossible to use. For example, if the new version of *number2* was `au_lname where au_lname like "[M-Z]%"`, view *number3* could no longer be used in a query, since it cannot derive the *phone* column from the object on which it depends. However, view *number3* would still exist, and in some systems would become usable again by dropping and recreating view *number2*, adding the *phone* column back to it.

In short, some systems allow you to change the definition of an intermediate view without affecting dependent views as long as the *target list* of the dependent views remains valid. If you violate this rule, a query that references the invalid view produces an error message.

DATA MODIFICATION THROUGH VIEWS

Changing data through views is a thorny issue. The general problem, as we'll demonstrate here, is that commands to change data in a view sometimes can't be understood by SQL in an unambiguous way. These updates are disallowed by every version of SQL. In other words, some views are inherently and logically not updatable.

There are other views that are logically updatable but that many versions of SQL rule non-updatable. Disallowing a wide range of data modification statements makes for more severe restrictions but simpler rules about what you can and cannot do. Other SQL implementations go to great lengths to let you make as many kinds of changes as possible, in spite of the complications inevitably introduced into rules about data modification.

The kinds of data modification statements that are allowed vary a great deal from SQL to SQL. So treat the rules we give here as guidelines, and check your system's reference manuals for details.

The Rules According to ISO/ANSI

The ISO/ANSI proposed standard is very restrictive on the matter of updating views. It declares that views are **read only** (not updatable) if the CREATE VIEW statement contains any of the following:

- DISTINCT in the select list
- Expressions (computed columns, aggregates, functions, etc.) in the select list
- References to more than one table, either in the FROM clause or in a subquery
- References to a view that is itself not updatable, either in the FROM clause or in a subquery
- A GROUP BY or HAVING clause

Some dialects of SQL are less restrictive than the ISO/ANSI proposed standard; others may be more restrictive. You can check your reference manual, or you can experiment. When you try to modify data through a view, SQL checks to make sure that no restrictions are violated. If it detects a violation, it rejects the data modification statement and informs you of an error.

The best way to understand the rationale for these restrictions is to look at some examples of non-updatable views. Let's start with the restriction that prohibits updating views with columns derived from computed columns. The *gross_sales* column in the view *accounts* is computed from the *price* and *ytd_sales* columns of the *titles* table:

```
SQL:
create view accounts (title, advance, gross_sales)
as
select title_id, advance, price * ytd_sales
from titles
where price > $15
   and advance > $5000
```

The rows visible through *accounts* are:

SQL:

```
select * from accounts
```

Results:

title	advance	gross_sales
PC1035	7,000.00	201,501.00
PC8888	8,000.00	81,900.00
PS1372	7,000.00	8,096.25
TC3218	7,000.00	7,856.25

```
(4 rows affected)
```

Think about what it would mean to update the *gross_sales* column. How could the system deduce the underlying values for price or year-to-date sales from any value you might enter? There's no way for the system to know, and no way for you to tell it. Thus, updates on this view are declared illegal.

Now let's turn to a view with a column derived from an aggregate—that is, a view whose definition includes a GROUP BY clause. Such views (and any view derived from them) are called **grouped views**. A variety of restrictions may apply to grouped views, depending on the particular version of SQL you're using. Here's the view definition statement:

SQL:

```
create view categories (Category, Average_Price)
as select type, avg(price)
from titles
group by type
```

Here's what the view looks like:

SQL:

```
select * from categories
```

Results:

Category	Average_Price
UNDECIDED	NULL

```
business           13.73
mod_cook           11.49
popular_comp       21.48
psychology         13.50
trad_cook          15.96
```

It would make no sense to insert rows into the view *categories*. To what group of underlying rows would an inserted row belong? Updates on the *Average_Price* column cannot be allowed either, because there is no way to know from any value you might enter there how the underlying prices should be changed. Theoretically, updates to the *Category* column and deletions could be allowed, but they are not supported by many versions of SQL.

Some SQL dialects place restrictions not only on updating grouped views, but also on querying through them. For example, the following query would be illegal in such SQLs:

```
SQL (possibly illegal):
select *
from categories
where Average_Price > $12.00
```

Such a query presents problems when it is translated or expanded: the SELECT statement that results is illegal because aggregates are not allowed in the WHERE clause. Here's what the (illegal) statement would look like:

```
SQL (illegal):
select type, avg(price)
from titles
where avg(price) > $12.00
group by type
```

Another restriction on view modifications disallows updates and insertions through a view if the statement would modify columns that are derived from more than one object. This is because updates and insertions on more than one object in a single statement are never allowed.

Some systems allow you to modify the view if you change columns from only one of the underlying tables. For example, if a view contains three columns from *titles* and two columns from *publishers*, these systems would allow an update operation on the view if it changed only the columns from *titles*. You couldn't write an update statement that changed one column from *titles* and one column from *publishers*.

CREATING COPIES OF DATA

We've stressed in this chapter that views are not copies of data, but rather are virtual tables with no physical data associated with them. If an independent copy of data is what you want, you need a SELECT INTO statement. Unlike a view, a table created with SELECT INTO is a separate, independent entity.

A SELECT INTO statement is just a SELECT statement that includes the INTO clause for specifying a name for the new table. The new table is based on the columns you specify in the select list, the table(s) you name in the FROM clause, and the rows you choose in the WHERE clause. The ISO-ANSI proposed standard says that GROUP BY and HAVING clauses cannot be used with a SELECT INTO statement, but some versions of SQL, including Transact-SQL, have no such restriction.

A SELECT INTO statement allows you to define a table and put data into it (based on existing definitions and data) without going through the usual data definition process.

As an example, imagine that you need a new table called *newbooks* that is made up of two of the columns in *titles* and a subset of its rows. Here's how you'd create it:

```
SQL:
select title_id, type
into newbooks
from titles
where price > $20
```

Here's what *newbooks* looks like:

```
SQL:
select *
from newbooks
```

```
Results:

title_id  type
--------  ------------
PC1035    popular_comp
PS1372    psychology
TC3218    trad_cook

(3 rows affected)
```

The new table, with a real (physical) copy of the data from the parent table, becomes part of the database. The data in the parent table is not affected in any way.

The SELECT INTO statement is useful for creating test tables, new tables that resemble existing tables, and tables that have some or all of the columns in several other tables.

You can also use a SELECT INTO statement to create a skeleton table with no data by putting a false condition in the WHERE clause. For example:

```
SQL:
select *
into newpubs
from publishers
where 1=2
```

```
SQL:
select *
from newpubs
```

```
Results:
pub_id    pub_name          city       state
------    --------------    --------   -----
```

DATABASE ADMINISTRATION ISSUES

The next chapter is a roundup of some remaining database management issues: security, transactions, performance, and integrity.

Chapter 10

Security, Transactions, Performance, and Integrity

DATABASE MANAGEMENT IN THE REAL WORLD

This chapter is devoted to four issues that are of particular importance in production-oriented, on-line database applications.

The first of these issues, security, is handled in nearly every relational database management system by two mechanisms: the assignment of **permissions** (also called **privileges**) with the SQL GRANT and REVOKE commands, and the creation of views (through which users can be granted selective access to the database). Different database management systems deal with the other three issues—transactions, performance, and integrity—in a wide variety of ways. For that reason, this chapter emphasizes concepts rather than syntax details in its discussion of them.

Security and one aspect of transaction management are primarily of concern in multi-user situations. Granting permissions to other users is an issue only when there are other users. Transaction management allows the database system to run interference among simultaneous requests for the same data from different users (a capability known as **concurrency control**). Database management systems also rely on transaction management for **recovery** purposes—in case of software or media failure. Recovery is important for both single-user and multi-user systems.

The integrity of data is important whether you're in a single-user system or a shared one. Performance is particularly critical in large multi-user database environments, but it also can become a problem in single-user systems.

In the past, performance was considered a weak point of the relational model. Now some relational products perform as well as or better than systems based on other data models. These high-performance relational systems tend to provide tools, some of them SQL-based, for monitoring and improving the speed and efficiency of data retrieval and modification.

Relational systems have also been criticized for failing to provide adequate assurances of data integrity. Unlike most of the critics of performance, however, the commentators most vocally addressing the integrity issue are strong relational supporters. In fact (as you may recall from Chapter 1), Dr. E.F. Codd, the originator of the relational model, has included stringent integrity requirements in his twelve rules for relational database systems. Currently, the majority of relational database systems provide little in the way of integrity guarantees. But the proposed ANSI-ISO standard includes language for defining integrity constraints, and a few vendors have enhanced their SQLs to meet integrity needs.

DATA SECURITY

Security is an important issue in database management because information is an important commodity. Much of the data worth entrusting to a database management system needs to be protected from unauthorized use—that is, from being seen, changed, or removed by anyone not certified to do so.

If you're the sole user of a database, the security issue boils down to figuring out how to protect the database as a whole—a project not in the province of SQL. With a personal computer, for example, your main line of defense may be as low-tech as a lock and key.

On the other hand, even if you're the only authorized user of a database, the database management system may be running in a shared environment (either on a multi-user computer or one that's linked into a network). Most such computers provide security facilities at the operating system level. Typically, they require passwords for logging on to the computer in the first place; often they flag each file according to which users have permission to read, write, and execute it.

When you're sharing a database with other users, you turn to SQL and the database management system to meet your security needs. Most SQL-based systems provide two major security mechanisms. The first is the control of privileges (also called permissions)—the use of the SQL GRANT and REVOKE commands to specify which users are to be allowed to perform which commands on which tables, views, and (in most versions of SQL) columns. A second security mechanism is the use of views in conjunction with GRANT and REVOKE to provide selective access to subsets of the data.

Both mechanisms assume the database system has a way to know who you are—to recognize its users and verify their identities.

User Identification and Special Users

Database management systems vary widely in their approaches to identifying users, both in basic concept and in detail. Not much can be said that applies across the board; a broad outline of the major variations is about the best that can be done.

Some systems rely on the user's identity at the operating system level: in other words, they recognize as an authorized user anyone who can log on to the computer. That's not to say, however, that anyone who can access the database system will be able to do much of anything in it.

More sophisticated database management systems have their own identification and authorization mechanisms, which require each user to have an established name (sometimes called an **account** or **login**) and password on the system itself and/or in each database on the system (assuming the system supports the concept of multiple interacting databases). Application programs can supply additional layers of protection.

What happens once the database management system recognizes your on-line identity and verifies it by requesting and receiving your password? At that point, what you can do depends on the kind of user you are and the permissions you've explicitly been granted by other users.

Most multi-user database management systems recognize at least two kinds of specially privileged users: a **super user** often known as the database administrator (DBA) or System Administrator, and the owners of database objects. Some database systems (like SYBASE) recognize additional special users and establish a hierarchy in which privileges to execute various commands are assigned to users depending on their position in the hierarchy.

The existence of the database administrator is established at the time the system is installed. The identity of the DBA is not exactly the same as that of ordinary mortals; DBA is actually a special role that can be (temporarily) filled by any user who knows the correct account name and password. In many database installations, the role of DBA is shared by several people. Each of these users might log in as DBA in order to accomplish administrative tasks, but use his or her own name for other functions in the database.

The DBA typically is blessed with many special privileges and burdened with many responsibilities for the maintenance and smooth operation of the database application. For the purposes of this discussion on security, the DBA (in most systems) automatically holds all permissions that the system recognizes, on all database objects and for all commands. Which of these permissions the DBA can pass along to other users varies from system to system.

The other special category of users that's important for security purposes is the owner of a table or view. In many systems, the user that creates a table or view is its owner. (Some systems support the additional concept of a database owner.) A table owner or view owner may automatically be entitled to do anything to the table or view, (usually) including the granting of permissions on it to other users.

Users other than the owners of a table or view (and the DBA) need explicit permission to perform any operation on it. These permissions are controlled with the SQL GRANT and REVOKE commands, which are supported by virtually every multi-user implementation of SQL.

Information about user identification and permissions may be stored in the data dictionary.

The GRANT and REVOKE Commands

The phrases "granting privileges" or "assigning permissions" are often associated with discussions of GRANT and REVOKE. In most implementations of SQL, you can't do anything for which you don't have explicit authorization—either by virtue of being an object owner or database administrator, or by virtue of having been granted authorization with the GRANT command.

The GRANT and REVOKE commands specify which users can perform which operations on which tables, views, or columns. In some versions of SQL, permission must also be explicitly granted (usually by the database administrator) in order to execute commands such as CREATE TABLE and DROP INDEX.

The operations associated with GRANT and REVOKE are (at a minimum) SELECT, UPDATE, INSERT, and DELETE. The database objects to which permissions for these operations apply are tables and views; some systems also provide for controlling permission at the level of columns. Authorization to grant these permissions originates with the object owner; in some SQLs permission to grant permissions is transferable along with the permission itself. Here's the syntax for the two commands that is typical of most SQL dialects:

```
GRANT {ALL | privilege_list}
ON {table_name [(column_list)] | view_name [(column_list)]}
TO {PUBLIC | user_list}

REVOKE {ALL | privilege_list}
ON {table_name [(column_list)] | view_name [(column_list)]}
FROM {PUBLIC | user_list}
```

As is often the case in SQL, the syntax looks much more complicated than the majority of statements you'll need to write. Before explaining it in detail, here's a simple example that grants permission to Mary to insert into and update the *titles* table:

```
grant insert, update
on titles
to mary
```

Here's one more that revokes Mary's permission to update the *advance* and *price* columns of the *titles* table:

```
revoke update
on titles(advance, price)
from mary
```

Now let's take a closer look at the GRANT and REVOKE syntax. The first line includes the keyword GRANT or REVOKE and either the keyword ALL or a list of (one or more) privileges being granted or revoked. If you include more than one privilege in the privilege list, separate them with commas. If the keyword ALL is used, every one of the privileges applicable to the object is granted or revoked (that is, every privilege held by the grantor or revoker).

The ON clause specifies the table or view for which the privilege is being granted or revoked—one table or one view per statement. Different versions of SQL allow the inclusion of somewhat different sets of privileges after the ON clause. SELECT, UPDATE, DELETE, and INSERT are always in that set, but SQLs differ in whether permissions for some, all, or none of these operations can be controlled on the level of columns as well as tables and views. When permissions are being granted on columns, the column name(s) are listed in parentheses after the table or view name.

Privileges can be granted for more than one column at a time, but all the columns must be in the same table, or in the same view. If you don't include a list of column names, the privilege is being granted or revoked for the entire table or view.

The next line in the syntax begins with the keyword TO (for the GRANT command) or FROM (for the REVOKE command). The keyword PUBLIC refers to all the users of the system. In Transact-SQL, granting privileges to PUBLIC includes both the user who issues the statement and all future users of the system.

The alternative to PUBLIC is a list of the names of the users to whom you want to grant the privileges (or from whom you want to revoke them). As always, each name in the list is separated from the next by a comma. Some SQL dialects support the concept of user groups; in these SQLs the name of a group can be included in the user list.

The syntax shown here does not include another optional clause—the WITH GRANT OPTION clause—that is part of the GRANT command in many SQL dialects, including the proposed ISO-ANSI SQL2. Granting a privilege with the grant option means that the grantee can in turn pass that privilege (with or without the grant option) on to other users. For example, here's a statement that grants Mary permission to SELECT from the *authors* table, and allows her to pass that privilege to other users:

```
grant select
on authors
to mary
with grant option
```

The implementations of SQL that do not provide the WITH GRANT OPTION clause, including Transact-SQL, have chosen to restrict the privilege of granting privileges to the owners of database objects and/or the DBA (called "System Administrator" in Transact-SQL).

In the ISO-ANSI proposed SQL standard, GRANT and REVOKE statements are issued as part of the schema creation (or database definition). Other SQL dialects don't include this built-in encouragement to consider the setting up of permissions as part of the database design process, but it's a good idea to do so (though you can issue GRANT and REVOKE statements at any time). Whenever you set up permissions on a table or view that you own, it's good practice to issue the GRANT and REVOKE commands according to a plan to which you've given some thought, rather than to GRANT and REVOKE haphazardly, on the spur of the moment.

Here are some examples that show how to use GRANT and REVOKE statements to set up permissions on a table. Suppose you are the owner of the *titles* table and that you've decided that most of the system's users should be allowed access to the table—except those columns dealing with money and sales. You want to restrict permission to modify those columns to three specific users (Sara, John, and Leslie).

In order to set up this situation, you can choose between two approaches. The most straightforward is to assign specific permissions to specific users—which in this case would mean writing several GRANT statements, including one with a very long user list. You'd need one statement to grant all the permissions to Sara, John, and Leslie:

```
grant select, insert, delete, update
on titles
to sara, john, leslie
```

Now you'd need a statement to grant SELECT permissions to all those other users:

```
grant select, insert, delete
on titles
to linda, pat, steve, chris, cathy, peter, lee, carl, karen
```

The list of users could be very long—and you still need another statement to grant all of them permission to modify all the columns in *titles* except *price* and *ytd_sales*:

```
grant update, insert, delete
on titles(title_id, title, type, pub_id,
  advance, contract, notes, pubdate)
to linda, pat, steve, chris, cathy, peter, lee, carl, karen
```

Since most users are going to be granted most privileges, it's easier to assign all permissions to all users and then revoke specific permissions from specific users. Here's how:

Begin with a statement that grants all users permission to SELECT from, INSERT into, DELETE from, and UPDATE *titles*:

```
grant all
on titles
to public
```

You've been very generous: now any user can modify *titles* at will. To protect the more sensitive columns, issue a statement to change the situation created by the previous statement. This statement revokes permission for all users to UPDATE, DELETE from, or INSERT into the *price* and *ytd_sales* columns of the *titles* table. The other privileges granted in the previous statement are unaffected.

```
revoke update, insert, delete
on titles (price, ytd_sales)
from public
```

Now, to give Sara, Leslie, and John permission to update those columns, you might issue this command:

```
grant update
on titles(price, ytd_sales)
to sara, john, leslie
```

You will want to include your own name in the user list as well, since the revocation from PUBLIC also applies to you.

Conflicting GRANT and REVOKE statements. As the previous examples imply, GRANT and REVOKE statements are order-sensitive (in most implementations of SQL). In case of a conflict, the most recently issued statement supersedes all others. So, for example, if PUBLIC has been granted SELECT permission on the *titles* table and then Joe's permission to SELECT the *advance* column has been revoked, Joe can SELECT all the columns except *advance*, while all the other users can still SELECT all the columns. Similarly, a GRANT or REVOKE statement issued to PUBLIC will change all previously issued permissions that conflict with the new regime.

The consequence of this rule is that the same GRANT and REVOKE statements issued in different orders can create entirely different situations. For example, this set of statements leaves Joe (who is, of course, part of PUBLIC) without any SELECT permission on *titles*:

```
grant select
on titles(title_id, title)
to joe

revoke select
on titles
from public
```

In contrast, consider the same statements issued in the opposite order:

```
revoke select
on titles
from public

grant select
on titles(title_id, title)
to joe
```

Now only Joe has SELECT permission, and only on the *title_id* and *title* columns.

Remember that when you use the keyword PUBLIC, you are including yourself. You could even deny yourself permission to modify your own table, while giving yourself permission to access a view built on it or a stored procedure that references it. (You can always change your mind and reinstitute the permission with a GRANT statement.) You will probably use PUBLIC more frequently as a quick way of revoking permissions and then defining some exceptions, as in the previous example.

Views as Security Mechanisms

The second major security mechanism in most relational database management systems involves using views in conjunction with GRANT and REVOKE. Permission to access the subset of data in a view must be explicitly granted or revoked, regardless of the set of permissions in force on the view's underlying table(s).

Through a view, users can query and modify only the data they can see. The rest of the database is neither visible nor accessible. For example, you might not want some users to be able to access the columns in the *titles* table that have to do with money and sales. You could create a view of the *titles* table that omits those columns (call it *bookview*), and then give all users permission on the view, but give only some members of the sales group permission on the table. Here's how:

```
grant all
on bookview
to public
```

```
grant all
on titles
to mccann, himmelwright, brady, mandelbaum
```

By defining different views and selectively granting permissions on them, a user (or any combination of users) can be restricted to different subsets of data:

- Access can be restricted to a subset of the rows of a base table (a value-dependent subset). For example, you might define a view that contains only the rows for business and psychology books, in order to keep information about other types of books hidden from some users.
- Access can be restricted to a subset of the columns of a base table (a value-independent subset). For example, you might define a view that contains all the rows of the *titles* table, but omits the *ytd_sales* and *advance* columns, since this information is sensitive.
- Access can be restricted to a row-and-column subset of a base table. For example, you might define a view that contains information only about business and psychology books, and only non-financial information about them.
- Access can be restricted to the rows that qualify for a join of more than one base table. For example, you might define a view that joins the *titles*, *authors*, and *titleauthors* table in order to display the names of the authors and the books they have written. This view would hide personal data about authors and financial information about the books.
- Access can be restricted to a statistical summary of data in a base table. For example, you might define a view that shows the average price of each type of book.
- Access can be restricted to a subset of another view, or of some combination of views and base tables. For example, you might define a view on the view described in the previous example, containing the average price of cooking and computer books.

Creating views and setting up authorizations on them and on base tables is often done as part of the data definition process. However, you can change the authorization scheme at any time, defining new views and writing new GRANT and REVOKE statements. For more details on views, you may want to review Chapter 9.

TRANSACTIONS

A **transaction** is a logical unit of work. **Transaction management** means ensuring that a set of SQL statements is treated as a unit—as an indivisible entity. In other words, transaction management guarantees either that all the operations within a set (a transaction) are completed or that none of them is completed: a transaction is an all-or-nothing proposition.

Transactions are necessary for the purposes of concurrency control (keeping users who are simultaneously accessing the database from colliding with each other) and recovery (allowing the database system to bring the database back to a consistent state after a software failure).

SQL automatically manages all commands, including single-step change requests, as transactions. Some implementations of SQL also allow users to group a set of SQL statements into a **user-defined transaction** with commands such as BEGIN TRANsaction and COMMIT TRANsaction.

Transactions and Concurrency

In multi-user systems, more than one user and/or transaction can access the same data at the same time. Preventing simultaneous transactions from interfering with each other—**controlling concurrency**—means making sure that data is never seen nor operated on by another user until a change is completed.

The purchase of airline tickets provides a classic example of one of the situations in which concurrency can be a problem. (It's so classic that it has a name—the **lost update problem**.)

Say you call your favorite airline and ask for a ticket to Tahiti. The ticketing clerk submits a query to the database that selects all the available seats, and tells you that there's one left on tonight's flight. As you ponder, another desperate tourist has called his travel agent to find out whether he can get to Tahiti tonight. The travel agent has submitted the query to the database—the same one submitted by your ticketing clerk—and gets the same results. The travel agent informs the customer of the availability of a single seat. By now you've made up your mind, and the airline's ticketing clerk updates the database to reflect the fact that the last seat has been sold. You start packing—unaware that the travel agent, who has no way to know about the update made by the ticketing clerk, has just sold the same ticket. In fact, the update made by the travel agent overwrites the update submitted by your ticketing clerk. When you get to the airport, no one has heard of you.

This example demonstrates one of the dangers posed by concurrency demands in large, shared database systems. To handle concurrency problems, most relational database management systems rely on a mechanism called **locking**. The details of locking are outside the scope of this book, especially since most database systems handle it automatically, leaving users little say (if any) about it. Therefore, only an overview of this mechanism will be given.

Locking.   Basically, the way locks work is that when a user selects some data from the database, the database management system automatically puts a lock on it so that no other user can update that data until the lock is released.

There are many kinds of locks, but the most important distinction to understand is the difference between an **exclusive** lock and a **shared** lock. Database systems apply exclusive locks during data modification (also called **write**) operations—UPDATE, INSERT, DELETE. When an exclusive lock is applied to a set of data, no other transaction can acquire any kind of lock on that data until the original lock is released at the end of the data modification transaction.

Shared locks are applied during non-update or read operations, usually SELECT. A shared lock on a set of data prevents a write operation from acquiring an exclusive lock on that data, but allows other read operations to acquire their own shared locks even though the first transaction hasn't completed.

For the most part, the database system handles the application and release of locks automatically—the whole mechanism is invisible to users. Some systems, however, let users control certain aspects of locking. They may provide SQL commands for choosing the level at which locking is automatically applied (for example, the table level or the row level), or the length of time that certain kinds of locks are held.

Transactions and Recovery

A transaction is not only a unit of work, but also a unit of recovery. Recovery refers to the database system's ability to get the database back on its feet after a system failure—that is, into the most current state of affairs that can be guaranteed to be consistent.

System failures are those that affect all transactions in progress but that don't damage the database physically. Physical damage to a database is caused by media failure; protection against this kind of failure is provided by regularly backing up your database and its **transaction log**. The SQL commands used for these purposes are discussed later in this chapter.

In the case of system failure, the problem facing the database system's recovery mechanism is to figure out:

* Which transactions were incomplete at the time of the failure, and should therefore be undone; and
* Which transactions were complete at the time of the failure, but had not yet been written from the system's internal buffers to the physical database itself, and should therefore be redone.

The recovery mechanism is largely invisible to users, though some systems give users a command such as CHECKPOINT, which forces the system to write to disk all the completed transactions in its buffers.

User-Defined Transactions

User-defined transactions allow users to instruct the database management system to process any number of SQL statements as a single unit. SQL commands that control user-defined transactions include BEGIN TRANsaction, COMMIT TRANsaction (or, in some systems, END TRANSACTION) ROLLBACK TRANsaction (sometimes ABORT TRANSACTION), and SAVE TRANsaction (sometimes SAVEPOINT). The keyword WORK is sometimes used in place of TRANsaction.

A classic illustration of the need for user-defined transactions is the situation faced by a bank when a customer transfers money from a savings account to a checking account. In database terms, this banking transaction consists of two operations: first updating the savings balance to reflect a debit, then updating the checking balance with the credit. Unless these two updates are treated as a single transaction to the database, the danger exists that some other user might submit a query during the interval between them. If a bank officer happened to submit a query requesting the customer's balance after the money was deducted from the savings account but before it was added to the checking account, the results would be incorrect. Putting the two operations into a user-defined transaction ensures that the transfer of money is either accomplished completely or not at all.

In addition to giving the user control over transaction management, user-defined transactions also improve performance, since system overhead is incurred only once for a set of transactions, rather than once for each individual command.

Certain SQL commands cannot be included inside user-defined transactions. Check your system's reference manuals for details.

BEGIN TRANsaction and COMMIT TRANsaction. The BEGIN TRANsaction and COMMIT TRANsaction commands can enclose any number of SQL statements. The syntax is simply:

```
BEGIN TRANsaction [transaction_name]

COMMIT TRANsaction
```

Here's a skeletal example:

```
begin tran
   statement
   statement
   statement
commit tran
```

Your system may require the transaction name to conform to its rules for identifiers.

ROLLBACK TRANsaction and SAVE TRANsaction. If a transaction must be canceled before it is committed—either because of some failure or because of a change of heart by the user—all of its statements that have been completed must be undone. A transaction can be canceled or rolled back with the ROLLBACK TRANsaction command at any time before the COMMIT TRANsaction command has been given. You can cancel either an entire transaction or part of it (if you have a savepoint mechanism). However, you can't cancel a transaction after it has been committed.

In most systems, the syntax of the ROLLBACK TRANsaction command looks something like this:

```
ROLLBACK TRANsaction [transaction_name | savepoint_name]
```

A savepoint is a marker that the user puts inside a transaction to indicate a point to which it can be rolled back (in addition to the beginning of the transaction). In Transact-SQL, savepoints are inserted by putting a SAVE TRANsaction command within the transaction. The syntax is:

```
SAVE TRANsaction savepoint_name
```

If no savepoint name or transaction name is given with the ROLLBACK TRANsaction command, the transaction is rolled back to the previous BEGIN TRANsaction point.

Here's how the SAVE TRANsaction and ROLLBACK TRANsaction commands might be used:

```
begin tran transaction_name
   statement
   statement
   save tran savepoint_name
   statement
rollback tran savepoint_name
   statement
   statement
rollback tran
```

The first ROLLBACK TRANsaction command rolls the transaction back to the savepoint inside the transaction. The second ROLLBACK TRANsaction rolls the transaction back to its beginning. If a transaction is rolled back to a savepoint, it must still proceed to completion or else be canceled altogether.

SQL considers all statements subsequent to BEGIN TRANSACTION to be part of the transaction, until it encounters a COMMIT TRANsaction. Check your reference manuals for information on your system's implementation of user transaction commands: it may vary from the examples given here.

Backup and Recovery

Backup and recovery are very system dependent. Here's a quick summary of how one system (SYBASE) handles them. Your system may approach these problems differently.

Every change to the database, whether it is the result of a single SQL update statement (a system-defined transaction) or a grouped set of SQL statements (a user-defined transaction), is automatically recorded in the transaction log, which is, in the SYBASE system, a table in the data dictionary.

The transaction log records data modification requests (UPDATE, INSERT, or DELETE statements) on a moment-to-moment basis. When a transaction begins, a BEGIN TRANsaction event is recorded in the log. As each data modification statement is received, it is recorded in the log.

In the SYBASE system, the change is recorded in the log before any change is made in the database itself. This type of log, called a write-ahead log, ensures that the database can be recovered completely in case of a failure.

When a failure occurs, the log can be played back against a copy of the database restored from a backup. Starting from the backup, all the transactions in the log can be redone. The SQL commands for backing up and restoring databases and their transaction logs are usually called something like DUMP DATABASE, DUMP TRANsaction, LOAD DATABASE, and LOAD TRANsaction. Once the appropriate LOAD commands are issued, the database system handles all aspects of the recovery process.

PERFORMANCE

Performance is a critical issue in relational database management systems. Multi-user, production-oriented applications are especially sensitive to performance problems: databases running on these systems tend to be larger, their operations tend to be more complex, the number of users and transactions puts heavy demands on the system, and the tasks for which the applications are responsible are often time-critical. However, performance sometimes becomes a matter of concern even for single-user database systems. No one wants to wait an unreasonable length of time for the results of a query or the execution of a data modification statement.

Unfortunately, many aspects of performance are outside the control of users. Instead, they depend on the features and capabilities built into the system by the vendor. If you're currently shopping for a relational database management system, you'll be particularly interested in the next section, which briefly discusses the use of **benchmarking** to compare the performance of different database systems. Benchmarking can also be used as a tool for evaluating the effect of different database designs and indexes on performance.

Following the discussion of benchmarking, the rest of this section mentions some of the ways that users can influence performance:

- A good logical database design can make a big difference in how well your system performs.
- In some implementations the way you structure your queries can affect performance.
- Some database systems provide tools for monitoring and fine-tuning performance, including some ways to tune physical design (where and how data is physically stored).

Performance is a huge subject. This book can only touch on it lightly, mainly in order to alert you to topics that you may need to research if performance becomes an issue for you.

Benchmarking

If you're in the market for a high-volume, production-oriented relational database management system, you've probably heard vendors making claims about the number of transactions per second their systems deliver. The numbers they bandy about are based on the results of benchmarks, or tests that measure the performance of a system in a controlled environment using a standard methodology.

Interpreting and analyzing claims about performance benchmarks is a notoriously difficult matter. Benchmarking is technically complex, and the results announced by vendors inevitably reflect the tendency of any interested party to show his or her product at its best. The technical details of benchmark evaluation are beyond the scope of this book, but you'll find some suggested readings in the bibliography.

Here are a few non-technical questions you can ask about performance claims based on benchmarking:

- Is one of the accepted standard tests (such as the DeWitt or TP1 benchmarks) used? Or has the vendor selected the test on the basis of how well its product does on it?
- Are the benchmark process and results validated by an independent and reputable organization?
- Is the hardware configuration that was used for the benchmark similar to what you'll be running on? Consider not only the type of computer, but how its memory is configured, whether it was in a network, and so on.

- Is the software that was used for the benchmark the commercially available version of the product, or was the benchmark test run on a pre-production or special release?
- Are the results of the benchmark consistent and repeatable?

Benchmarks are typically associated with database systems that will be used for mission-critical applications involving dozens to hundreds of users and very large databases—hundreds of megabytes. They are used not only for making performance comparisons among products, but also for planning the kind of hardware you'll need for a given level of performance, and for making decisions about database design and indexing. Two versions of a database design, for example, can be created and tested against a benchmark to determine which is best for your purposes.

Design and Indexing

You can greatly enhance performance by paying close attention to logical database design. The importance of design for performance (as well as in other areas) belies the often-repeated notion that with a relational database system, you need only specify what you want, not how to get it. Relational expert Robert Epstein goes so far as to call this a "myth" and to state that "the relational database is no smarter than the design you came up with."

Chapters 2 and 3 explain how to analyze your data and make use of the normalization guidelines in order to wind up with a good clean database design. You may remember from the discussion in these chapters that indexes speed retrieval considerably while slowing down data modification to some extent, and that splitting tables for the purposes of normalization can slow the retrieval of data when a query that could have been answered by looking at one table now requires the system to look at more than one. Multi-table queries can adversely affect performance for several reasons. Since the data is dispersed among several tables, additional disk reads may be required to find it. Then, once the data is located, the system must join it. Finally, accessing more tables incurs the overhead of setting more locks.

Thus, with respect to performance, the basic principle is to consider how the database will primarily be used. If the number of queries to be run far surpasses the number of data modification statements, build a lot of indexes and minimize the number of joins that are required by designing fewer and larger tables. More specifically, find out which queries will be run often and put all the columns used by a given query in the same table. For the fastest response to data modification statements, use as few indexes as possible and feel free to normalize.

Queries

When you submit a SQL statement to the database management system, a lot of work gets done that you don't see. In fact, SQL is considered a **non-procedural language** precisely because it does not require the user to specify the steps the system must take to execute the command. Instead, the user simply states what is being sought.

The strength of the non-procedural approach is the same as its drawback. Stating it in the positive light, the system does the work for you. The bad news is that, once you're committed to a particular database design, you usually have no choice but to trust the system's intelligence rather than your own.

The part of the database management system responsible for analyzing a SQL statement is called the **query optimizer**. The query optimizer decomposes each query into its constituent parts and rearranges it to run as efficiently as possible. It evaluates several search strategies or access paths, deciding on the most useful indexes to use and on the path that requires the smallest number of logical page accesses. In other words, the query optimizer generates a plan, determining the most efficient path between the user's SQL statement and the data needed to carry out the assigned task.

The query optimizers of various relational database management systems have at their disposal a library of standard query processing strategies (for example, to use the column's clustered index) that are applied in various query situations. If none of the strategies known to the system apply to the SQL statement being examined, the system resorts to the default strategy of reading every row of the table(s) referenced by the query. Whole-table scans always produce the desired results, but on a table of any size at all, they are horribly slow.

Some implementations provide SQL with no built-in protection against inefficient structuring of queries by users. In a few systems, the placement of parentheses or the order in which tables are referenced in the table list can make a crucial difference in the amount of time the system takes to perform the requested operations. Ideally, the query optimizer is smart enough to "rephrase" SQL statements into the form that runs most efficiently.

Some commercial systems, including Transact-SQL, support **precompiled queries** (Transact-SQL calls them **stored procedures**). These are named collections of SQL statements for which access plans have already been figured out. Stored procedures are invoked with or without parameters given by the user at execution time. Since much of the query processing work has been carried out in advance, the performance of stored procedures is considerably faster than if the SQL statements were submitted ad hoc.

Other Tools for Monitoring and Boosting Performance

Relational database management systems that have been developed for production-oriented, multi-user, on-line applications often provide a variety of tools for monitoring and fine-tuning performance. Many of these features are outside the province of SQL *per se*; some systems expect you to accomplish these tasks using operating system facilities rather than facilities provided by the database system. A sampling of performance tools is mentioned briefly here in order to give you a flavor of the facilities that may be available.

Caches. The configuration of your computer's internal memory, especially the amount of memory allocated to the **data cache** or **buffer cache**, can markedly affect performance. The cache is the area of memory where the most recently used data pages and index pages are stored. The database system always looks in the cache first for a page that it needs; if it finds what it's looking for there it saves itself a disk access. In other words, holding commonly used pages in a cache boosts performance by minimizing disk accesses.

Data caches are usually managed in what is called a **LRU-MRU** (least recently used, most recently used) fashion: the most recently used pages are put into the cache, displacing the least recently used ones. It makes sense to experiment with the data cache—increasing its size may speed up your application. Some systems also allow you to adjust the size of a page to your application. The smaller the page, the more of them the cache can hold.

Logging. Most relational database management systems allow you to turn off the logging of database transactions, which speeds updates by saving the time it takes to enter the changes in the log. Of course, without logging you can't rely on the database system to recover any of the changes that have been made in case of a media failure.

It makes sense to suspend logging temporarily before you load a large amount of data into the database—if the operation can be easily repeated if a media failure occurs. But remember to make a backup copy before you begin, so that you can easily start over.

Monitoring Execution Plans.   Transact-SQL provides SQL keywords for setting options that allow you to display a query's execution plan without actually executing it. You can use this tool to check on SQL's work, and to see how its plan varies depending on where you put indexes and how you have written the statement.

Other monitoring tools could display information about how a given SQL statement was processed: how many table scans, logical accesses (cache reads) and physical accesses (disk reads) the system did for each table or view that is referenced in a query; how many pages it wrote for each data modification command; how much CPU time it took to parse and compile each command or to execute each step of the command.

Index Statistics.   Many systems provide a SQL command called UPDATE STATISTICS that you can issue in order to help the database system make the best decisions about which indexes to use when it processes a query.

Some versions of the UPDATE STATISTICS command examine an index to determine its minimum value, maximum value, and the number of distinct values. In Transact-SQL and some other SQL dialects, UPDATE STATISTICS calculates the distribution of index key values in the specified index.

Whether SQL calculates simple statistics or distribution statistics for an index, it stores this information in order to estimate how long a search using that index will take. By ranking the indexes for which it compiles statistics, the system can intelligently select the best one to use.

Statistics based on the distribution of key values give a much better estimate of retrieval time than simple statistics, which assume that the index's key values are uniformly distributed. If you're using a version of SQL that uses distribution statistics, it's important to remember to re-issue the UPDATE STATISTICS command whenever you've added, deleted, or modified a bunch of new data, since those actions are likely to change the distribution of the index keys. If the system's information about key distribution is not kept up to date, it uses the old information and may make a bad choice about how to process a query.

Index Fillfactor.   An indexing option provided by Transact-SQL allows you to control how full to make each page of a new index. This number (called the **fillfactor** in Transact-SQL) affects performance because of the time it takes for the system to split index pages when they become one hundred percent full. Setting the fillfactor for a new index does not mean that the index will be maintained at that level of fullness, but only that it is created at that level. Smaller fillfactor values make sense when you are creating an index on a table that you know contains a small portion of the data it will eventually hold.

Another reason to use a feature like fillfactor is to physically spread the data in small but frequently accessed tables and thus cut down on lock contention. Let's say an important table takes up only a couple of data pages, and locking is on the page level. Specifying a clustered index with a small fillfactor distributes the data over many more pages and decreases competition for locks.

The disadvantage of small fillfactor values is that each index takes more storage space.

DATA INTEGRITY

Broadly speaking, data integrity refers to the accuracy and consistency of the data in the database. Ideally, database software would provide a variety of mechanisms for checking on data integrity; unfortunately, several important kinds of integrity are unsupported by most relational systems.

In practice, requirements for integrity are often met through special-purpose application code. The disadvantages of assigning the task of integrity control to application programs include the amount of extra work involved in writing and maintaining integrity-checking code, the potential for both replicating work and introducing inconsistencies when more than one application uses the same database, and the ease with which constraints coded into applications can be bypassed by users with access to the underlying database.

There are several kinds of data integrity. At the most basic level, all database systems (not just relational ones) should be able to guarantee that a value being entered is the correct datatype and that it's within the range of values supported by the system. Different relational systems provide different assortments of datatypes, but all of them check values being entered and reject the data modification statement if the values are wrong for the specified datatype. The null status of the column is also checked on data entry. Finally, certain datatypes—usually character types—can (or must) be associated with user-specified lengths. Some systems reject data entries that exceed the maximum length for the datatype; others truncate the entered value to fit.

Three other kinds of integrity are discussed in this section:

- Domain constraints
- Entity integrity
- Referential integrity

Domain Constraints

A **domain** is the set of logically related values from which the value in a particular column can be drawn. Here are some examples of domains in the *bookbiz* database:

- The domain of the *authors.au_id* column is all the social security numbers issued by the U.S. government.
- The domain of the *authors.city* and *publishers.city* columns is all the cities in the U.S.; for *authors.state* and *publishers.state* it's all the states in the U.S. (Note the assumption that all authors live in the U.S.)
- The domain of *titles.type* is the following set of values: *business, popular_comp, psychology, mod_cook, trad_cook.*
- The domain of *titles.title_id* is the set of values with the following format: the first two characters are capitalized letters of the alphabet from the set *BU, PC, PS, MC, TC*; the next four characters are integers between 0 and 9, inclusive.
- The domain of *titleauthors.royaltyshare* is all numbers between 0 and 1, inclusive.

Notice the different kinds of logical relationships among the values in these domains. Some of the domains represent application-determined constraints—that is, business rules and regulations. For example, the constraints on the format of the title ID numbers were determined by someone in the publishing company. The publisher might also decide that the prices of books must be no less than $1.99 and no greater than $99.99; dollar-and-cents amounts between those two values would then be the domain for *titles.price.*

Other domains are based not on business rules but on physical or mathematical constraints. The values in *titleauthors.royaltyshare*, for example, represent percentages, so they must be numbers between 0 and 1. As another example, suppose the publisher wanted to record the sex of each author in the database. The domain for that column would be limited by (widely accepted interpretations of) human biology to the values *female, male, unknown*.

The descriptions of the domains in the list above were deduced from an examination of the values in the *bookbiz* database. Unfortunately, deduction is too often the process by which domains are determined, since many implementations of SQL still offer no way to specify them. Without language to describe domains and the capacity to store their specifications in the data dictionary, the database system has no way to make sure that values being entered meet the desired domain constraints for that column.

Transact-SQL is one implementation of SQL that does support a generalized mechanism for specifying domains, the CREATE RULE command. A **rule** is a named database object that can be associated with any number of columns or with all columns of a specified datatype. The rule definition can include any expression that is valid in a WHERE clause— arithmetic operators, comparison operators, LIKE, IN, BETWEEN, and so on. This flexibility in defining rules allows you to base domains on lists of values (like the domain for *titles.type*), ranges (like the domain for *titleauthors.royaltyshare*), or format (like the domain for *titles.title_id*).

The Transact-SQL rule mechanism is limited, however, in that the rule definition cannot reference another column in the database. A couple of examples (unrealistic though they be): you can't define a rule that requires the price of a book must be less than the advance paid to an author, or one that limits the royalty share for authors living in Cleveland to less than 50%.

Other database systems provide mechanisms for specifying range constraints (every value in a column must fall within a specified range) and format constraints (every value in a column must adhere to a specified pattern). These are more commonly supported than are general domain constraints.

One last note: recall from Chapter 7 that if the values in two columns have the same domains, joins between these columns are usually logical. For example, *publishers.city* and *authors.city* have the same domain (all cities in the United States); therefore it would be meaningful to join on them.

Entity Integrity

Entity integrity requires that no component of a primary key be allowed to have a null value. That is, a single-column primary key can't accept nulls, nor can any of the columns in a composite primary key.

The entity integrity constraint derives from the relational model, not from the requirements of any particular application. Nor is entity integrity a concern in other models of database management, the way domain constraints are. The requirement that no primary key contain a null value is based on the fact that real-world entities are distinguished from each other by primary keys that serve as unique identifiers. In fact, entity integrity is as much a design issue as it is an integrity issue.

You may recall from Chapter 2 that most SQL implementations provide no language for specifying primary keys. However, you can (and by all means should) guarantee entity integrity by designating a primary key that will not accept null values when you design your database. In your SQL data definition statements, you can't represent your decision about which column or combination of columns serves as the primary key. But nearly all dialects of SQL enable you to guarantee the uniqueness of a primary key by building a unique index on it, and by assigning it "not null" status.

Referential Integrity

Informally speaking, referential integrity concerns the relationship between the values in logically related tables. In the relational model, it means guaranteeing the logical consistency of the database by making sure that the values of a primary key and the foreign keys that point to it always match.

Here's E.F. Codd's definition: "For each distinct non-null foreign key value in a relational database, there must exist a matching primary key value from the same domain."

Chapter 2 explains that foreign key-primary key relationships are planned during the design of a database; that they represent the logical relationships among data (although their presence in no way limits the possible access paths among the data). In considering referential integrity, the question is what the database system can do to guarantee the maintenance of matching values between foreign keys and the primary key to which they point (that is, that referential constraints are not violated).

One possibility is to treat all violations of referential integrity just the way violations of domain constraints and entity integrity are treated: the system simply rejects the offending data modification operation and (in many systems) displays an error message advising the user of the rejection and the reason for it. For example, changing an author ID would not be allowed, since the alteration would destroy the connection between the *authors*, *titles*, and *titleauthors* tables. Nor would deleting or updating a publisher ID be permitted if there were books in the *titles* table that reference the old ID.

In addition to rejecting (or restricting) operations that would violate a referential constraint, there are a couple other possibilities. One applies to attempts to delete or update a primary key value pointed to by one or more foreign key values. In this situation, the system could (if it had such powers) automatically "cascade" the update or delete operation to the matching foreign keys. For example, if a publisher's ID number changes, the system would change the matching ID's in *titles.pub_id* in exactly the same way, without intervention by the user.

Another possibility is to accept data modification operations to primary key values even if they upset referential integrity, but first to change the matching foreign key values to NULL. (Of course, if the foreign key has been defined so as not to accept null values, this course of action is out.) Using a variation on the previous example: in response to a DELETE command that removes the row for Algodata Infosystems from the *publishers* table, the *titles.pub_id* values for all books published by Algodata would be set to NULL.

To summarize briefly, there are in general three possible responses to an attempt to delete or update a primary key to which a foreign key points:

- **Cascade**—the DELETE or UPDATE operation is automatically applied to the foreign keys whose values matched the "old" value of the deleted or updated primary key.
- **Restrict**—the DELETE or UPDATE operation on the primary key is rejected unless there are no matching foreign key values.
- **Nullify**—before the DELETE or UPDATE operation on the primary key is committed, the value(s) of matching foreign key(s) are set to NULL.

Unfortunately, many SQL dialects do not provide mechanisms for controlling referential integrity. In these cases, the closest you can come to guaranteeing referential integrity is to REVOKE all permissions for deleting and updating to a primary key column.

However, as the importance of referential integrity becomes more and more widely recognized, vendors are beginning to address it. The proposed 1988 ISO-ANSI SQL standard includes language for a referential integrity mechanism called a **trigger**, and Transact-SQL has already implemented such a mechanism. While the details of the Transact-SQL trigger mechanism are not important for our purposes, the description in the next section gives an idea of how triggers can be used to enforce referential integrity.

Triggers.   A Transact-SQL trigger is a named collection of SQL statements that describes an action to be carried out when a specified data modification operation is attempted on a given column or table.

Triggers are automatic. They work no matter what causes the data modification—a clerk's entry, an application action, a report calculation. Each trigger is specific to one or more of the data modification operations—UPDATE, INSERT, or DELETE.

Creating a trigger involves specifying the data modification command that "fires" the trigger, the table that is its "target," and the action or actions the trigger is to take. Here's the CREATE TRIGGER syntax:

```
CREATE TRIGGER trigger_name
  ON table_name
  FOR {INSERT | UPDATE | DELETE}
    [, {INSERT | UPDATE | DELETE}]...
  AS SQL_statements
    [IF UPDATE (column_name)
    [{AND | OR} UPDATE (column_name)]...]
```

The ON clause gives the name of the table that activates the trigger—the trigger table. The FOR clause specifies which data modification command(s) on the trigger table activate the trigger.

The SQL statements in the AS clause specify **trigger actions** and **trigger conditions**. The trigger actions can consist of any number and any kind of SELECT statements, including the control-of-flow language that is part of Transact-SQL.

Trigger conditions can specify additional criteria that determine whether the attempted INSERT, DELETE, or UPDATE will cause the trigger action(s) to be carried out. Trigger conditions often include a subquery preceded by the keyword IF. The IF UPDATE(column_name) clause tests whether the specified column has been modified, allowing trigger actions to be associated with changes to particular columns.

The names of two logical (or conceptual) tables—*deleted* and *inserted*—are used in CREATE TRIGGER statements. When a DELETE command is issued on a trigger table (for example, an attempt is made to remove primary key values), the deleted rows are removed from the trigger table and transferred to the *deleted* table. Then the trigger can examine the rows in *deleted* to determine whether or how the trigger action(s) should be carried out.

When an INSERT or UPDATE command is attempted, rows representing the new values are added to the trigger table and to *inserted* at the same time. The rows in *inserted* can then be examined by trigger mechanism.

Here's an example of a trigger that performs a cascading delete when a primary key value in *titles* is deleted. When a DELETE statement on *titles* is executed, the trigger removes the row from *titles* and adds it to *deleted*. Then it checks the tables—*titleauthors*, *salesdetails*, and *roysched* to see if they have any rows with a foreign key *title_id* that matches the *title_id* removed from *titles* (now stored in the *deleted* table). If the trigger finds any such rows, it removes them.

```
create trigger delcascadetrig
on titles
for delete
as

delete titleauthors
from titleauthors, deleted
where titleauthors.title_id = deleted.title_id
        /* Remove titleauthors rows
        ** that match deleted (titles) rows.*/

delete salesdetails
from salesdetails, deleted
where salesdetails.title_id = deleted.title_id
        /* Remove sales order rows
        ** that match deleted (titles) rows.*/

delete roysched
from roysched, deleted
where roysched.title_id = deleted.title_id
        /* Remove roysched rows
        ** that match deleted (titles) rows.*/
```

Here's another example of a referential control trigger. This one is not absolute, however: it prevents updates to the primary key column of the *titles* table on certain days of the week. (Such a trigger might be desirable for any type of column, not just for a primary key.)

The IF UPDATE clause focuses this trigger on a particular column, *titles.title_id*. Modifications to that column cause the trigger to go into action, canceling the update and printing a message.

```
create trigger stopupdatetrig
on titles
for update
as
if update (title_id)
    and datename(dw, getdate())
    in ("Saturday", "Sunday")
begin
    rollback transaction
    print "We don't allow monkeying with primary keys on the weekend!"
end
        /* If titles.title_id changes on
        ** Saturday or Sunday, cancel the update. */
```

As illustrated, above, Transact-SQL triggers are often used to control referential integrity threatened by updates or deletions to a primary key. However, triggers actually represent a more generalized method for dealing with integrity issues:

- Triggers are often used with updates or insertions of a foreign key value to make sure that there is a matching primary key value. For example, inserting a row into *salesdetails* with a title ID that is not listed in *titles* doesn't make any sense—you can't sell a book you don't have. A trigger could reject all such insertions. Similarly, updating *titles.pub_id* with a publisher ID not known to the system (that is, one that doesn't exist in the *publishers* table) could be prohibited.
- Triggers can enforce restrictions much more complex than those defined with rules. Unlike rules, triggers can reference columns or database objects. For example, a trigger can reject updates that attempt to increase a book's price by more than 1% of its advance, or prevent all price increases greater than 100%.
- Triggers can be used to recalculate ongoing tallies. For example, you might write a trigger that updates the *ytd_sales* column in the *titles* table whenever a row is added to the *salesdetails* table.

FROM GENERIC SQL TO THE REAL WORLD

The concluding chapter has brought the discussion of generic SQL closer to the real world by touching on topics such as performance, transaction control, and tools for maintaining referential integrity. We will not explore these issues further, since relational database management systems differ widely from each other in their implementations of backup and recovery tools, transaction control, and access strategies.

Appendix A

Syntax Summary for the SQL Used in this Book

SYNTAX CONVENTIONS

Key

BIG	Caps means it's a keyword (command).
MIXed	Caps mixed with lowercase letters means it's a keyword and you can type either the full word or just the part in caps.
little	Lowercase words are variables; supply your own.
{ }	Curly braces mean you must choose at least one of the enclosed options.
[ ]	Brackets mean choosing one or more of the enclosed options is optional.
( )	Parentheses are actually typed as part of the command (unlike curly braces and brackets, which are syntax symbols).
|	The vertical bar means you choose a maximum of one option.
,	The comma means you choose as many options as you like, and separate your choices with commas that you type as part of the command.
. . .	The ellipses mean you can do it again, whatever it was.

FORMATTING

SQL is a free-form language, meaning there are no rules about how many words you can put on a line or where you need to break a line. However,

for readability, all examples and syntax statements in this manual are formatted so that each clause of a statement begins on a new line. Clauses
that have more than one part extend to additional lines, which are
indented.

Case

```
SELECT column_name
FROM table_name
WHERE search_conditions
```

In syntax statements, keywords (commands) are in uppercase letters
and identifiers and user-supplied words are in lowercase letters. Type the
keywords just as you see them, disregarding case. (Keywords with some
uppercase and some lowercase letters mean you can use either the full
word or abbreviate by using only the uppercase part of it.)

```
SELECT is the same as Select is the same as select
```

Case is significant for identifiers and user-supplied words.

```
Column_name is not the same as column_name or COLUMN-NAME
```

Obligatory Options {You Must Choose At Least One}

Curly Braces and Vertical Bars.   Choose *one and only one* option.

```
{die_on_your_feet | live_on_your_knees | live_on_your_feet}
```

Curly Braces and Commas.   Choose *one or more* options. If you choose
more than one, separate your choices with *commas*.

```
{cash , check , credit}
```

Optional Options [You Don't Have to Choose Any]

One Item in Square Brackets.   You don't have to choose it.

```
[severe_depression]
```

Square Brackets and Vertical Bars.   Choose *none or one* (only).

```
[beans | rice | sweet_potatoes]
```

Square Brackets and Commas.   Choose *none, one, or more* options. If you choose more than one, separate your choisces with *commas.*

```
[extra_cheese , avocados , sour_cream]
```

Ellipses: Do it Again (and Again)...

The ellipses (three dots) mean that you can *repeat* the last unit as many times as you like. In this syntax statement, BUY is a required keyword:

```
BUY thing = price [cash | check | credit]
    [, thing = price [cash | check | credit]]...
```

You must buy at least one thing and give its price. You may choose a method of payment—one of the items enclosed in square brackets. You may also choose to buy additional things—as many of them as you like. For each thing you buy, give its name, its price, and (optionally) a method of payment.

STATEMENTS

ALTER DATABASE database_name

ALTER TABLE table_name
  (various options)

BEGIN TRANsaction [transaction_name]

COMMIT TRANsaction

CREATE DATABASE database_name

CREATE [UNIQUE] [CLUSTERED |
  NONCLUSTERED] INDEX index_name
  ON table_name
  (column_name [, column_name]...)

CREATE TABLE table_name
  (column_name datatype [NOT NULL | NULL]
  [, column_name datatype [NOT NULL | NULL]]...)

CREATE VIEW [owner.]view_name
  [(column_name [, column_name]...)]
  AS select_statement
  [WITH CHECK OPTION]

DELETE FROM
    {table_name | view_name}
  [WHERE search_conditions]

DROP DATABASE database_name

DROP INDEX
  table_name.index_name [, table_name.index_name]...

DROP TABLE table_name

DROP VIEW [owner.]view_name [, [owner.]view_name]...

DUMP DATABASE database_name
  TO device_name

DUMP TRANsaction database_name
  TO device_name

GRANT {ALL | privilege_list}
  ON {table_name [(column_list)] |
    view_name [(column_list)}
  TO {PUBLIC | name_list}

GRANT {ALL | command_list}
  TO {PUBLIC | name_list}

INSERT [INTO]
    {table_name | view_name}
      [(column_list)]
  {VALUES (constant_expression
    [, constant_expression]...) | select_statement}

LOAD DATABASE database_name

```
    FROM device_name
LOAD TRANsaction database_name
    FROM device_name
REVOKE {ALL | privilege_list}
    ON {table_name [(column_list)] |
      view_name [(column_list)]}
    FROM {PUBLIC | name_list}
REVOKE {ALL | command_list}
    FROM {PUBLIC | name_list}
ROLLBACK TRANsaction
      [transaction_name | savepoint_name]
SAVE TRANsaction [savepoint_name]
SELECT [DISTINCT] select_list
    [INTO table_name]
    [FROM
      {table_name | view_name},
        [{table_name | view_name}]...
    [WHERE search_conditions]
    [GROUP BY [ALL] column_name
        [, column_name]...
      [HAVING search_conditions]
    [ORDER BY
        [{table_name. | view_name.}]
          column_name |
        select_list_number | expression} [ASC | DESC]
        [,{[table_name. | view_name.}]
          column_name |
        select_list_number | expression} [ASC | DESC]]...]
UPDATE {table_name | view_name}
    SET [{table_name. | view_name.}]
      column_name1 = {expression1 | NULL | (select_statement)}
      [, column_name2 = {expression2 | NULL | (select_statement)}]...
    [FROM {table_name | view_name}
      [, {table_name | view_name}]...
    [WHERE search_conditions]
UPDATE STATISTICS
      table_name [index_name]
```

Appendix B

Industry SQL Equivalents

SYNTAX COMPARISON

In this appendix, you'll find popular SQL commands (CREATE and DROP, GRANT, REVOKE, SELECT, INSERT, UPDATE, DELETE) for DB2, INFORMIX, INGRES, ORACLE, SQL/DS, and SYBASE. All of the versions are represented with the syntax conventions described in this manual, though in some cases the syntax has been simplified slightly to make the entries easier to read and compare. You'll notice that basic command syntax, overall, is very similar. However there are some caveats to keep in mind when reviewing this list:

- Not all vendors offer every item in even this basic set.
- There are some differences in options in those commands that are universally present.
- There may be underlying semantic content that make two apparently identical commands rather different in meaning (*i.e.*, the definitions of terms like *subselect* or *expression* for particular vendors)
- Vendors do modify existing SQL commands and add new ones as they refine their products—items on this list may not represent the latest version.

DB2 syntax is based on release 3, INFORMIX on version 2.10, INGRES on version 5.0, Oracle on version 5.1, SQL/DS on release 3, and SYBASE on version 3.4.

The statements are divided into three groups: data definition, data administration, and data manipulation.

DATA DEFINITION

These commands deal with creating and dropping databases, specifying the active database, and creating and dropping database objects (indexes, tables, and views).

Database Statements

Most systems have commands for creating and dropping databases, though some use operating system commands. Only Sybase and Informix have commands for choosing a database.

CREATE DATABASE

DB2
CREATE DATABASE db_name
STOGROUP storage_group_name
BUFFERPOOL buffer_pool_name

INFORMIX
CREATEDB db_name
  (WITH LOG IN "pathname")

INGRES
operating system level command

ORACLE
operating system level command

SQL/DS
n/a

SYBASE
CREATE DATABASE db_name
  (ON {DEFAULT l disk_name} (=size)
  (,disk_name(=size))...)

DROP DATABASE

DB2
DROP DATABASE db_name

INFORMIX
DROP DATABASE db_name

INGRES
operating system command

ORACLE
operating system command

SQL/DS
DROP DBSPACE dbspace_name

SYBASE
DROP DATABASE db_name

Choose Database
DB2
n/a

INFORMIX
DATABASE db_name (EXCLUSIVE)

INGRES
operating system command

ORACLE
operating system command

SYBASE
USE db_name

SQL/DS
n/a

Creating and Dropping Database Objects

Database objects include indexes, tables, and views. Each CREATE statement is followed by its DROP.

CREATE INDEX
DB2
CREATE (UNIQUE) INDEX index_name
  ON table_name
    (column_name(ASC I DESC)(,column_name (ASC I DESC))...)

INFORMIX
CREATE (UNIQUE I DISTINCT)(CLUSTER) INDEX index_name
  ON table_name
    (column_name(ASC I DESC)(,column_name (ASC I DESC))...)

INGRES
CREATE INDEX (locationname:)index_name
  ON table_name
    (column_name(,columnname)...)

ORACLE
CREATE (UNIQUE) INDEX index_name
  ON table_name
    (column_name(,columnname)...)
  ({COMPRESS | NOCOMPRESS})

SQL/DS
CREATE (UNIQUE) INDEX index_name
  ON (creator.)table_name
    (column_name(ASC | DESC)(,column_name (ASC | DESC))...)

SYBASE
CREATE (UNIQUE)(CLUSTERED | NONCLUSTERED) INDEX index_name
  ON ((db.)owner.)table_name
    (column_name(,column_name)...)
  (WITH {FILLFACTOR=x, IGNORE DUP_KEY,
    (IGNORE DUP_ROW | ALLOW DUP_ROW)}

DROP INDEX
DB2
DROP INDEX index_name

INFORMIX
DROP INDEX index_name

INGRES
DROP index_name
  (,index_name)...

ORACLE
DROP INDEX index_name

SQL/DS
DROP INDEX index_name

SYBASE
DROP INDEX table_name.index_name
  (,table_name.index_name)...

CREATE TABLE
DB2
CREATE TABLE table_name
  (column_name datatype (NOT NULL)
    (,column_name datatype (NOT NULL))...)

INFORMIX
CREATE (TEMP) TABLE table_name
  (column_name datatype (NOT NULL)

    (,column_name datatype (NOT NULL))...)
    (IN "directory_name")

INGRES
CREATE TABLE (locationname:)table_name
    ((column_name format
    (,column_name format)...)
    (WITH JOURNALING)
CREATE TABLE (locationname:)tabl_ename
    ((column_name
    (,column_name)...)
    AS SUBSELECT

ORACLE
CREATE TABLE table_name
    (column_name datatype (NOT NULL)
    (,column_name datatype (NOT NULL))...)
    (SPACE ALLOCATION)

SQL/DS
CREATE TABLE table_name
    (column_name datatype (NOT NULL)
    (,column_name datatype (NOT NULL))...)
    (IN dbspace_name)

SYBASE
CREATE TABLE ((db.)owner.)table_name
    (column_name datatype (NOT NULL | NULL)
    (,column_name datatype (NOT NULL | NULL))...)

DROP TABLE
DB2
DROP TABLE table_name

INFORMIX
DROP TABLE table_name

INGRES
DROP table_name (,table_name)...

ORACLE
DROP TABLE table_name

SQL/DS
DROP TABLE table_name

SYBASE
DROP TABLE ((database.)owner.)table_name
(,((database.)owner.)table_name)...

CREATE VIEW
DB2
CREATE VIEW view_name
  ((column_name(,column_name)...))
 AS subselect
 (WITH CHECK OPTION)

INFORMIX
CREATE VIEW view_name
  ((column_name(,column_name)...))
 AS select_statement
 (WITH CHECK OPTION)

INGRES
CREATE VIEW view_name
  ((column_name(,column_name)...))
 AS subselect

ORACLE
CREATE VIEW view_name
  ((column_name(,column_name)...))
 AS subselect

SQL/DS
CREATE VIEW view_name
  ((column_name(,column_name)...))
 AS subselect

SYBASE
CREATE VIEW (owner.)view_name
  ((column_name(,column_name)...))
 AS select_statement

DROP VIEW
DB2
DROP VIEW view_name

INFORMIX
DROP VIEW view_name

INGRES
DROP view_name
 (,view_name)...

ORACLE
DROP VIEW view_name

SQL/DS
DROP VIEW view_name

SYBASE
DROP VIEW (owner.)view_name
  (,(owner.)viewname)...

DATA ADMINISTRATION

Data administration commands include GRANT and REVOKE.

GRANT
DB2
GRANT {ALL (PRIVILEGES)
  | ALTER, DELETE,INDEX, INSERT, SELECT,UPDATE ((column_list))}
  ON (TABLE) table/view_list
  TO {user_list | PUBLIC}
  (WITH GRANT OPTION)
GRANT db_privileges
  ON DATABASE database_name (,database_name)...
  TO {user_list | PUBLIC}
  (WITH GRANT OPTION)
GRANT system_privileges
  TO {user_list | PUBLIC}
  WITH GRANT OPTION

INFORMIX
GRANT table_privileges
  ON table_name
  TO {user_list | PUBLIC}
  (WITH GRANT OPTION)
GRANT db_privileges
  TO {user_list | PUBLIC}

INGRES
n/a

ORACLE
GRANT {table_privilege_list | ALL}
  ON table_name
  TO {user_list | public}
  (WITH GRANT OPTION)
GRANT {CONNECT, RESOURCE, DBA}
  TO {user_list | PUBLIC}

SQL/DS
GRANT {ALL I privilege_list}
  ON (creator.) {table_name I view_name}
  TO {user_list I PUBLIC}
  (WITH GRANT OPTION)
GRANT {DBA, CONNECT, RESOURCE, SCHEDULE}
  TO user_list (IDENTIFIED BY pswd_list)

SYBASE
GRANT {ALL I privilege_list}
  ON {table_name ((column_list) I view_name ((column_list)) I stored_procedure}
  TO {user_list I PUBLIC}
GRANT {ALL I command_list}
  TO {user_list I PUBLIC}

REVOKE
DB2
REVOKE {ALL (PRIVILEGES)
  I ALTER, DELETE,INDEX, INSERT, SELECT, UPDATE}
  ON (TABLE) table/view_list
  FROM {user_list I PUBLIC}
  BY {user_list I ALL}
REVOKE db_privileges
  ON DATABASE database_name (,database_name)...
  FROM {user_list I PUBLIC}
  BY {user_list I ALL}
REVOKE system_privileges
  FROM {user_list I PUBLIC}
  BY {user_list I ALL}

INFORMIX
REVOKE {table_privilege_list
  ON table_name
  I db_privilege}
  FROM {user_list I PUBLIC}

INGRES
n/a

ORACLE
REVOKE {table_privilege_list I ALL}
  ON table_name
  FROM {user_list I public}
REVOKE {CONNECT, RESOURCE, DBA}
  FROM {user_list I PUBLIC}

SQL/DS
REVOKE {privilege_list | ALL}
  ON (creator.) {table_name | view_name}
  FROM {user_list | PUBLIC}
REVOKE {DBA, CONNECT, RESOURCE, SCHEDULE}
  FROM user_list

SYBASE
REVOKE {table_privilege_list | ALL}
  ON {table/view_name((column_list)) | stored_procedure}
  FROM {user_list | PUBLIC}

DATA MANIPULATION

Data manipulation commands include DELETE, INSERT, SELECT, and UPDATE.

DELETE
DB2
DELETE FROM {table_name | view_name} (correlation_name)
  (WHERE search_condition)

INFORMIX
DELETE FROM table_name
  (WHERE search_condition)

INGRES
DELETE FROM table_name (corr_name)
  (WHERE search_condition)

ORACLE
DELETE FROM (creator.)table_name
  (WHERE search_condition)

SQL/DS
DELETE FROM (creator.)table_name
  (WHERE search_condition)

SYBASE
DELETE (FROM) ((database.)owner) {table_name | view_name}
  (FROM((database.(owner.){table_name | view_name}
    (,((database.(owner.){table_name | view_name})...)
  (WHERE search_condition)

INSERT

DB2
INSERT INTO table_name
  ((column_list))
  {VALUES (constant_list)
  | subquery}

INFORMIX
INSERT INTO table_name
  ((column_list))
  {VALUES (value_list)
  | select_statement}

INGRES
INSERT INTO table_name
  ((column_list))
  {VALUES (expression_list)
  | subquery}

ORACLE
INSERT INTO (creator.)table_name
  ((column_list))
  {VALUES (value_list)
  | select_statement}

SQL/DS
INSERT INTO (creator.)table_name | view_name}
  ((column_list))
  VALUES (data_list)

SYBASE
INSERT (INTO) ((database.(owner.){table_name | view_name}
  ((column_list))
  {VALUES(constant_expr(,constant_expr)...)
  | select_statement}

SELECT

DB2
SELECT {ALL | DISTINCT} select_list
  FROM {table_name | view_name} (corr_name)
    (,{table_name | view_name} (corr_name))...
  (WHERE search_condition)
  (GROUP BY column_name (,column_name)...)
  (HAVING search_condition)
  (ORDER BY {column_name | select_list_number}(ASC | DESC)
    (,{column_name | select_list_number}(ASC | DESC))...)

INFORMIX
SELECT (ALL I DISTINCT I UNIQUE) select_list
  FROM {table_name I OUTER table_name I OUTER(table_expression}
    (,{table_name I OUTER table_name I OUTER(table_expression})...
  (WHERE search_condition)
  (GROUP BY column_name (,column_name)...)
  (HAVING search_condition)
  (ORDER BY {column_name I select_list_number}(ASC I DESC)
    (,{column_name I select_list_number}(ASC I DESC))...)
  {INTO TEMP table_name)

INGRES
SELECT {ALL I DISTINCT} select_list
  FROM table_name (corr_name)
    (, table_name {corr_name))...
  (WHERE search_condition)
  (GROUP BY column_name (,column_name)...)
  (HAVING search_condition)

ORACLE
SELECT {ALL I DISTINCT} select_list
  FROM (creator.)table_name
    (,(creator.)table_name)...
  (WHERE search_condition)
  (CONNECT BY search_condition
    START WITH condition))
  (GROUP BY expr (,expr)...)
  (HAVING search_condition)
  ({UNION I INTERSECT I MINUS} SELECT)
  (ORDER BY {expr I select_list_number}(ASC I DESC)
    (,{expr I select_list_number}(ASC I DESC))...)
  (FOR UPDATE OF column_list (NOWAIT)

SQL/DS
SELECT {ALL I DISTINCT} select_list
  FROM (creator.) table_name
  (WHERE search_condition)
  (GROUP BY column_name (,column_name)...)
  (HAVING search_condition)
  (ORDER BY {column_name I select_list_number}(ASC I DESC)
    (,{column_name I select_list_number}(ASC I DESC))...)

SYBASE
SELECT (ALL I DISTINCT) select_list
  (INTO ((database.)owner.)table_name)
  (FROM ((database.)owner.){table_name I view_name}
    (HOLDLOCK)

```
(,((database.)owner.){table_name I view_name}(HOLDLOCK))...
(WHERE search_condition)
(GROUP BY (ALL)aggregate_free_expression
  (,aggregate_free_expression)...
(HAVING search_condition)
(ORDER BY {((((database.(owner.){table_name. I view_name.})
  column_name I select_list_number I expression}(ASC I DESC)
  (,{((((database.(owner.){table_name I view_name})
    column_name I select_list_number I expression}(ASC I DESC))...)
(COMPUTE row_aggregate (column_name)
  (,row_aggregate (column_name))...
  (BY column_name (,column_name)...))
(FOR BROWSE)
```

UPDATE

DB2

```
UPDATE {table_name I view_name} (correlation_name)
  SET
  column_name = {expression I NULL}
  (,column_name = {expression I NULL})...
  (WHERE search_condition)
```

INFORMIX

```
UPDATE table_name
  SET
  {column_name =expression
    (,column_name= expression)...
      I {(column_list) I *}=(expr_list)}
  (WHERE search_condition)
```

INGRES

```
UPDATE table_name (corr_name)
  SET column_name = expression
    (,column_name = expression)...
  (WHERE search_condition)
```

ORACLE

```
UPDATE (creator.) table_name
  SET
  {column_name =expression
    (,column_name= expression)...
      I (column_list) = (subquery)}
  (WHERE search_condition)
```

SQL/DS

```
UPDATE (creator.) table_name
  SET
```

```
column_name =expression
  (,column_name= expression)...
(WHERE search_condition)
```

SYBASE
```
UPDATE {((database.(owner.) {table_name I view_name}
  SET(((database.(owner.){table_name. I view_name.})
  column_name= {expression I NULL I select_statement}
    (,column_name= {expression I NULL I select_statement})...
  (FROM ((database.(owner.){table_name I view_name}
    (,((database.(owner.){table_name I view_name})...
  (WHERE search_condition)
```

Appendix C

Glossary

access strategy
The method by which a database management system locates physical data.

aggregate functions
Often used with the GROUP BY and HAVING clauses, aggregate functions generate one summary value from a group of values in a specified column. Aggregate functions include AVG, COUNT, COUNT(*), MIN, and MAX.

alias
A temporary name given to a table (in the FROM clause). Here are two examples of how it can be used:

```
select au_id, a.city, p.city, pub_id
from authors a, publishers p
where au_lname like "P%"

select a.au_id, b.au_id
from authors a, authors b
where a.zip = b.zip
```

In the first example, the alias eliminates the need to type the whole table name as a qualifier for each column name that could belong to either table in the FROM clause. In the second example, aliases allow a self join—the *authors* table takes on two identities, *a* and *b*.

argument
A value (also called "parameter") supplied to a function.

arithmetic operators
Addition (+), subtraction (-), multiplication (*), and division (/) are arithmetic operators. They can be used with all numeric columns. Some systems also supply modulo (%), for finding the integer remainder after a division operation on two integers.

association
A many-to-many relationship between entities.

attribute
A data value that describes one characteristic of an entity. It is also called a "field" or a "column."

base table
A permanent database table on which a view is based. It is also called a virtual table.

benchmarking
The process of testing a piece of hardware or software to determine its general or specific performance characteristics.

binary datatype
A datatype provided by some systems for storing bit patterns.

bit datatype
A datatype provided by some systems for storing true/false data.

Boolean expressions
Expressions that evaluate as "true" or "false" rather than returning a specific value.

buffer cache
Memory allocated for data storage.

Cartesian product
All the possible combinations of rows from the tables. Such a result is generally caused by not including all the necessary joins.

cascade
Propagation of an update or delete through related tables in a database.

character datatype
A datatype used to store character data such as letters, numbers, and special characters.

clustered index
An index in which the bottom, or leaf level, is the data itself. A table can have only one clustered index.

column
One particular attribute or characteristic of the entity that is the subject of a table; also called a "field."

command
Any SQL statement, such as INSERT or CREATE DATABASE.

comparison operators
Operators used for comparing one expression to another in a WHERE or HAVING clause. Comparison operators include equal to (=), greater than (>), less than (<), greater than or equal to (>=), less than or equal to (<=), and not equal to (!= or <>).

composite indexes
Indexes based on more than one column in a table.

comprehensive data sublanguage
A single language that handles all communications with the database.

concurrency control
Strategies such as locking that prevent two or more users from changing the same piece of data concurrently.

connecting column
A column that participates in a join, allowing one table to link with another or with itself. Connecting columns are columns from one or more tables that contain similar values.

correlated subquery
A subquery that cannot be evaluated independently, but that depends on the outer query for its results. Also called a repeating subquery, since the subquery is executed once for each row that might be selected by the outer query.

data administration
One of the three general categories for which SQL is used. The other two are data definition and data manipulation. Data administration includes activities such as granting and revoking permissions to users.

data cache
The area of memory allocated for data storage.

data control
Another term for data administration.

data definition
The process of creating (or removing) a database and its objects.

data dictionary
The system tables that contain descriptions of the database objects and how they are structured.

data manipulation
Retrieving and modifying data, through SQL statements SELECT, INSERT, DELETE, and UPDATE.

data modification
Changing data, through SQL statements INSERT, DELETE, and UPDATE.

data retrieval
Finding and displaying data in the database via queries (SELECT statements).

data structure diagram
A diagram that shows how the objects in a database fit together.

database
A collection of related tables containing data and definitions of database objects.

database administrator
See **system administrator**.

database design
The process of setting up the objects in the database (principally, but not exclusively, tables and their columns).

database device
The physical or logical device on which a database is stored.

database owner
The creator or owner of a database, a concept most useful in systems that allow more than one database.

date datatype
A datatype used for storing date information.

decimal datatype
A datatype used for storing decimal data.

default
A value entered by the system for specified columns when the user supplies no explicit value.

derived tables
A name sometimes applied to views, which are also known as "virtual tables."

designations
One-to-many relationships among data.

difference
A set operation that displays rows that two tables do not have in common.

distinguished nulls
Unknown pieces of information whose values are not precisely known, but some things about the values are known.

domain
The set of all legal or valid values for a particular column.

entity
The object or thing that a table describes; the subject of the table.

entity integrity
An integrity rule requiring that each row have a primary key and that no primary key allow nulls.

entity-relationship modeling
Identifying the important subjects about which information will be stored; identifying their attributes; and identifying the relationships among these entities. Also known as entity modeling.

equijoin
Joining columns on the basis of equality, where values match exactly; see also **natural join**.

exclusive lock
Sometimes called a "write" lock, it gives one user exclusive use of a row, page, or table during data modification activities.

expression
A constant, column name, function, or any combination thereof connected by arithmetic (and sometimes bitwise) operators.

field
An attribute of an entity, a column of a table.

file
Often used as equivalent to "table."

fillfactor
An indexing option provided by Transact-SQL that allows you to control how full to make each page of a new index. This number (called the fillfactor in Transact-SQL) affects performance because of the time it takes for the system to split index pages when they become one hundred percent full.

first normal form
First of the five normal forms. It requires that each row have a fixed number of columns and that there be no repeating groups.

fixed length
Some datatypes can have either fixed or variable length. Choosing the correct one may have storage and performance implications.

foreign key
A column in a table that matches a primary key column in another table.

grouped view
A view with a GROUP BY clause in its definition.

identifier
The name of a database or database object.

inclusive range
A range, specified with the keyword BETWEEN, in which you search for the lower value and upper value of the range as well as the values included in the range.

index
A mechanism for locating data.

instance
Each row in a table represents an occurrence or instance of the entity.

intersection
A set operation that displays rows that two or more tables have in common.

join
Selecting from more than one table by comparing values in specified columns.

join column
A column used to set conditions for a join.

join-compatable columns
columns holding similar kinds of data values.

key values
Primary keys uniquely identify a row, while foreign keys provide a way to refer to those unique values from another table.

keyword
Word used as part of SQL syntax, also called "reserved word."

locking
A concurrency-control mechanism to protect data from being modified by more than one user at a time and from being read while a transaction is in progress.

logical independence
The concept that relationships among tables, columns, and rows can change without impairing the function of application programs and *ad hoc* queries.

logical operators
AND (joins two or more conditions and returns results when all the conditions are true) OR (connects two or more conditions and returns results when any of the conditions is true), and NOT (negates a condition).

lost update problem
Multi-user updates can overwrite each other is a database has no concurrency control.

LRU-MRU
Least-recently-used most-recently-used: an algorithm often used in data caching. Most recently used items are put in the cache, displacing least recently used ones.

many-to-many
Relationships such as those between *authors* and *titles* in which an author can have several books and a book can have several authors.

MIS specialist
See **system administrator**.

modulo
An arithmetic operator which gives the integer remainder after a division operation on two integers. For example, 21 modulo 9 is 3, because 21 divided by 9 equals 2 with a remainder of 3.

money datatype
A datatype used for representing decimal currency values.

natural join
A display of only one from each pair of columns whose matching values created the join on the basis of equality. See also **equijoin**.

nested query
See **subquery**.

nested sort
A sort within another sort.

non-loss decomposition
The process of splitting a table into smaller tables without losing any information.

non-procedural language
A language that allows you to specify the results you want without describing the method for getting them.

normal forms
See **normalization**.

normalization
Normalization guidelines are a set of data design standards called the normal forms. Five normal forms are widely accepted, although more have been proposed.

null
A NULL represents a missing or inapplicable value in a column of a database table.

occurrence
Each row in a table is an occurrence or instance of the entity.

one-to-many
A master-detail relationship in which one row in the first table may relate to many in the second, but a row in the second table can only relate to one row in the first.

outer join
A join that displays non-joining rows from either one or the other of a pair of joined tables.

owner
The creator of a database object is the owner of that object, and usually has full privileges on that object.

permissions
Authority to run certain actions on certain database objects or to run certain commands.

physical data independence
The independence of the physical storage of data from a database's logical design.

precompiled queries
In Transact-SQL, named collections of SQL statements for which execution plans have already been figured out.

primary key
The column or columns whose values uniquely identify a row in a table.

privileges
See **permissions**.

projection
Listing the columns that will be included in the results of a selection from the database.

qualifications
Conditions on the rows to be retrieved, described in the WHERE or HAVING clause.

queries
Requests for retrieval of data from the database; sometimes also used to refer to SQL statements in general.

query optimizer
The part of the DBMS that calculates the most efficient way to perform a given query.

record
A set of related fields that describes a specific entity. Also called "tuple" or "row."

recovery
Restoring the database to a consistent state after a software or hardware failure.

referential integrity
The rules governing data consistency, specifically the requirement that a foreign key must either match its primary key exactly, or else be completely null.

relation
Synonym for table.

repeating subquery
See **correlated subquery**.

restrict
See **restriction**.

restriction
One of the basic query operations in a relational system, also called selection. A restriction determines which rows will be selected from a table.

rows
The set of data values associated with one instance of the entity that the table describes: one set of columns.

rule
A specification that controls what data may be entered in a particular column.

scalar aggregate
An aggregate function that produces a single value from a SELECT statement. See also vector aggregate.

second normal form
Requires that all the non-primary key columns relate to the entire primary key and not just to one of its components.

selection
Specifying conditions for retrieving rows from a table. See also restriction.

self-join
Selecting from a table by comparing values in one or more columns of the same table.

shared lock
A lock created by non-update ("read") operations. Other users may read the data concurrently, but no transaction can acquire an exclusive lock on the data until all the shared locks have released.

SQL
A unified language for defining, querying, modifying, and controlling the data in a relational database (originally an acronym for Structured Query Language).

statement
A SQL data definition, data manipulation, or data administration command.

stored procedures
See **precompiled queries**.

strings
Groups of one or more letters, numbers, or special characters (such as the question mark or asterisk).

subquery
A SELECT statement that nests inside the WHERE clause of another statement.

system administrator
The person who has overall responsibility for the data in the database, and for its consistency and integrity.

system catalog
The system tables containing descriptions of the database objects and how they are structured.

system tables
See system catalog.

table
A rectangular display of data values as rows and columns.

theta join
A join based on any valid comparison operator, such as equal (=), greater than (>), or not less than (!<).

third normal form
Third normal form requires that each nonkey column give information about the key column. A nonkey column may not describe another nonkey column.

three-valued logic
Logic that allows yes, no, and maybe responses to questions. Two-valued logic permits only yes and no.

time datatype
A datatype that stores time information.

transaction
A mechanism for ensuring that a set of actions is treated as a single unit of work.

transaction log
A log in which changes to the database are recorded, (usually for recovery purposes). The method is implementation dependent.

transaction management
Ensuring that transactions are either completed or cancelled so that the database is never left in an inconsistent state.

trigger
Meaning can vary from system to system. In Transact-SQL, a special form of stored procedure that goes into effect when a user gives a data modification command on a specified table or column.

trigger actions
In Transact-SQL, the actions for which a trigger is specified.

trigger conditions
In Transact-SQL, the conditions which cause a trigger to take effect.

tuple
A set of related attributes that describes a specific entity. Also called row or record.

unique indexes
An index with no duplicate primary keys.

unmodified comparison operator
A comparison operator not followed by ANY or ALL.

user-defined datatypes
In Transact-SQL, datatypes created by the user, defined in terms of the system datatypes, with characteristics such as NULL status and length (where appropriate). Users can apply rules and defaults to these datatypes.

user tables
Tables that contain the information that is the database management system's reason for existing.

validation rules
A rule specifies what data may be entered in a particular column: it is a way of defining the domain of the column. Rules are sometimes referred to as validation rules, since they allow the system to check whether a value being entered in a column falls within the column's domain.

vector aggregates
Aggregates that return an array of values, one per set.

view
An alternative way of looking at the data in one or more tables.

virtual table
See view.

whole number
A number with no fraction or decimal value.

wildcards
Special characters used with the SQL LIKE keyword that can represent one character (underscore, _) or any number of characters (percent sign, %).

Appendix D

The *Bookbiz* Sample Database

This is the sample database *bookbiz*. The names of the tables are *authors, publishers, roysched, titleauthors, titles, editors, titleditors, sales, and salesdetails.*

The header for each column lists the datatypes (including the user defined datatypes *id* and *tid,*) and its null/not null status. Defaults, rules, triggers, and indexes are noted where they apply.

publishers				
pub_id char(4) not null clust, uniq	pub_name varchar(40) null	address varchar(40) null	city varchar(20) null	state char(2) null
0736 0877 1389	New Age Books Binnet & Hardley Algodata Infosystems	1 1st St 2 2nd Ave. 3 3rd Dr.	Boston Washington Berkeley	MA DC CA

authors							
au_id char(11) not null clust, uniq	au_lname varchar(40) not null nonclust	au_fname varchar(20) not null	phone char(12) null	address varchar(40) null	city varchar(20) null	state char(2) null	zip char(5) null
172-32-1176 213-46-8915 238-95-7766 267-41-2394 274-80-9391 341-22-1782 409-56-7008 427-17-2319 472-27-2349 486-29-1786	White Green Carson O'Leary Straight Smith Bennet Dull Gringlesby Locksley	Johnson Marjorie Cheryl Michael Dick Meander Abraham Ann Burt Chastity	408 496-7223 415 986-7020 415 548-7723 408 286-2428 415 834-2919 913 843-0462 415 658-9932 415 836-7128 707 938-6445 415 585-4620	10932 Bigge Rd. 309 63rd St. 589 Darwin Ln. 22 Cleveland Av. 5420 College Av. 10 Misisipi Dr. 6223 Bateman St. 3410 Blonde St. PO Box 792 18 Broadway Av.	Menlo Park Oakland Berkeley San Jose Oakland Lawrence Berkeley Palo Alto Covelo San Francisco	CA CA CA CA CA KS CA CA CA CA	94025 94618 94705 95128 94609 66044 94705 94301 95428 94130

authors, continued							
au_id char(11) not null clust, uniq	au_lname varchar(40) not null nonclust	au_fname varchar(20) not null	phone char(12) null	address varchar(40) null	city varchar(20) null	state char(2) null	zip char(5) null
527-72-3246	Greene	Morningstar	615 297-2723	22 Graybar Rd.	Nashville	TN	37215
648-92-1872	Blotchet-Halls	Reginald	503 745-6402	55 Hillsdale Bl.	Corvallis	OR	97330
672-71-3249	Yokomoto	Akiko	415 935-4228	3 Silver Ct.	Walnut Creek	CA	94595
712-45-1867	del Castillo	Innes	615 996-8275	2286 Cram Pl.	Ann Arbor	MI	48105
722-51-5454	DeFrance	Michel	219 547-9982	3 Balding Pl.	Gary	IN	46403
724-08-9931	Stringer	Dirk	415 843-2991	5420 Telegraph Av.	Oakland	CA	94609
724-80-9391	MacFeather	Stearns	415 354-7128	44 Upland Hts.	Oakland	CA	94612
756-30-7391	Karsen	Livia	415 534-9219	5720 McAuley St.	Oakland	CA	94609
807-91-6654	Panteley	Sylvia	301 946-8853	1956 Arlington Pl.	Rockville	MD	20853
846-92-7186	Hunter	Sheryl	415 836-7128	3410 Blonde St.	Palo Alto	CA	94301
893-72-1158	McBadden	Heather	707 448-4982	301 Putnam	Vacaville	CA	95688
899-46-2035	Ringer	Anne	801 826-0752	67 Seventh Av.	Salt Lake City	UT	84152
998-72-3567	Ringer	Albert	801 826-0752	67 Seventh Av.	Salt Lake City	UT	84152

titles									
title_id char(6) not null clust, uniq	title varchar(80) not null nonclust	type char(12) null	pub_id char(4) null	price money null	advance money null	ytd_sales int null	contract bit not null	notes varchar(200) null	pubdate datetime null
BU1032	The Busy Executive's Database Guide	business	1389	$19.99	$5000.00	4095	1	An overview of available database systems with emphasis on common business applications. Illustrated.	Jun 12 1985 12:00AM
BU1111	Cooking with Computers: Surreptitious Balance Sheets	business	1389	$11.95	$5000.00	3876	1	Helpful hints on how to use your electronic resources to the best advantage.	Jun 9 1985 12:00AM
BU2075	You Can Combat Computer Stress!	business	0736	$2.99	$10125.00	18722	1	The latest medical and psychological techniques for living with the electronic office. Easy-to-understand explanations.	Jun 30 1985 12:00AM

titles, continued									
title_id char(6) not null clust, uniq	title varchar(80) not null nonclust	type char(12) null	pub_id char(4) null	price money null	advance money null	ytd_sales int null	contract bit not null	notes varchar(200) null	pubdate datetime null
BU7832	Straight Talk About Computers	business	1389	$19.99	$5000.00	4095	1	Annotated analysis of what computers can do for you: a no-hype guide for the critical user.	Jun 22 1985 12:00AM
MC2222	Silicon Valley Gastronomic Treats	mod_cook	0877	$19.99	$0.00	2032	1	Favorite recipes for quick, easy, and elegant meals, tried and tested by people who never have time to eat, let alone cook.	Jun 9 1985 12:00AM
MC3021	The Gourmet Microwave	mod_cook	0877	$2.99	$15000.00	22246	1	Traditional French gourmet recipes adapted for modern micro-wave cooking.	Jun 18 1985 12:00AM
MC3026	The Psychology of Computer Cooking	NULL	0877	NULL	NULL	NULL	0	NULL	NULL
PC1035	But Is It User Friendly?	popular_comp	1389	$22.95	$7000.00	8780	1	A survey of software for the naive user, focusing on the 'friendliness' of each.	Jun 30 1985 12:00AM

titles, continued									
title_id char(6) not null clust, uniq	title varchar(80) not null nonclust	type char(12) null	pub_id char(4) null	price money null	advance money null	ytd_sales int null	contract bit not null	notes varchar(200) null	pubdate datetime null
PC8888	Secrets of Silicon Valley	popular_comp	1389	$20.00	$8000.00	4095	1	Muckraking reporting by two courageous women on the world's largest computer hardware and software manufacturers.	Jun 12 1985 12:00AM
PC9999	Net Etiquette	popular_comp	1389	NULL	NULL	NULL	0	A must-read for computer conferencing debutantes!	NULL
PS1372	Computer Phobic and Non-Phobic Individuals: Behavior Variations	psychology	0736	$21.59	$7000.00	375	1	A must for the specialist, this book examines the difference between those who hate and fear computers and those who think they are swell.	Oct 21 1985 12:00AM
PS2091	Is Anger the Enemy?	psychology	0736	$10.95	$2275.00	2045	1	Carefully researched study of the effects of strong emotions on the body. Metabolic charts included.	Jun 15 1985 12:00AM
PS2106	Life Without Fear	psychology	0736	$7.00	$6000.00	111	1	New exercise, meditation, and nutritional techniques that can reduce the shock of daily interactions. Popular audience. Sample menus included, exercise video available separately.	Oct 5 1985 12:00AM

titles, continued									
title_id char(6) not null clust, uniq	title varchar(80) not null nonclust	type char(12) null	pub_id char(4) null	price money null	advance money null	ytd_sales int null	contract bit not null	notes varchar(200) null	pubdate datetime null
PS3333	Prolonged Data Deprivation: Four Case Studies	psychology	0736	$19.99	$2000.00	4072	1	What happens when the data runs dry? Searching evaluations of information-shortage effects on heavy users.	Jun 12 1985 12:00AM
PS7777	Emotional Security: A New Algorithm	psychology	0736	$7.99	$4000.00	3336	1	Protecting yourself and your loved ones from undue emotional stress in the modern world. Use of computer and nutritional aids emphasized.	Jun 12 1985 12:00AM
TC3218	Onions, Leeks, and Garlic: Cooking Secrets of the Mediterranean	trad_cook	0877	$20.95	$7000.00	375	1	Profusely illustrated in color, this makes a wonderful gift book for a cuisine-oriented friend.	Oct 21 1985 12:00AM

titles, continued									
title_id char(6) not null clust, uniq	title varchar(80) not null nonclust	type char(12) null	pub_id char(4) null	price money null	advance money null	ytd_sales int null	contract bit not null	notes varchar(200) null	pubdate datetime null
TC7777	Sushi, Anyone?	trad_cook	0877	$14.99	$8000.00	4095	1	Detailed instructions on improving your position in life by learning how to make authentic Japanese sushi in your spare time. 5-10% increase in number of friends per recipe reported from beta test.	Jun 12 1985 12:00AM

titleauthors			
au_id char(11) not null nonclust uniq, clust, composite	title_id char(6) not null nonclust	au_ord tinyint null	royaltyshare float null
172-32-1176	PS3333	1	1.000000000
213-46-8915	BU1032	2	0.400000000
213-46-8915	BU2075	1	1.000000000
238-95-7766	PC1035	1	1.000000000
267-41-2394	BU1111	2	0.400000000
267-41-2394	TC7777	2	0.300000000
274-80-9391	BU7832	1	1.000000000
409-56-7008	BU1032	1	0.600000000
427-17-2319	PC8888	1	0.500000000
472-27-2349	TC7777	3	0.300000000
486-29-1786	PC9999	1	1.000000000
486-29-1786	PS7777	1	1.000000000
648-92-1872	TC4203	1	1.000000000
672-71-3249	TC7777	1	0.400000000
712-45-1867	MC2222	1	1.000000000
722-51-5454	MC3021	1	0.750000000
724-80-9391	BU1111	1	0.600000000
724-80-9391	PS1372	2	0.250000000
756-30-7391	PS1372	1	0.750000000
807-91-6654	TC3218	1	1.000000000
846-92-7186	PC8888	2	0.500000000
899-46-2035	MC3021	2	0.250000000
899-46-2035	PS2091	2	0.500000000
998-72-3567	PS2091	1	0.500000000
998-72-3567	PS2106	1	1.000000000

sales			
sonum int not null	stor_id char(4) not null	ponum varchar(20) not null	date datetime null
1	7066	QA7442.3	Sep 13 1985 12:00AM
2	7067	D4482	Sep 14 1985 12:00AM
3	7131	N914008	Sep 14 1985 12:00AM
4	7131	N914014	Sep 14 1985 12:00AM
5	8042	423LL922	Sep 14 1985 12:00AM
6	8042	423LL930	Sep 14 1985 12:00AM
7	6380	722a	Sep 13 1985 12:00AM
8	6380	6871	Sep 14 1985 12:00AM
9	8042	P723	Mar 11 1988 12:00AM
19	7896	X999	Feb 21 1988 12:00AM
10	7896	QQ2299	Oct 28 1987 12:00AM
11	7896	TQ456	Dec 12 1987 12:00AM
12	8042	QA879.1	May 22 1987 12:00AM
13	7066	A2976	May 24 1987 12:00AM
14	7131	P3087a	May 29 1987 12:00AM
15	7067	P2121	Jun 15 1987 12:00AM

salesdetails				
sonum int not null	qty_ordered smallint not null	qty_shipped smallint null	title_id char(6) not null	date_shipped datetime null
1	75	75	PS2091	Sep 15 1985 12:00AM
2	10	10	PS2091	Sep 15 1985 12:00AM
3	20	20	PS2091	Sep 18 1985 12:00AM
4	25	20	MC3021	Sep 18 1985 12:00AM
5	15	15	MC3021	Sep 14 1985 12:00AM
6	10	3	BU1032	Sep 22 1985 12:00AM
7	3	3	PS2091	Sep 20 1985 12:00AM
8	5	5	BU1032	Sep 14 1985 12:00AM
9	25	5	BU1111	Mar 28 1988 12:00AM
19	35	35	BU2075	Mar 15 1988 12:00AM
10	15	15	BU7832	Oct 29 1987 12:00AM
11	10	10	MC2222	Jan 12 1988 12:00AM
12	30	30	PC1035	May 24 1987 12:00AM
13	50	50	PC8888	May 24 1987 12:00AM
14	20	20	PS1372	May 29 1987 12:00AM
14	25	25	PS2106	Apr 29 1987 12:00AM
14	15	10	PS3333	May 29 1987 12:00AM
14	25	25	PS7777	Jun 13 1987 12:00AM
15	40	40	TC3218	Jun 15 1987 12:00AM
15	20	20	TC4203	May 30 1987 12:00AM
15	20	10	TC7777	Jun 17 1987 12:00AM

editors								
ed_id char(11) not null clust, uniq	ed_name varchar(40) not null nonclust, composite	ed_fname varchar(20) not null	ed_pos varchar(12) null	phone char(12) null	address varchar(40) null	city varchar(20) null	state char(2) null	zip char(5) null
234-88-9720	Hunter	Amanda	acquisition	617 432-5586	18 Dowdy Ln.	Boston	MA	02210
321-55-8906	DeLongue	Martinella	project	415 843-2222	3000 6th St.	Berkeley	CA	94710
723-48-9010	Sparks	Manfred	copy	303 721-3388	15 Sail	Denver	CO	80237
777-02-9831	Samuelson	Bernard	project	415 843-6990	27 Yosemite	Oakland	CA	94609
777-66-9902	Almond	Alfred	copy	312 699-4177	1010 E. Devon	Chicago	IL	60018
826-11-9034	Himmel	Eleanore	project	617 423-0552	97 Bleaker	Boston	MA	02210
885-23-9140	Rutherford-Hayes	Hannah	project	301 468-3909	32 Rockbill Pike	Rockbill	MD	20852
943-88-7920	Kaspchek	Chistof	acquisition	415 549-3909	18 Severe Rd.	Berkeley	CA	94710
993-86-0420	McCann	Dennis	acquisition	301 468-3909	32 Rockbill Pike	Rockbill	MD	20852

titleditors		
ed_id char(11) not null clust, uniq, composite	title_id char(6) not null	ed_ord tinyint null
321-55-8906	BU1032	2
321-55-8906	BU1111	2
321-55-8906	BU2075	3
321-55-8906	BU7832	2
321-55-8906	PC1035	2
321-55-8906	PC8888	2
777-02-9831	PC1035	3
777-02-9831	PC8888	3
826-11-9034	BU2075	2
826-11-9034	PS1372	2
826-11-9034	PS2091	2
826-11-9034	PS2106	2
826-11-9034	PS3333	2
826-11-9034	PS7777	2
885-23-9140	MC2222	2
885-23-9140	MC3021	2
885-23-9140	TC3218	2
885-23-9140	TC4203	2
885-23-9140	TC7777	2
943-88-7920	BU1032	1
943-88-7920	BU1111	1
943-88-7920	BU2075	1
943-88-7920	BU7832	1
943-88-7920	PC1035	1
943-88-7920	PC8888	1
993-86-0420	MC2222	1
993-86-0420	MC3021	1
993-86-0420	PS1372	1
993-86-0420	PS2091	1
993-86-0420	PS2106	1
993-86-0420	PS3333	1
993-86-0420	PS7777	1
993-86-0420	TC3218	1
993-86-0420	TC4203	1
993-86-0420	TC7777	1

roysched			
title_id char(6) not null nonclust	lorange int null	hirange int null	royalty float null
BU1032	0	5000	0.100000
BU1032	5001	50000	0.120000
PC1035	0	2000	0.100000
PC1035	2001	4000	0.120000
PC1035	4001	50000	0.160000
BU2075	0	1000	0.100000
BU2075	1001	5000	0.120000
BU2075	5001	7000	0.160000
BU2075	7001	50000	0.180000
PC9999	0	50000	0.100000
PS2091	0	1000	0.100000
PS2091	1001	5000	0.120000
PS2091	5001	50000	0.140000
PS2106	0	2000	0.100000
PS2106	2001	5000	0.120000
PS2106	5001	50000	0.140000
MC3021	0	1000	0.100000
MC3021	1001	2000	0.120000
MC3021	2001	6000	0.140000
MC3021	6001	8000	0.180000
MC3021	8001	50000	0.200000
TC3218	0	2000	0.100000
TC3218	2001	6000	0.120000
TC3218	6001	8000	0.160000
TC3218	8001	50000	0.180000
PC8888	0	5000	0.100000
PC8888	5001	50000	0.120000
PS7777	0	5000	0.100000
PS7777	5001	50000	0.120000
PS3333	0	5000	0.100000
PS3333	5001	50000	0.120000
MC3026	0	1000	0.100000
MC3026	1001	2000	0.120000
MC3026	2001	6000	0.140000
MC3026	6001	8000	0.180000
MC3026	8001	50000	0.200000
BU1111	0	4000	0.100000
BU1111	4001	8000	0.120000
BU1111	8001	50000	0.140000
MC2222	0	2000	0.100000
MC2222	2001	4000	0.120000
MC2222	4001	8000	0.140000
MC2222	8001	12000	0.160000
TC7777	0	5000	0.100000
TC7777	5001	15000	0.120000
TC4203	0	2000	0.100000
TC4203	2001	8000	0.120000
TC4203	8001	16000	0.140000
BU7832	0	5000	0.100000
BU7832	5001	50000	0.120000
PS1372	0	50000	0.100000

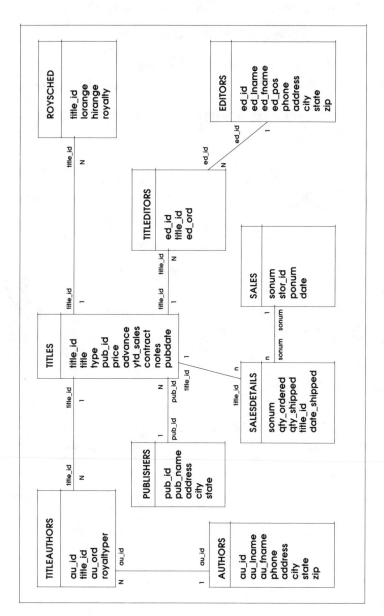

Figure D–1. Data Structure Diagram for the Sample Database *bookbiz*

CREATE AND INSERT STATEMENTS FOR THE
BOOKBIZ DATABASE

The CREATE and INSERT statements for creating the *bookbiz* database on the SYBASE system are provided for your reference in recreating this database on your system. These sample statements are not guaranteed to work with the SQL you are using: they are provided for reference purposes only.

```
use master
go
   drop database bookbiz
go
print 'Creating the "bookbiz" database'
create database bookbiz
go
use bookbiz
go
   create table authors
   (au_id char(11) not null,
   au_lname varchar(40) not null,
   au_fname varchar(20) not null,
   phone char(12) null,
   address varchar(40) null,
   city varchar(20) null,
   state char(2) null,
   zip char(5) null)
go
grant select on authors to public
go
   create table publishers
   (pub_id char(4) not null,
   pub_name varchar(40) null,
   address varchar(40) null,
   city varchar(20) null,
   state char(2) null)
go
grant select on publishers to public
go
   create table roysched
   (title_id char(6) not null,
   lorange int null,
   hirange int null,
   royalty float null)
go
grant select on roysched to public
go
   create table titleauthors
   (au_id char(11) not null,
   title_id char(6) not null,
   au_ord tinyint null,
```

```
   royaltyshare float null)
go
grant select on titleauthors to public
go
   create table titles
   (title_id char(6) not null,
   title varchar(80) not null,
   type char(12) null,
   pub_id char(4) null,
   price money null,
   advance money null,
   ytd_sales int null,
   contract bit not null,
   notes varchar(200) null,
   pubdate datetime null)
go
grant select on titles to public
go

create table editors
   (ed_id char(11) not null,
   ed_lname varchar(40) not null,
   ed_fname varchar(20) not null,
   ed_pos varchar(12) null,
   phone char(12) null,
   address varchar(40) null,
   city varchar(20) null,
   state char(2) null,
   zip char(5) null)
go
grant select on editors to public
go

create table titleditors
   (ed_id char(11) not null,
   title_id char(6) not null,
   ed_ord tinyint null)
go
grant select on titleditors to public
go

create table sales
   (sonum int not null,
   stor_id char(4) not null,
   ponum varchar(20) not null,
   date datetime null)
go
grant select on sales to public
go

create table salesdetails
   (sonum int not null,
   qty_ordered smallint not null,
   qty_shipped smallint null,
   title_id char(6) not null,
```

```
    date_shipped datetime null)
go
grant select on salesdetails to public
go


create unique clustered index pubind
on publishers (pub_id)
go
create unique clustered index auidind
on authors (au_id)
go
create nonclustered index aunmind
on authors (au_lname, au_fname)
go
create unique clustered index titleidind
on titles (title_id)
go
create nonclustered index titleind
on titles (title)
go
create unique clustered index taind
on titleauthors (au_id, title_id)
go
create nonclustered index auidind
on titleauthors (au_id)
go
create nonclustered index titleidind
on titleauthors (title_id)
go
create unique clustered index edind
on editors (ed_id)
go
create nonclustered index ednmind
on editors (ed_lname, ed_fname)
go
create unique clustered index teind
on titleditors (ed_id, title_id)
go
create nonclustered index titleidind
on roysched (title_id)
go


insert authors
values('409-56-7008', 'Bennet', 'Abraham',
'415 658-9932', '6223 Bateman St.', 'Berkeley', 'CA', '94705')
go
insert authors
values ('213-46-8915', 'Green', 'Marjorie',
'415 986-7020', '309 63rd St.', 'Oakland', 'CA', '94618')
go
insert authors
values('238-95-7766', 'Carson', 'Cheryl',
'415 548-7723', '589 Darwin Ln.', 'Berkeley', 'CA', '94705')
go
```

```
insert authors
values('998-72-3567', 'Ringer', 'Albert',
'801 826-0752', '67 Seventh Av.', 'Salt Lake City', 'UT', '84152')
go
insert authors
values('899-46-2035', 'Ringer', 'Anne',
'801 826-0752', '67 Seventh Av.', 'Salt Lake City', 'UT', '84152')
go
insert authors
values('722-51-5454', 'DeFrance', 'Michel',
'219 547-9982', '3 Balding Pl.', 'Gary', 'IN', '46403')
go
insert authors
values('807-91-6654', 'Panteley', 'Sylvia',
'301 946-8853', '1956 Arlington Pl.', 'Rockville', 'MD', '20853')
go
insert authors
values('893-72-1158', 'McBadden', 'Heather',
'707 448-4982', '301 Putnam', 'Vacaville', 'CA', '95688')
go
insert authors
values('724-08-9931', 'Stringer', 'Dirk',
'415 843-2991', '5420 Telegraph Av.', 'Oakland', 'CA', '94609')
go
insert authors
values('274-80-9391', 'Straight', 'Dick',
'415 834-2919', '5420 College Av.', 'Oakland', 'CA', '94609')
go
insert authors
values('756-30-7391', 'Karsen', 'Livia',
'415 534-9219', '5720 McAuley St.', 'Oakland', 'CA', '94609')
go
insert authors
values('724-80-9391', 'MacFeather', 'Stearns',
'415 354-7128', '44 Upland Hts.', 'Oakland', 'CA', '94612')
go
insert authors
values('427-17-2319', 'Dull', 'Ann',
'415 836-7128', '3410 Blonde St.', 'Palo Alto', 'CA', '94301')
go
insert authors
values('672-71-3249', 'Yokomoto', 'Akiko',
'415 935-4228', '3 Silver Ct.', 'Walnut Creek', 'CA', '94595')
go
insert authors
values('267-41-2394', "O'Leary", 'Michael',
'408 286-2428', '22 Cleveland Av.', 'San Jose', 'CA', '95128')
go
insert authors
values('472-27-2349', 'Gringlesby', 'Burt',
'707 938-6445', 'PO Box 792', 'Covelo', 'CA', '95428')
go
insert authors
values('527-72-3246', 'Greene', 'Morningstar',
'615 297-2723', '22 Graybar Rd.', 'Nashville', 'TN', '37215')
```

```
go
insert authors
values('172-32-1176', 'White', 'Johnson',
'408 496-7223', '10932 Bigge Rd.', 'Menlo Park', 'CA', '94025')
go
insert authors
values('712-45-1867', 'del Castillo', 'Innes',
'615 996-8275', '2286 Cram Pl.', 'Ann Arbor', 'MI', '48105')
go
insert authors
values('846-92-7186', 'Hunter', 'Sheryl',
'415 836-7128', '3410 Blonde St.', 'Palo Alto', 'CA', '94301')
go
insert authors
values('486-29-1786', 'Locksley', 'Chastity',
'415 585-4620', '18 Broadway Av.', 'San Francisco', 'CA', '94130')
go
insert authors
values('648-92-1872', 'Blotchet-Halls', 'Reginald',
'503 745-6402', '55 Hillsdale Bl.', 'Corvallis', 'OR', '97330')
go
insert authors
values('341-22-1782', 'Smith', 'Meander',
'913 843-0462', '10 Misisipi Dr.', 'Lawrence', 'KS', '66044')
go

insert publishers
values('0736', 'New Age Books', '1 1st St', 'Boston', 'MA')
go
insert publishers
values('0877', 'Binnet & Hardley','2 2nd Ave.', 'Washington', 'DC')
go
insert publishers
values('1389', 'Algodata Infosystems', '3 3rd Dr.', 'Berkeley', 'CA')
go

insert roysched
values('BU1032', 0, 5000, .10)
go
insert roysched
values('BU1032', 5001, 50000, .12)
go
insert roysched
values('PC1035', 0, 2000, .10)
go
insert roysched
values('PC1035', 2001, 4000, .12)
go
insert roysched
values('PC1035', 4001, 50000, .16)
go
insert roysched
values('BU2075', 0, 1000, .10)
go
insert roysched
```

```
values('BU2075', 1001, 5000, .12)
go
insert roysched
values('BU2075', 5001, 7000, .16)
go
insert roysched
values('BU2075', 7001, 50000, .18)
go
insert roysched
values('PC9999', 0, 50000, .10)
go
insert roysched
values('PS2091', 0, 1000, .10)
go
insert roysched
values('PS2091', 1001, 5000, .12)
go
insert roysched
values('PS2091', 5001, 50000, .14)
go
insert roysched
values('PS2106', 0, 2000, .10)
go
insert roysched
values('PS2106', 2001, 5000, .12)
go
insert roysched
values('PS2106', 5001, 50000, .14)
go
insert roysched
values('MC3021', 0, 1000, .10)
go
insert roysched
values('MC3021', 1001, 2000, .12)
go
insert roysched
values('MC3021', 2001, 6000, .14)
go
insert roysched
values('MC3021', 6001, 8000, .18)
go
insert roysched
values('MC3021', 8001, 50000, .20)
go
insert roysched
values('TC3218', 0, 2000, .10)
go
insert roysched
values('TC3218', 2001, 6000, .12)
go
insert roysched
values('TC3218', 6001, 8000, .16)
go
insert roysched
values('TC3218', 8001, 50000, .16)
```

```
go
insert roysched
values('PC8888', 0, 5000, .10)
go
insert roysched
values('PC8888', 5001, 50000, .12)
go
insert roysched
values('PS7777', 0, 5000, .10)
go
insert roysched
values('PS7777', 5001, 50000, .12)
go
insert roysched
values('PS3333', 0, 5000, .10)
go
insert roysched
values('PS3333', 5001, 50000, .12)
go
insert roysched
values('MC3026', 0, 1000, .10)
go
insert roysched
values('MC3026', 1001, 2000, .12)
go
insert roysched
values('MC3026', 2001, 6000, .14)
go
insert roysched
values('MC3026', 6001, 8000, .18)
go
insert roysched
values('MC3026', 8001, 50000, .20)
go
insert roysched
values('BU1111', 0, 4000, .10)
go
insert roysched
values('BU1111', 4001, 8000, .12)
go
insert roysched
values('BU1111', 8001, 50000, .14)
go
insert roysched
values('MC2222', 0, 2000, .10)
go
insert roysched
values('MC2222', 2001, 4000, .12)
go
insert roysched
values('MC2222', 4001, 8000, .14)
go
insert roysched
values('MC2222', 8001, 12000, .16)
go
```

```
insert roysched
values('TC7777', 0, 5000, .10)
go
insert roysched
values('TC7777', 5001, 15000, .12)
go
insert roysched
values('TC4203', 0, 2000, .10)
go
insert roysched
values('TC4203', 2001, 8000, .12)
go
insert roysched
values('TC4203', 8001, 16000, .14)
go
insert roysched
values('BU7832', 0, 5000, .10)
go
insert roysched
values('BU7832', 5001, 50000, .12)
go
insert roysched
values('PS1372', 0, 50000, .10)
go

insert titleauthors
values('409-56-7008', 'BU1032', 1, .60)
go
insert titleauthors
values('486-29-1786', 'PS7777', 1, 1.00)
go
insert titleauthors
values('486-29-1786', 'PC9999', 1, 1.00)
go
insert titleauthors
values('712-45-1867', 'MC2222', 1, 1.00)
go
insert titleauthors
values('172-32-1176', 'PS3333', 1, 1.00)
go
insert titleauthors
values('213-46-8915', 'BU1032', 2, .40)
go
insert titleauthors
values('238-95-7766', 'PC1035', 1, 1.00)
go
insert titleauthors
values('213-46-8915', 'BU2075', 1, 1.00)
go
insert titleauthors
values('998-72-3567', 'PS2091', 1, .50)
go
insert titleauthors
values('899-46-2035', 'PS2091', 2, .50)
go
```

```
insert titleauthors
values('998-72-3567', 'PS2106', 1, 1.00)
go
insert titleauthors
values('722-51-5454', 'MC3021', 1, .75)
go
insert titleauthors
values('899-46-2035', 'MC3021', 2, .25)
go
insert titleauthors
values('807-91-6654', 'TC3218', 1, 1.00)
go
insert titleauthors
values('274-80-9391', 'BU7832', 1, 1.00)
go
insert titleauthors
values('427-17-2319', 'PC8888', 1, .50)
go
insert titleauthors
values('846-92-7186', 'PC8888', 2, .50)
go
insert titleauthors
values('756-30-7391', 'PS1372', 1, .75)
go
insert titleauthors
values('724-80-9391', 'PS1372', 2, .25)
go
insert titleauthors
values('724-80-9391', 'BU1111', 1, .60)
go
insert titleauthors
values('267-41-2394', 'BU1111', 2, .40)
go
insert titleauthors
values('672-71-3249', 'TC7777', 1, .40)
go
insert titleauthors
values('267-41-2394', 'TC7777', 2, .30)
go
insert titleauthors
values('472-27-2349', 'TC7777', 3, .30)
go
insert titleauthors
values('648-92-1872', 'TC4203', 1, 1.00)
go

insert titles
values ('PC8888', 'Secrets of Silicon Valley',
'popular_comp', '1389', $20.00, $8000.00, 4095, 1,
"Muckraking reporting by two courageous women on
the world's largest computer hardware and software manufacturers.",
'06/12/85')
go
```

```
insert titles
values ('BU1032', "The Busy Executive's Database Guide",
'business', '1389', $19.99, $5000.00, 4095, 1,
"An overview of available database systems with emphasis
on common business applications.  Illustrated.",
'06/12/85')
go

insert titles
values ('PS7777', 'Emotional Security: A New Algorithm',
'psychology', '0736', $7.99, $4000.00, 3336, 1,
"Protecting yourself and your loved ones from undue emotional stress
in the modern world.  Use of computer and nutritional aids emphasized.",
'06/12/85')
go

insert titles
values ('PS3333', 'Prolonged Data Deprivation: Four Case Studies',
'psychology', '0736', $19.99, $2000.00, 4072, 1,
'What happens when the data runs dry?  Searching evaluations
of information-shortage effects on heavy users.',
'06/12/85')
go

insert titles
values ('BU1111', 'Cooking with Computers: Surreptitious Balance Sheets',
'business', '1389', $11.95, $5000.00, 3876, 1,
'Helpful hints on how to use your electronic resources to
the best advantage.', '06/09/85')
go

insert titles
values ('MC2222', 'Silicon Valley Gastronomic Treats',
'mod_cook', '0877', $19.99, $0.00, 2032, 1,
'Favorite recipes for quick, easy, and elegant meals,
tried and tested by people who never have time to eat, let alone cook.',
'06/09/85')
go

insert titles
values ('TC7777', 'Sushi, Anyone?',
'trad_cook', '0877', $14.99, $8000.00, 4095, 1,
'Detailed instructions on improving your position in life
by learning how to make authentic Japanese sushi in your spare time.
5-10% increase in number of friends per recipe reported from beta test.',
'06/12/85')
go
insert titles
values ('TC4203', 'Fifty Years in Buckingham Palace Kitchens',
'trad_cook', '0877', $11.95, $4000.00, 15096, 1,
"More anecdotes from the Queen's favorite cook
describing life among English royalty.
Recipes, techniques, tender vignettes.",
'06/12/85')
go
```

```
insert titles
values ('PC1035', 'But Is It User Friendly?',
'popular_comp', '1389', $22.95, $7000.00, 8780, 1,
"A survey of software for the naive user,
focusing on the 'friendliness' of each.",
'06/30/85')
go
insert titles
values('BU2075', 'You Can Combat Computer Stress!',
'business', '0736', $2.99, $10125.00, 18722, 1,
'The latest medical and psychological techniques
for living with the electronic office.
Easy-to-understand explanations.',
'06/30/85')
go

insert titles
values('PS2091', 'Is Anger the Enemy?',
'psychology', '0736', $10.95, $2275.00, 2045, 1,
'Carefully researched study of the effects of
strong emotions on the body.  Metabolic charts included.',
'06/15/85')
go

insert titles
values('PS2106', 'Life Without Fear',
'psychology', '0736', $7.00, $6000.00, 111, 1,
'New exercise, meditation, and nutritional techniques
that can reduce the shock of daily interactions.
Popular audience.  Sample menus included, exercise video
available separately.',
'10/05/85')
go
insert titles
values('MC3021', 'The Gourmet Microwave',
'mod_cook', '0877', $2.99, $15000.00, 22246, 1,
'Traditional French gourmet recipes
adapted for modern microwave cooking.',
'06/18/85')
go

insert titles
values('TC3218',
'Onions, Leeks, and Garlic: Cooking Secrets of the Mediterranean',
'trad_cook', '0877', $20.95, $7000.00, 375, 1,
'Profusely illustrated in color, this makes a wonderful
gift book for a cuisine-oriented friend.',
'10/21/85')
go

insert titles (title_id, title, pub_id, contract)
values('MC3026', 'The Psychology of Computer Cooking', '0877', 0)
go
```

```
insert titles
values ('BU7832', 'Straight Talk About Computers',
'business', '1389', $19.99, $5000.00, 4095, 1,
'Annotated analysis of what computers can do for you:
a no-hype guide for the critical user.',
'06/22/85')
go

insert titles
values('PS1372',
'Computer Phobic and Non-Phobic Individuals: Behavior Variations',
'psychology', '0736', $21.59, $7000.00, 375, 1,
'A must for the specialist, this book examines
the difference between those who hate and fear computers
and those who think they are swell.',
'10/21/85')
go
insert titles (title_id, title, type, pub_id, contract, notes)
values('PC9999', 'Net Etiquette', 'popular_comp', '1389', 0,
'A must-read for computer conferencing debutantes!')
go

insert editors
values ("321-55-8906","DeLongue","Martinella","project",
"415 843-2222","3000 6th St.","Berkeley","CA","94710")
insert editors
values ("723-48-9010","Sparks","Manfred","copy",
"303 721-3388","15 Sail","Denver","CO","80237")
insert editors
values ("777-02-9831","Samuelson","Bernard","project",
"415 843-6990","27 Yosemite","Oakland","CA","94609")
insert editors
values ("777-66-9902","Almond","Alfred","copy",
"312 699-4177","1010 E. Devon","Chicago","IL","60018")
insert editors
values ("826-11-9034","Himmel","Eleanore","project",
"617 423-0552","97 Bleaker","Boston","MA","02210")
insert editors
values ("885-23-9140","Rutherford-Hayes","Hannah","project",
"301 468-3909","32 Rockbill Pike","Rockbill","MD","20852")
insert editors
values ("993-86-0420","McCann","Dennis","acquisition",
"301 468-3909","32 Rockbill Pike","Rockbill","MD","20852")
insert editors
values ("943-88-7920","Kaspchek","Chistof","acquisition",
"415 549-3909","18 Severe Rd.","Berkeley","CA","94710")
insert editors
values ("234-88-9720","Hunter","Amanda","acquisition",
"617 432-5586","18 Dowdy Ln.","Boston","MA","02210")
go

insert titleditors values
("826-11-9034","BU2075", 2)
insert titleditors values
("826-11-9034","PS2091", 2)
```

```
insert titleditors values
("826-11-9034","PS2106", 2)
insert titleditors values
("826-11-9034","PS3333", 2)
insert titleditors values
("826-11-9034","PS7777", 2)
insert titleditors values
("826-11-9034","PS1372", 2)
insert titleditors values
("885-23-9140","MC2222", 2)
insert titleditors values
("885-23-9140","MC3021", 2)
insert titleditors values
("885-23-9140","TC3218", 2)
insert titleditors values
("885-23-9140","TC4203", 2)
insert titleditors values
("885-23-9140","TC7777", 2)
insert titleditors values
("321-55-8906","BU1032", 2)
insert titleditors values
("321-55-8906","BU1111", 2)
insert titleditors values
("321-55-8906","BU7832", 2)
insert titleditors values
("321-55-8906","PC1035", 2)
insert titleditors values
("321-55-8906","PC8888", 2)
insert titleditors values
("321-55-8906","BU2075", 3)
insert titleditors values
("777-02-9831","PC1035", 3)
insert titleditors values
("777-02-9831","PC8888", 3)
insert titleditors values
("943-88-7920","BU1032", 1)
insert titleditors values
("943-88-7920","BU1111", 1)
insert titleditors values
("943-88-7920","BU2075", 1)
insert titleditors values
("943-88-7920","BU7832", 1)
insert titleditors values
("943-88-7920","PC1035", 1)
insert titleditors values
("943-88-7920","PC8888", 1)
insert titleditors values
("993-86-0420","PS1372", 1)
insert titleditors values
("993-86-0420","PS2091", 1)
insert titleditors values
("993-86-0420","PS2106", 1)
insert titleditors values
("993-86-0420","PS3333", 1)
```

```
insert titleditors values
("993-86-0420","PS7777", 1)
insert titleditors values
("993-86-0420","MC2222", 1)
insert titleditors values
("993-86-0420","MC3021", 1)
insert titleditors values
("993-86-0420","TC3218", 1)
insert titleditors values
("993-86-0420","TC4203", 1)
insert titleditors values
("993-86-0420","TC7777", 1)
go

insert sales
values(1,'7066', 'QA7442.3', '09/13/85')
go
insert sales
values(2,'7067', 'D4482', '09/14/85')
go
insert sales
values(3,'7131', 'N914008', '09/14/85')
go
insert sales
values(4,'7131', 'N914014', '09/14/85')
go
insert sales
values(5,'8042', '423LL922', '09/14/85')
go
insert sales
values(6,'8042', '423LL930', '09/14/85')
go
insert sales
values(7,'6380', '722a', '09/13/85')
go
insert sales
values(8,'6380', '6871', '09/14/85')
go
insert sales
values(9,'8042','P723', '03/11/88')
go
insert sales
values(19,'7896','X999', '02/21/88')
go
insert sales
values(10,'7896','QQ2299', '10/28/87')
go
insert sales
values(11,'7896','TQ456', '12/12/87')
go
insert sales
values(12,'8042','QA879.1', '5/22/87')
go
insert sales
values(13,'7066','A2976', '5/24/87')
```

```
go
insert sales
values(14,'7131','P3087a', '5/29/87')
go
insert sales
values(15,'7067','P2121', '6/15/87')
go

insert salesdetails
values (1, 75, 75, 'PS2091', '9/15/85')
go
insert into salesdetails values
(2, 10, 10, 'PS2091','9/15/85')
go
insert into salesdetails values
(3, 20, 20, 'PS2091', '09/18/85')
go
insert into salesdetails values
(4,25,20,'MC3021','09/18/85')
go
insert into salesdetails values
(5,15,15,'MC3021','09/14/85')
go
insert into salesdetails values
(6,10,3,'BU1032', '09/22/85')
go
insert into salesdetails values
(7,3,3, 'PS2091', '09/20/85')
go
insert into salesdetails values
(8,5, 5,'BU1032', '09/14/85')
go
insert into salesdetails values
(9,25,5, 'BU1111','03/28/88')
go
insert into salesdetails values
(19, 35, 35, 'BU2075', '03/15/88')
go
insert into salesdetails values
(10,15,15, 'BU7832', '10/29/87')
go
insert into salesdetails values
(11,10, 10, 'MC2222', '1/12/88')
go
insert into salesdetails values
(12,30, 30, 'PC1035', '5/24/87')
go
insert into salesdetails values
(13,50,50, 'PC8888','5/24/87')
go
insert into salesdetails values
(14,20,20, 'PS1372','5/29/87')
go
insert into salesdetails values
(14, 25, 25, 'PS2106', '4/29/87')
```

```
go
insert into salesdetails values
(14, 15, 10, 'PS3333', '5/29/87')
go
insert into salesdetails values
(14, 25, 25, 'PS7777', '6/13/87')
go
insert into salesdetails values
(15,40,40,'TC3218','6/15/87')
go
insert into salesdetails values
(15, 20, 20, 'TC4203', '5/30/87')
go
insert into salesdetails values
(15, 20, 10, 'TC7777', '6/17/87')
go

create view titleview
as
select title, au_ord, au_lname,
price, ytd_sales, pub_id
from authors, titles, titleauthors
where authors.au_id = titleauthors.au_id
and titles.title_id = titleauthors.title_id
go
```

Appendix E

Bibliography

ISO-ANSI SQL Standard.
A working draft of the 1988 ISO-ANSI SQL2 standard (March 1988) is available through ANSI as document X3H2-88-72 and through ISO as document DBL CPH-2. ANSI is located at 1430 Broadway, New York, NY 10018. Telephone (212) 354-3300 or (212) 642-4900.

Codd, E.F.
"A Relational Model of Data for Large Shared Data Banks," *Communications of the ACM*, Vol. 13, No. 6, June 1970.

———.
"Is Your DBMS Really Relational?," *Computerworld*, October 14, 1985: 1-9. Author proposes twelve criteria for testing relational database management systems.

———.
"Does Your DBMS Run By the Rules?," *Computerworld*, October 21, 1985: 49-55. Details the 30 essential features of the relational model. No current implementation of SQL—nor the ISO-ANSI SQL standard—is completely faithful to Codd's model.

Darnovsky, Marcy and Bowman, Judy.
Transact-SQL User's Guide. Emeryville, CA: Sybase, Inc., 1988.

Date, C.J.
Database: A Primer. Reading, MA: Addison-Wesley Publishing Company, 1983.

————.

A Guide to the SQL Standard. Reading, MA: Addison-Wesley Publishing Company, 1987.

————.

An Introduction to Database Systems, Volume I, Fourth Edition. Reading, MA: Addison-Wesley Publishing Company, 1986.

————.

An Introduction to Database Systems, Volume II. Reading, MA: Addison-Wesley Publishing Company, 1983.

————.

Relational Database: Selected Writings. Reading, MA: Addison-Wesley Publishing Company, 1986. The article "A Practical Approach to Database Design" is very clear and useful, and helped us to organize our thinking on the subject.

Epstein, Robert.
Relational Performance: Understanding the Performance of Relational DBMSs. Emeryville, CA: Sybase, Inc., 1986.

Gane, Chris.
Developing Business Systems in SQL Using ORACLE on the IBM-PC New York, NY: Rapid System Development, Inc., 1986.

IBM Corporation
SQL/Data System Terminal User's Reference for VSE". Endicott, NY: IBM Corporation, 1984.

Kent, William.
"A Simple Guide to Five Normal Forms in Relational Database Theory," *Communications of the ACM,* Vol.20, No. 2 (February, 1983): 120-125.

Larson, Bruce L.
The Database Expert's Guide to Database 2. New York, NY: McGraw-Hill Book Company, 1988.

Perkinson, R.C.
Data Analysis: the Key to Data Base Design. Wellesley, MA: QED Information Sciences, Inc., 1984.

Relational Database Systems, Inc.
INFORMIX-SQL Reference Manual. Menlo Park, CA: Relational Database Systems, Inc., 1986.

Relational Technology
INGRES Quick Reference Summary SQL Release 5.0. Alameda, CA: Relational Technology, 1986.

Ross, Ronald G.
Entity Modeling: Techniques and Application. Boston: Database Research Group, Inc., 1987.

Sachs, Jonathon, *et al.*
*SQL*Plus Reference Guide.* Belmont, CA: ORACLE Corporation, 1987.

van der Lans, Rick F.
Introduction to SQL. Reading, MA: Addison-Wesley Publishing Company, 1988.

Index